HENRY N. COBB

WORDS & WORKS

Piazza San Marco, Venice: author's poster-color painting, 1935.

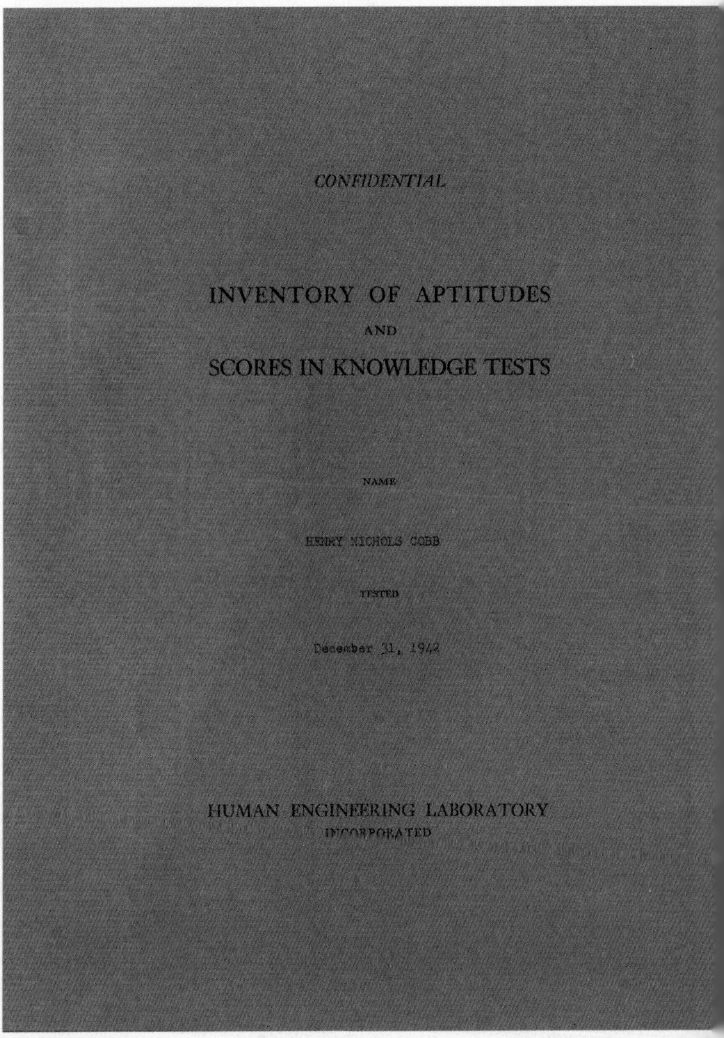

CONFIDENTIAL

INVENTORY OF APTITUDES

AND

SCORES IN KNOWLEDGE TESTS

NAME

HENRY NICHOLS COBB

TESTED

December 31, 1942

HUMAN ENGINEERING LABORATORY

INCORPORATED

Assessment of author's career prospects, 1942.

HENRY NICHOLS COBB

Up until we gave you our test for creative imagination, you scored exactly like successful architects, namely, objective personality, high structural visualization, and a large English vocabulary. However, you scored low in creative imagination unlike the architect. Actually, with your aptitudes, manufacturing executive's work would be ideal for you. Thus we recommend that you do not attempt to do straight architectural planning, but head for executive work such as manufacturing prefabricated houses. You spoke of an interest in prefabricated houses which, we feel, would be an ideal field for you. From an amateur's point of view the Laboratory feels that prefabricated houses have gone bad for two reasons; people with too little knowledge have undertaken this work and architects with too high creative imagination have raised havoc with them. Thus, you with low creative imagination and sound architectural background could effectively attack this problem. To obtain such a position you must have an architectural background which means taking a straight architectural course in college. You may find these courses difficult because of your creative imagination, but we feel that any boy who has the large English vocabulary that you have and who can do so well in languages despite your high structural visualization certainly will not find this obstacle too difficault to overcome.

Because you are low in accounting aptitude and high in English vocabulary, the Laboratory suggests that you plan to attend a small, old college. St. John's College, founded in 1784 with an enrollment of 175 persons, which you asked about, would be perfect.

Keep your vocabulary at the same high level it is now and take as many sciences as necessary to enter a technical school with an eye to someday directing the production of architectural works.

M:E — Carolyn Manning, Test Administrator

Test Administrators:
Carolyn Manning
Johnson O'Conner
Margaret D. Waterman

I have written so little that I am afraid you may be concerned about the success of the trip... I assure you that my experiences of the past weeks will be of incalculable value to me in determining the course of my career. It is not too much to say that the ideas which I have encountered in England, Czechoslovakia and

Author's letter to his parents, 1947.
Warsaw, Poland: author's photograph, 1947.

particularly Poland may form the basis from which to develope an entirely new approach to architecture and physical planning. You may infer (quite correctly) that I find myself in sympathy with leftist elements in all the aforementioned countries. I have acquired new confidence in necessity for an essentially social approach to any profession

Outhouse, North Haven, Maine: author's first built work, 1948.
Watercolor by author's father, Charles K. Cobb, circa 1960.

For

Joan

Sara, Emma, Pamela

Julia, Elizabeth, Elsie

HENRY N. COBB
WORDS & WORKS

1948 —— 2018

Scenes From a Life in Architecture

THE MONACELLI PRESS

Words: Conversations

Henry N. Cobb

Words: Lectures, Writings

Works

INDIA WHARF, BOSTON

Waterfront Apartments: Harvard Graduate School of Design Thesis Project, 1948–49

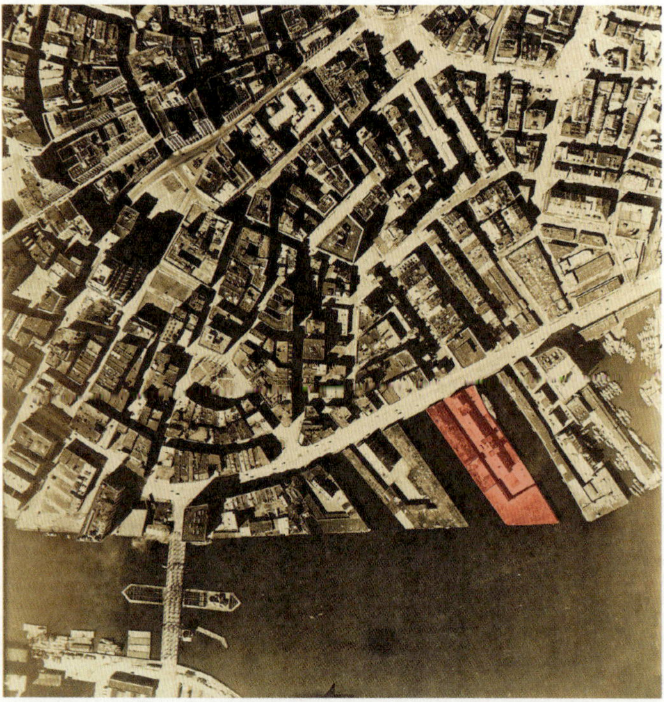

When, in the early fall of 1948, I was compelled after months of dilly-dallying to settle at last on a program and site for my thesis project at Harvard's Graduate School of Design, my thoughts naturally turned toward the Boston waterfront. There were two reasons for this, one stemming from caution and the other from ambition. I wanted my project to be located in a place that I knew well enough so that I could feel confident in making my mark there. This suggested someplace in or around my hometown. But I also wanted to be liberated from unwelcome constraints imposed by the preexisting fabric of a city that seemed to me full, self-satisfied, and deeply resistant to change. This drew me to the waterfront—a well-defined edge beyond which I would be free to explore the limitless possibilities of modern architecture. Furthermore, I saw the harbor, with its openness to sea and sky, as a habitat profoundly stirring to the imagination of an architect.

As it happened, there were few parts of Boston that I knew better than its waterfront. My father, a lifelong sailor and lover of all things nautical, had taken me often to shop for gear in the ship chandleries that once lined Atlantic Avenue and to walk the wharves from which, in my childhood, a substantial fishing fleet still went daily out to sea. Among the wharf buildings, Charles Bulfinch's India Wharf Stores, though by then reduced to a fraction of its original size, was still the noblest of all. When completed in 1807, this 425-foot-long, four-story structure had been the centerpiece of a bold speculative enterprise that swept away the old wooden docks, replacing them with the stone-faced piers and brick warehouses that enabled Boston merchants to welcome the burgeoning China trade. Less than three-quarters of a century later, India Wharf was itself sliced in half by Atlantic Avenue,

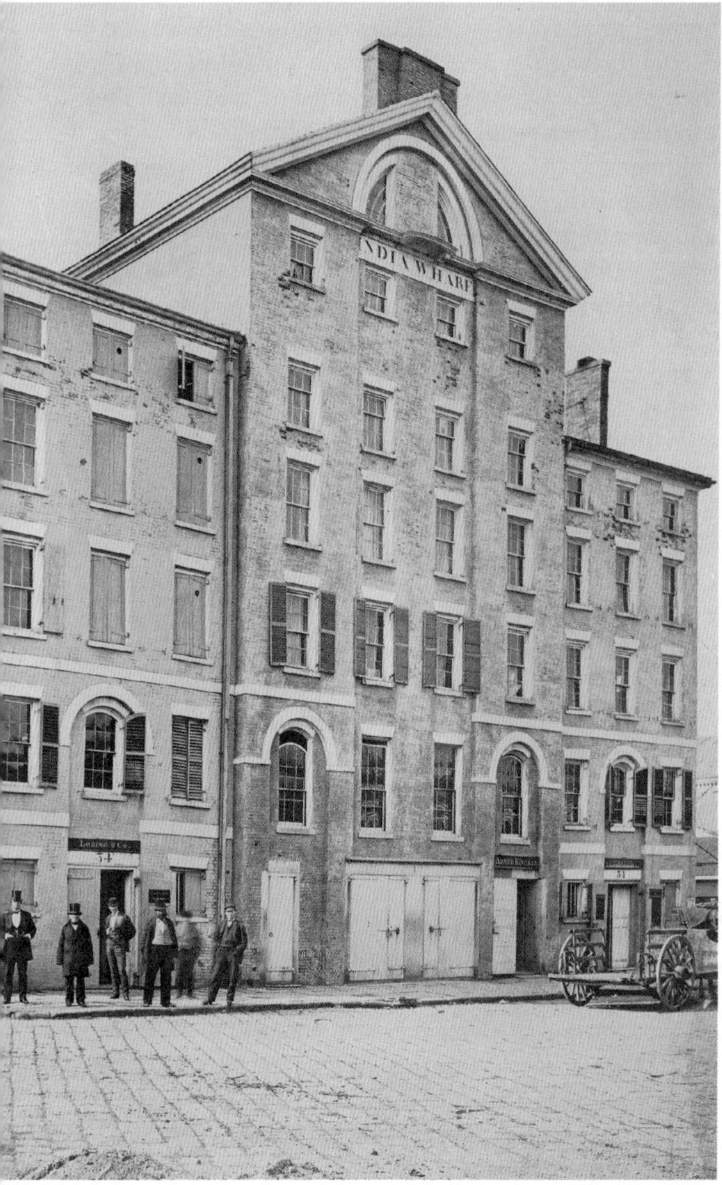
NDIA WHARF
LORING & CO.
54
31

built in response to the pressing need for a direct rail connection between depots at the north and south ends of the peninsula. By the time I appeared on the scene, the wharf had been rendered largely obsolete, and the remaining fragment of its warehouse was only sparsely occupied. I had more than once been led upstairs by my father to a modest fourth-floor room, lying just behind Bulfinch's stately eastern front, where the members of a small dining club met from time to time to enjoy good food, good wine, and each other's good company, while reminiscing nostalgically on the good old days when men went "down to the sea" in sailing ships.

Yet for my immediate purpose, this familiarity with a place and building so rich in history counted for almost nothing. In my preoccupation with the new, I saw India Wharf not as a place to be valued for the evocative residue of its history but merely as a site where, having imagined the removal of everything that had gone before, I would find a liberating tabula rasa on which to project my dream of the New Architecture.

To understand my frame of mind at that time, it is only necessary to recall that I am one of a very small number of architects still practicing—or even living, for that matter—who were trained under the teaching program established and led by Walter Gropius at Harvard from 1937 to 1952. I was the beneficiary or victim, depending on how you look at it, of an ideologically driven pedagogy that, through its mistreatment of history as much as through the methodology of its design studios, profoundly shaped the practice of architecture, especially in North America, during the decades immediately following World War II.

In characterizing the handling of history at Harvard under Gropius as "mistreatment," I do not mean to imply that the abuse of history in schools of architecture was at that time unprecedented or even unusual. As a matter of fact, throughout the three and a half centuries since formal professional training was first introduced in France, there has never been a time when history has not been in some way misused as an instrument for placing the practice of architecture in the service of a prevailing ideology. But unlike earlier pedagogies, which often privileged one historical period or style over others, the pedagogy of the modern movement, as practiced by Gropius, sought to protect the student from contamination by *all* of history. This erasure of the past was intended to clear the way for an entirely "New Architecture," liberated from the tyranny of dead styles, in which art, technology, and social purpose would be powerfully joined for the benefit of humanity. This attitude toward history is elegantly summed up in one of Franz Kafka's most memorable aphorisms. "The decisive moment of human development," he wrote, "is continually at hand. This is why those movements of revolutionary thought that declare everything preceding to be an irrelevance are correct—because as yet nothing has happened."[1]

The perfect architectural analogue to this aphorism—an analogue that cast a powerful spell on the imagination of my generation of students—was Le Corbusier's Plan Voisin of 1925. He proposed to eradicate the historic center of Paris, sparing only a few monuments, and replace it with an array of cruciform towers set in a vast green space. This tabula rasa approach to city building, which had a wide influence at mid-century, was reflected in an extraordinary proposal by one of my own professors at Harvard, Martin Wagner. In response to

1 Franz Kafka, *The Zürau Aphorisms*, trans. Michael Hoffman (New York: Schocken, 2006), 8.

a call for "the best planning ideas for renewing Boston," he suggested, in 1944, that the entire downtown be erased and replaced with a single building in the shape of a gigantic question mark, as if to ask, "Why bother to renew it when you can just as well remove it?" As a student I was wildly enthusiastic about Professor Wagner's proposal. It perfectly catered to my frustration and disgust with what I perceived to be the hopeless backwardness of my hometown. At the same time it nourished my generation's hubristic confidence that we could, we should, and we would remake the world.

My Harvard thesis project, while much more modest in scale, displayed an almost equal disregard for the historic fabric of Boston. Rather than work within that fabric, I chose to cast my proposal for urban housing as an aloof and autonomous cluster of towers rising out of the water, adjacent to but disengaged from the city itself. In the accompanying text, I wrote:

> The project is envisaged as part of an overall redevelopment scheme for a semi-blighted waterfront area. The site is ideally suited to apartment-type housing: located immediately adjacent to the business center, it is nonetheless well insulated from the hubbub of commercial traffic and offers a vantage point from which the city can be viewed in a clear perspective seldom glimpsed from the close disorder of the street. For here the sea, timeless and unencumbered, has penetrated deeply into man's temporal chaos, endowing the urban landscape with the dignity of distances and the reassurance of horizons. The wealth of visual "raw material" thus discovered is the basic element out of which this project attempts to fashion a fresh concept of urban living.

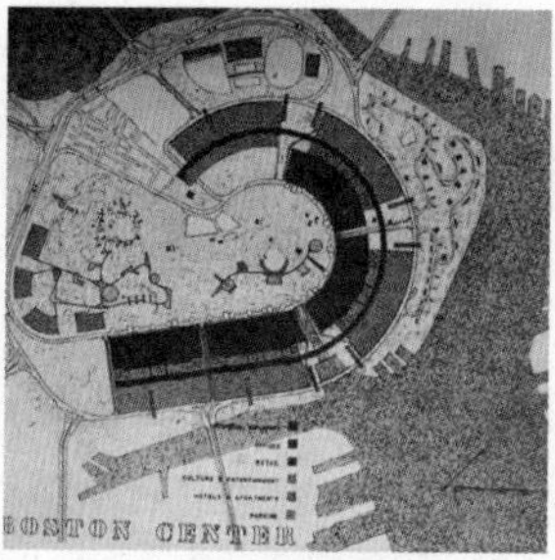

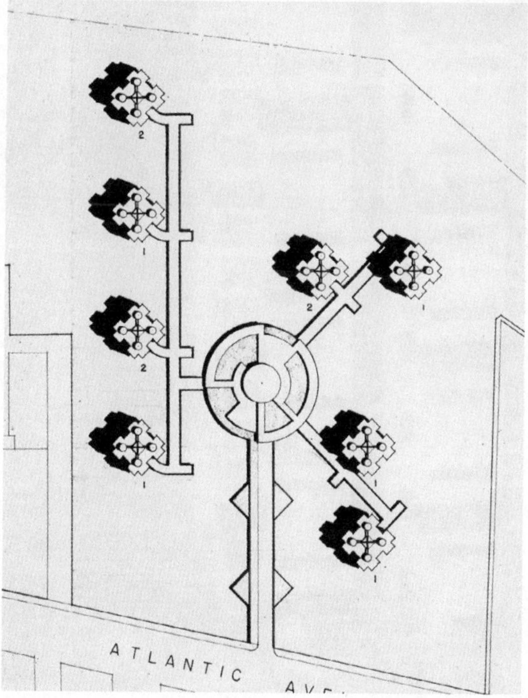

Top Left Martin Wagner, proposal for Boston, 1944. **Top Right** Le Corbusier, Plan Voisin, Paris, 1925. **Above** Site plan of waterfront apartments. **Pages 18–19** Charles Bulfinch, India Wharf Stores, 1804 (photograph circa 1862).

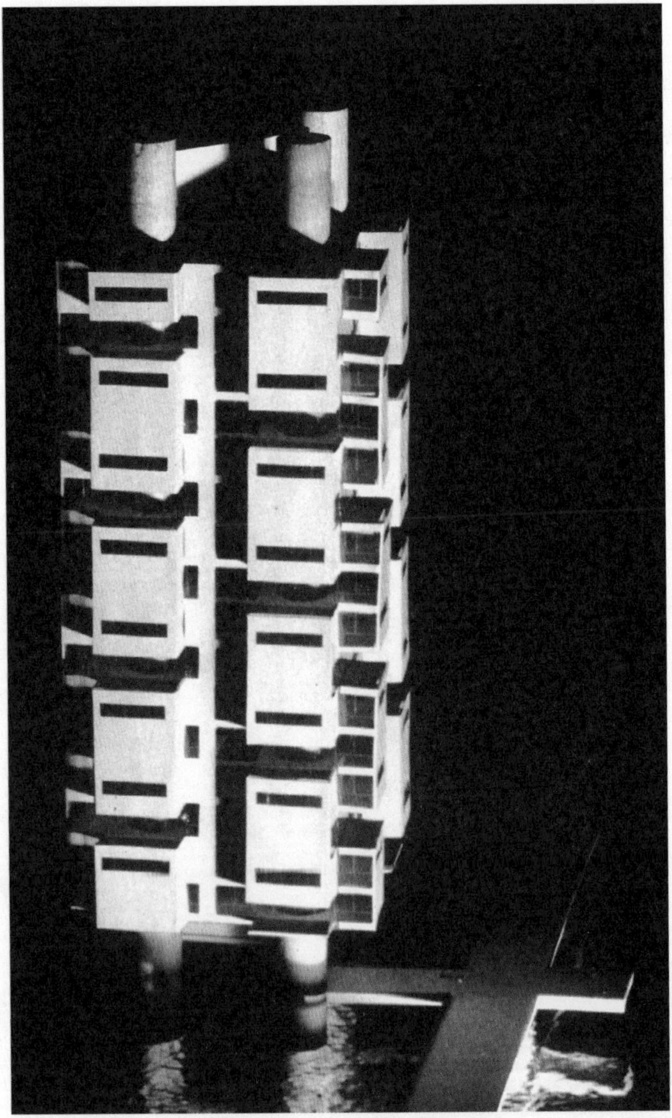

Above Model of typical apartment tower.

The narrative included phrases that I had encountered and underlined some years earlier in chapter 13 of *The Ambassadors*. The relevant passage reads, "The court was large and open, full of revelations, for our friend, of the habit of privacy, the peace of intervals, the dignity of distances and approaches." Evidently, my enthusiasm for the New Architecture had not entirely erased an innate susceptibility to the sensibility and style of Henry James; and that was perhaps a portent of things to come.

Aside from its naively utopian and socially problematic ambitions as urban design, my proposed cluster of eight apartment towers was first and foremost an effort to achieve a formal integration between structure and program, such that with the sole exception of the curtain wall enclosure, virtually nothing extraneous to the building's structure would be required to define and serve the living spaces within. As I further explained:

> The sixteen floors of each building are cantilevered from four reinforced-concrete "stems," which rise through the entire structure to a total height of 310 feet above bedrock. This system was developed directly from the necessity of giving sufficient stiffness to foundation piers, which could depend on very little lateral support for a distance of a hundred feet below water level. The resulting cylinder-shell achieved the desired rigidity with the greatest possible economy of material, and it was then only logical to allow the system to attain its maximum effectiveness by carrying it though the entire structure.... In every case the cylinder-shell serves as the major, and often as the only, interior partition, so that the sense of the structure is strongly felt in each unit; and in every case all utility spaces are concentrated within the stem.

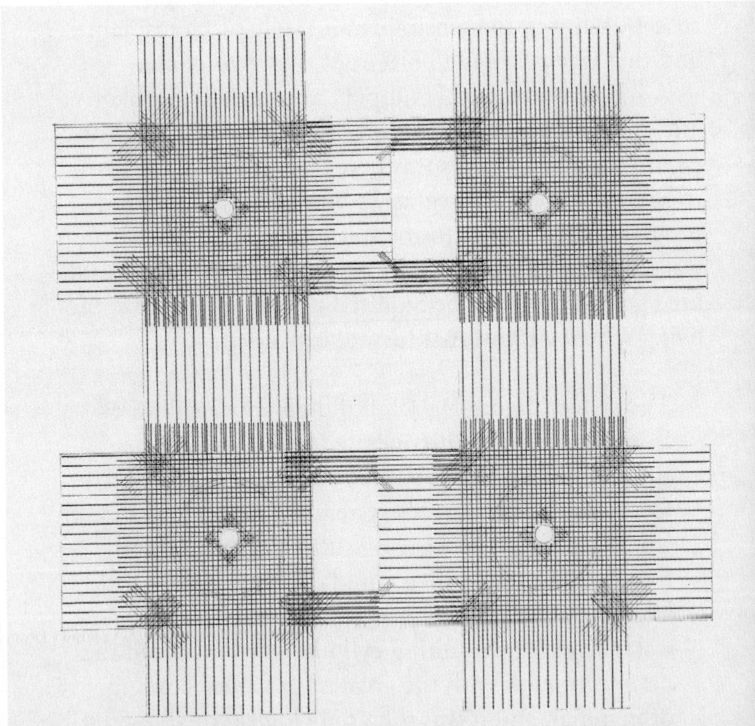

Above Plan of reinforcing steel.
Opposite Perspective sketch by Ulrich Franzen.

My enthusiasm for making architecture out of structure is perhaps most evident in the loving attention that I gave to the plan of reinforcing steel in the tower floors, just as my desire to escape the "close disorder of the street" is most vividly shown in the perspective sketch dashed off for me during the last hours of charrette by my good friend and fellow student Ulrich Franzen.

By the time I submitted this project in March of 1949, I had already convinced myself that Boston was hopelessly moribund—socially, economically, culturally, politically—and that nothing of interest to me was likely to happen there in my lifetime. So after a few months of employment at the office of Hugh Stubbins, I abandoned my hometown and hurried off to New York to join I. M. Pei in his then-fledgling practice under the auspices of the legendary developer William Zeckendorf, Sr. Ironically, the reward for my early infidelity was a series of challenges that brought me repeatedly back to Boston and obliged me to think deeply about my erstwhile hometown throughout much of the ensuing seven decades.

THE SCHOOL OF GROPIUS

Conversation with Paolo Conrad Bercah
New York City, February 1998

Hardly a day has gone by since the start of your practice when you have not had to solve problems related to the design of tall buildings. In fact, your involvement with these issues goes back to your days as a student at Harvard, where your thesis project consisted of a novel proposal for a group of apartment towers rising out of Boston Harbor. This early effort prefigures not only a major architectural preoccupation of your career, the tall building, but also a major urban one, Boston. What first attracted you to this sort of problem?

My choice of high-rise housing responded to something that was fairly explicit in the Gropius pedagogy, which is the idea that architecture should address social problems. Yet the project was very far removed from so-called social housing. The cluster of apartment towers was designed to serve a cultural and economic elite—sophisticated people who worked downtown and wanted to live downtown. So my thesis project in one way reflected and in another way took exception to the Gropius agenda.

In retrospect, I'd say that this choice was also my attempt to compensate for a void in the pedagogical program of the Graduate School of Design. The program was based on the idea that architecture was now liberated from the tyranny of dead styles, but beyond that simplistic polemic and an affirmation of the social responsibility of architects, it contained alarmingly little substance or coherence. Other than a poorly taught "basic design" course that was a pale reflection of its Bauhaus forebears, there was an absence of the kind of disciplined training that is the traditional precursor of achieving mastery in any field.

By the time I reached the thesis project, I knew that something was missing. I understood that I did not possess a nucleus of ideas or skills that could propel me into practice. What I did have—and it was the result of my interest in planning and social issues—was the sense that problems of aggregation were going to be significant for architecture. I was attracted not so much to an architecture of one beautiful object as to an architecture that comes from an interesting assemblage of many parts. I was eager to tackle large-scale problems, problems of aggregation and socially useful architecture. At the same time, I lacked the formal discipline that equips one to deal with those problems. This left me looking for a thesis subject containing an inherent discipline or imperative that would help me fill the void and get a leg up, so to speak.

In spite of its pedagogical weaknesses, did the GSD offer anything positive?

Oh, yes. From my perspective the most important thing it offered was the contact with my fellow students, among whom were some extraordinarily gifted people. This was just after the war, and many of them were four or five years older than I. They had returned from what was, to say the least, a maturing experience, and this made them for me in many ways more significant mentors than the professors. I was invigorated by being a part of a group of people I looked up to as my elders and betters, and from whom I learned a lot. I received much more interesting critiques from them than from the faculty—with the notable exception of I. M. Pei, the youngest and best of our design critics.

During my years at the GSD, Professor Gropius limited his teaching activity to his master class of fifteen students. So although he was the reason that we all came to Harvard, most of us had scarcely any contact with him. This was deeply disappointing. In fact, I was so offended by his absence from studio reviews that when I returned thirty years later as department chair, I vowed to attend at least part of every final review. And I did so throughout my five-year term.

Were any of the so-called masters of the modern movement particularly influential?

The strongest influence on students at that time came from those first-generation modernists who both built and published. Le Corbusier and Wright were the great architect-polemicists. After them came Mies, who didn't write much but conveyed through his built works a powerful ethic as much as an aesthetic. Among those three, the dominant figure for students was Le Corbusier; he embodied the full spectrum of modernist ambitions, from *l'art pour l'art* to social housing to the remaking of cities to reconstructing the whole world.

The "architecture or revolution" thing.

Yes: *I choose architecture.* Le Corbusier published, doing so in a very polemical fashion that joined theory and practice. At that time, the first three volumes of the *Oeuvre Complète* had appeared. What you see in his publications—and what is so engaging from the point of view of the student—is a powerful theoretical proposition joined to an equally powerful formal development of that proposition. The same could be said about Wright. But Wright was perceived to be resisting rather than embracing the zeitgeist, and indeed he was; he abhorred the European modernism that Gropius had brought. As a result, very few students at the GSD embraced Wright, and those who did never found fertile ground there.

I gather that Marcel Breuer was no longer a faculty member when you were a student.

No, by then he had had a falling out with Gropius and had stopped teaching. Breuer was a good teacher because he was a good architect, and I'm sure I would have benefited greatly from having him as a critic. But I absorbed him anyway, because he was the one acknowledged master whose buildings were close at hand. For me, his houses around Boston were absolute icons. At the time, I had never seen a Wright house or a Mies building. I had visited one Le Corbusier building, the Swiss Pavilion, and had been enchanted. The Swiss Pavilion was another icon for us at school, especially for me because it dealt with a problem of aggregation. But in terms of built works around Boston, Breuer's were by far the most admired. Students could visit the Chamberlain Cottage, that wonderful little house in Wayland, or his own house in Lincoln.

Above Marcel Breuer, Chamberlain Cottage, Wayland, Massachusetts, 1940.

In spite of your admiration for Breuer's houses, you were drawn to problems of aggregation.

Yes. I saw that when you put things together, there has to be a certain rationality in the way they're joined. It was a way, I suppose, of compensating for my lack of intuitive genius as a form maker. I also consoled myself with the notion that problems of aggregation were socially important. But I was also looking for a discipline, an imperative. I was attracted to the tall building because of the necessity it imposed to think about structure in a rational way. The tall building by its nature imposes a discipline you don't find when you aggregate things horizontally.

This was before Mies had completed any high-rise projects. It was before the Seagram Building, before the Lake Shore Drive Apartments.

True, but it was not before his designs for the Friedrichstrasse. I was very excited by his drawings of those two wonderful towers, but I didn't really understand them. Compared with the formal aspect, the systemic aspect of Mies's early tower projects, particularly the wiggly one, is relatively weak. It is an exercise in form, and I was not ready for that. I was not sufficiently gifted to play with form independent of some discipline. The major influence in my thesis project came, in fact, not from Mies or Le Corbusier but from Wright.

Above Mies van der Rohe, Friedrichstrasse Skyscraper proposal, Berlin, 1921.

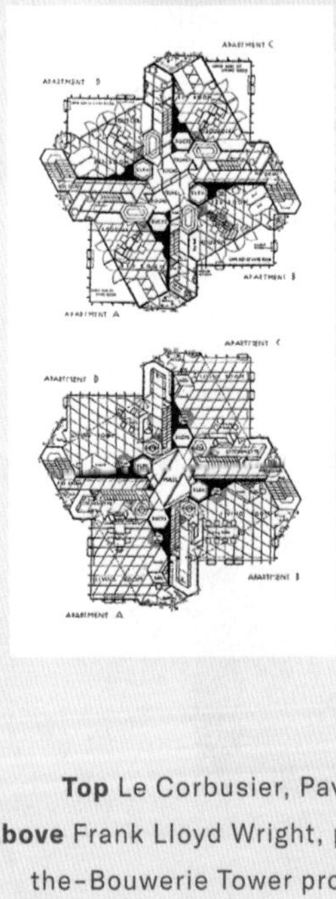

Top Le Corbusier, Pavillon Suisse, Paris, 1932.
Above Frank Lloyd Wright, plans and model, St. Mark's-in-the-Bouwerie Tower proposal, New York City, 1929.

Because of the St. Mark's-in-the-Bouwerie Tower?
That was the most obvious influence, and it was certainly the building that I looked at most while I was working on the thesis. But the idea of a cantilever, of the building as a tree, of part of a building carrying compression and part of it hanging, of the interlocking aspect—all those concepts that are so prevalent in Wright's work were influential. I had also been impressed by Le Corbusier's Unité d'Habitation in Marseilles, which had not yet been built but had been published as a project.

Your apartment towers seem suspended. They don't even touch the ground.
That reflects the influence of both Wright and Le Corbusier, but it also reflects an incipient sensibility of my own. I've always been attracted to what I call levitation, things that float. For example, the Swiss Pavilion, a building I enormously admired, demonstrated that buildings can transcend their condition of being locked to the ground, that they are capable of floating above the city. A decade later, I would find myself enchanted by Yona Friedman's Ville Spatiale. The appeal of levitation stemmed from the fact that it opened up new possibilities. As a strategy, it was totally unreflective and unironic. It was unburdened by history.

And the fact that you envisioned your project in Boston? How did that come about?
I wanted to be in the city yet not in the city, so I chose the Boston waterfront, which was decayed and no longer useful commercially. At the time there was already talk about what would happen to it. I'd been on India Wharf a number of times, and I'd spent a lot of time on the water. I think I intuitively understood that I needed

all the help I could get. I needed a place that I knew, a place that was exciting, and a site that was dramatic; and I needed a problem that would contain the seeds of a discipline out of which I could make an architecture. The choice of site was an effort to make the best of what was available to me.

Looking at a photograph of Boston in the late 1940s, one can see how revolutionary your proposal was. Apart from the Custom House tower and the new Suffolk County Courthouse, there were no tall buildings, so you did set some sort of precedent.
Yes, but I didn't think of it that way. You have to remember the mentality of the student: we were all trying to do something exceptional to launch our careers. I imagined that I was showing how Boston could be made more exciting, but it certainly was not part of a social program other than the idea that it would be nice to live downtown.

Did anybody remark upon that?
I vaguely remember that Gropius, who actually did attend my thesis review, was mildly critical of it as being housing for the rich. Nonetheless, it was seen as an interesting project. I never imagined that it could be built in Boston; I didn't think Boston would be hospitable to it. Despite the project being located in Boston, it was in a certain way anti-Boston. It's deliberately provocative.

How do you feel about the project now?
In their arrangement the towers make some acknowledgment of the site, but they remain completely self-referential. They are omnidirectional, and the site allows them to be that way. The architecture comes entirely out of the interpretation of the structural imperative and in that

sense is autonomous; it could be anywhere. While the location and the nature of the project certainly reflect my interest in aggregation and in reshaping the city, the tall building is seen here as the product of its internal logic. In this respect it has a kind of a purity; it's innocent. It is unburdened by any sense of history, any sense of irony, any sense of a relationship to the past or to the city next to which it stands. It's just an invention that is as self-referential as a building can be.

Unlike most of your subsequent tall buildings, your thesis project is a housing complex, not an office tower. Would you say those are two different types?
Definitely. I never would have done an office building for my school thesis. You choose problems that you think you can master in some way or another. At the time I knew nothing about office buildings. But I did know that an apartment had a kitchen, a bathroom, and so on. Beyond this, an apartment tower is presumably more socially useful and engaging. In any case, I certainly did not foresee that I would spend so much of my life designing office buildings!

But did you imagine that you would return to the site of your thesis twenty years later to design Harbor Towers?
I certainly did not, and if I could have foreseen how that project would play out, I would have done everything to avoid it. But let's not spoil this conversation by talking about a built work that is so much less interesting than my unbuilt thesis. Let's end on a positive note. My thesis was one of only a few student projects to be given a full page in the February 1950 issue of *L'Architecture d'Aujourd'hui*, which was devoted in its entirety to a celebration of "Gropius et Son École." So it turned out to be a better launch than I had dared to hope for.

383 MADISON AVENUE, NEW YORK CITY

Wine Cabinet for William Zeckendorf, Sr., 1951–52

The top floor of an unremarkable but well-located Manhattan office block was the birthplace of our practice, and the roof above was the site of its first built work. Here, in September 1948, I. M. Pei, at age thirty-one, took up his position as director of the newly created architectural research division of Webb & Knapp, Inc., a real estate development company headed by the brilliant and charismatic entrepreneur William Zeckendorf, Sr. For the previous two years, Pei had been teaching at Harvard, where I had had the good fortune to be his student and to become his friend. During his first months at Webb & Knapp, Pei had no staff, and when he needed help in documenting his first major project, the Helix Apartment Tower, he called on me to organize a group of students in Cambridge to make presentation drawings and a model. In the spring of 1950, after Zeckendorf commissioned Pei to design Webb & Knapp's new penthouse offices, I. M. invited me to join the small

Top William Zeckendorf's private dining pavilion, above Webb & Knapp penthouse, with author reclining on roof, 1952. **Above Left and Right** Wine cabinet, with doors closed and opened, installed in dining pavilion.

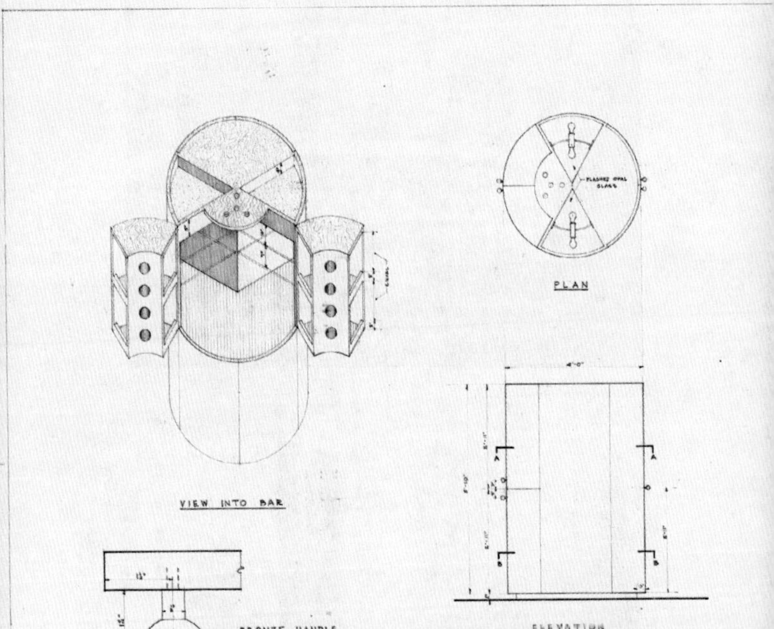
VIEW INTO BAR
PLAN
FLASHED OPAL GLASS
ELEVATION
4'-0"
BRONZE HANDLES
FULL SIZE

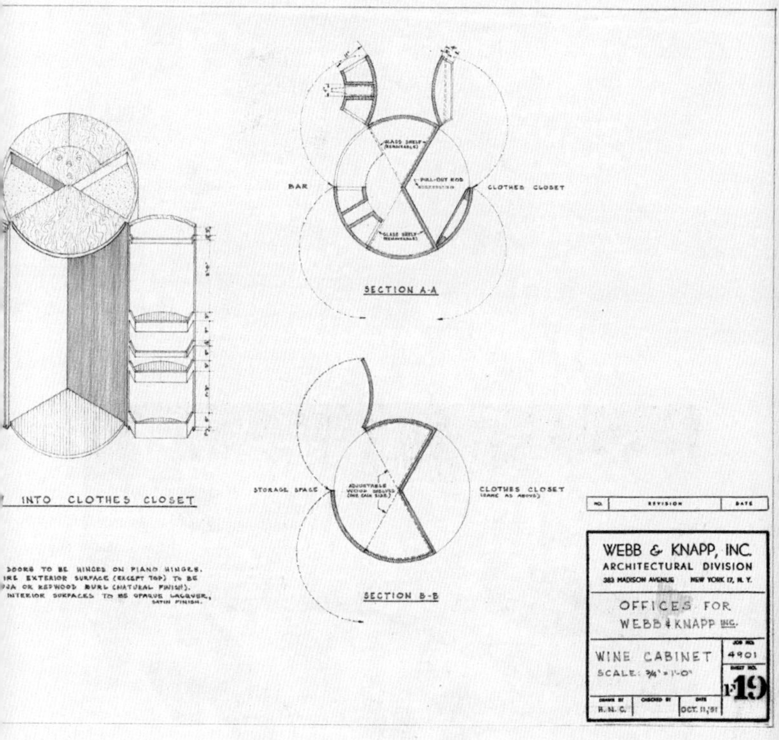

Above Wine cabinet plan, elevation, sections, and axonometric views. Drawing by author, 1951.

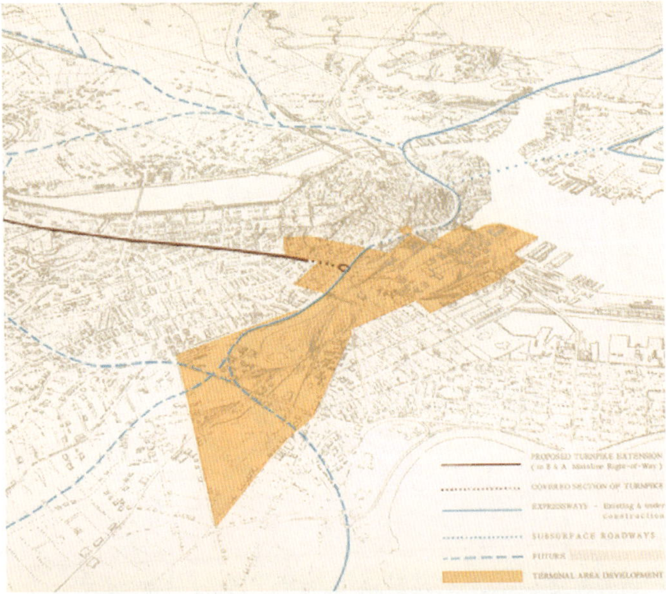

Top Terminal Area Development proposal, Boston, 1957.
Above Model, Century City proposal, Los Angeles, 1958.

staff, composed mostly of former Harvard students, that he was assembling for this purpose. My role in the project was modest, as befitted a recent graduate with little experience, but I was happy to be entrusted with the design of a cylindrical wine cabinet that would become the focal point of a semicircular private dining room hovering above the new penthouse and its surrounding roof garden.

William Zeckendorf, Sr., was a man of large and varied appetites, among which were a taste for fine wine on one end of the spectrum and for transformative urban development on the other. Throughout the ten years of our employment at Webb & Knapp, we had ample exposure to both of these happily coexisting if seemingly disparate aspects of his character. Hence, not long after I finished selecting thuja-burl flitches for the wine cabinet, I found myself planning a nine-hundred-acre mixed-use development in Boston, and a few years later a fifteen-hundred-foot-long apartment building for the property that would subsequently become Century City in Los Angeles. Although neither of these ambitious projects reached fruition, they bear witness to the important fact that 383 Madison Avenue was not just the site of our first built work; it was also the site of an intensive postgraduate education in the role of speculative enterprise as a catalyst in the ever-shifting interplay of competing interests that shape the city.

THE SCHOOL OF ZECKENDORF

Conversation with Paolo Conrad Bercah
New York City, February 1998

In 1950 you were invited to join the newly formed architectural division of the real estate firm of Webb & Knapp, headed by I. M. Pei and sponsored by the developer William Zeckendorf, Sr. At the time it was very unusual for an architect to be in the employ of a single developer. What drew you to that situation?

When I accepted the offer, the most attractive aspect of it was certainly the opportunity to work with I. M. Pei. He had been the best of my studio critics at Harvard, and because he taught second-year studio when I was in second year and third-year studio when I was in third year, I got to know him quite well. He became a mentor and a friend. It was clear, by the time he left Harvard in the summer of 1948 to come to New York, that we shared certain enthusiasms and aspirations. It was therefore natural that he should call on me to help him with the presentation of his Helix project, an apartment building that Zeckendorf hoped to build in Manhattan. At the time I was living in Boston and working for Hugh Stubbins, and I still had access to a network of GSD students who could be mobilized to help with models and drawings. Then, when it appeared that the architectural research division of Webb & Knapp might be called upon to do significant built work, it was natural for Pei to invite me to join him.

Behind the opportunity to work with Pei was the opportunity to work with Zeckendorf. I knew something about Zeckendorf's vision and imagination because the Helix had been not only sponsored but in a rather direct way provoked by him. He had made a sketch of a tree with branches, saying something to the effect of "I would like to make an apartment house like a tree." At that time, though, Zeckendorf was otherwise unknown to me except as someone who promised to offer what both Pei and I were interested in, namely, the opportunity to tackle large undertakings. But what those would be we did not know. Indeed, the specific occasion for my coming to New York, which was to work on the offices of Webb & Knapp, could hardly be categorized as a large undertaking; it was more like an interior remodeling with some minor new construction. It occupied us from the spring of 1950 to the beginning of 1952. During that period Pei was undoubtedly in conversation with Zeckendorf about bigger things, but the rest of us were entirely focused on designing everything from the ashtrays on up. There was talk of exciting projects in the future but nothing specific in sight.

After I had agreed to come to New York, I was invited to a dinner party for Pei and his group that Zeckendorf gave at his apartment on East Seventy-Second Street. I came down from Boston just for that dinner, and I remember it vividly. Zeckendorf made some kind of inspirational hortatory remarks reflecting his excitement at having his own architects. He had tapped into the youth, the energy, and perhaps even the prestige of having around him these young people, mostly from Harvard, headed by someone who was already being taken seriously as a very promising and accomplished designer.

How much power did he have at the time?

Zeckendorf never held a position that was in itself powerful. But he knew how to leverage power. He understood the mechanisms of power, and he had a remarkable capacity to manipulate those mechanisms in a way that enabled him to achieve things that those who did hold power would never have achieved, or even aspired to, by themselves.

The truth is—and this is something that I learned from watching Zeckendorf—power in itself is the enemy of architecture, and indeed the enemy of culture and civilization. Entrepreneurial initiative, which is a destabilizing force because it always wants to change something, is the essential fuel for architecture. This applies to all building types, not only commercial. If power is not put in motion by energy that is entrepreneurial in nature, there is unlikely to be an opportunity for architecture. Furthermore, while accumulation of power is not an essential precondition, manipulation of power is. An important aspect of the manipulation of power—something that, again, I began to learn from Zeckendorf and confirmed in my own experience of life—is what I would call indirect manipulation. This starts from an understanding that neither architects nor developers in themselves possess power.

In the sense that they are instruments?

Yes, but if they are merely instruments of power, the results are likely to be disastrous. Somehow they have to make power into the instrument for their enterprises, but often this can be accomplished only indirectly. The art in the manipulation of power resides in bringing competing powers into a relationship that creates destabilization, which allows something to happen in the cracks between power systems. In other words, while a direct appeal to any one power system is unlikely to produce an opportunity for innovation or advancement of the arts, the coexistence of competing power systems, neither one of which is in itself open to innovation, can by their mutual juxtaposition create opportunities.

My friends who were involved in socialist planning in England regarded with disapproval, if not horror, the idea that things would be made to happen through such a process rather than through the direct expression of the will of the people, transformed by means of bureaucratic planning into a prescribed outcome. But the problem with socialist planning is that it is profoundly anti-urban; it tends to suppress and suffocate the natural interaction of competing interests that make a city an exciting place to be.

So a certain degree of conflict is actually desirable?
Yes. What makes cities alive is the perpetual interplay of competing interests. Without that interplay, cities would be very boring places.

Yet it also makes the architect's job more complicated.
It does. But the essential lesson I learned from Zeckendorf is that while architects (and, for that matter, developers) never will have the direct capacity to exercise power, they do have the capacity to find openings created by the juxtaposition of competing interests to add something that could never be made through a frontal attack on any one system of power.

This is a highly pragmatic view, to say the least. But Zeckendorf must have been very idealistic as well.
Yes, although his idealism was of a kind that would not have been acknowledged by my socialist friends. They regarded him as somebody who was simply thinking of how to make money. But for Zeckendorf, money was never the end; it was simply the means.

How did other architects feel about your association with Zeckendorf?

They were appalled. At that time it was still a violation of professional ethics to practice architecture as an employee of a developer, and the AIA was very unhappy about it. It was not a "good" thing to do, especially for people with the kind of aspirations we had. People said we were thumbing our noses at the profession, and indeed we were.

What was Zeckendorf like as a person?

He had an oversized ego, as you would expect, but also great charisma and charm, accompanied by a chameleon quality: he could change his personality in a second—very useful when negotiating a business deal. And he carried himself in an extraordinary way. When he entered or moved across a room, he seemed to precede himself, with the result that his every step constituted a sort of one-man procession. This impression was enhanced by the fact that despite his portliness, he was exceptionally graceful in his movements. I have always thought that if Fellini had made a film for which he needed a pope—Leo X, for example—he would surely have tried to cast William Zeckendorf in the part.

CANADIAN NATIONAL RAILWAYS CENTRAL STATION, MONTREAL

Place Ville Marie, 1955–62
with Vincent Ponte (planning), Pershing Wong

William Zeckendorf's largest fully realized urban development project, and coincidentally the first major built work for which I assumed principal responsibility as an architect, was a four-million-square-foot, mixed-use building complex rising above the railroad tracks that had, for almost half a century, occupied a seven-acre pit fifty feet below the surrounding streets in the heart of Montreal. In his autobiography, Zeckendorf later recalled a key episode in the evolution of this characteristically—some would say recklessly—bold speculative enterprise.

> By late winter and early spring of 1956, Cobb was ready with preliminary plans for Montreal. He and Vincent Ponte, our city planner, as well as some *Look* magazine people who were doing a story on Webb & Knapp, flew up to Montreal with me in our DC-3. Circling the city at a few thousand feet, I looked over the site while studying Cobb's designs. Because we were concerned about the conservative atmosphere that pervaded Montreal, Cobb had prepared a step-by-step design.

Above Cruciform tower at Place Ville Marie, viewed from Rue Victoria.

Above Author presenting an early scheme for Place Ville Marie to William Zeckendorf, Sr., in June 1956, aboard the latter's DC-3. Vincent Ponte is at right.

On an elevated platform plaza over the "hole," he set two rectangular towers plus a number of lower, subsidiary buildings. In this way, only after the first tower was successful would we need to put money down for the second structure. It was a competent and a pleasant design, but as I stood up in the steeply banked airplane, and looked out of the windows to the winter-gripped city below, I was dissatisfied. Something was missing. Here lay this unexploited but potentially fabulous site which only we could develop, but what we proposed to develop lacked power. As I began to sense what was missing, I said, "Harry, I want to tell you something...you don't make 'melly' out of a blue white diamond." The minute I explained that "melly" are merely the bits and chips left over when a great diamond has been cut, he saw what I meant. He, too, recognized that we needed something with enough critical mass to force changes on Montreal. By critical mass I mean not only the physical but also the emotional and the aesthetic impact of a truly successful building complex. We then and there set out the final specifications, within which Cobb was free to design as his genius dictated. I told him we wanted a major building of at least 1.5 million square feet total area, with at least 35,000 square feet per floor. It must be designed to provide corporate identity for more than one major tenant. Given these directions, Cobb went off to produce the plans of the great cruciform building that now so powerfully dominates downtown Montreal. This was the design that I took to Gordon. What we determined on that airplane was the most crucial decision of the whole Montreal project.[1]

1 William Zeckendorf, *Zeckendorf* (New York: Holt, Rinehart and Winston, 1970), 170–71.

When completed in 1962, the Royal Bank of Canada tower was the largest and tallest office building in Canada. Aside from its clearly derivative and oddly hybrid character—a body by Le Corbusier decked out in Miesian drag—two qualities of this early work deserve mention: first, that it adheres strictly to the modernist conception of the tall building as a resolutely autonomous, self-referential organism shaped entirely by its own internal needs and systems; and second, that the huge urban building project of which it is the centerpiece was very much the kind of opportunity that I had left Boston in search of—that is to say, a building project of a scale that invited radical reordering of the spatial, volumetric, and circulatory systems of the city.

It was gratifying to the ego of a young architect to have his very first building appear on a postage stamp together with the cathedral of Montreal. But in truth the aspect of this tower that I consider most worthy of note is not the way it meets the sky but the way it meets the ground: a levitational inversion of solid and void that prefigures my lifelong preoccupation with the question of how towers can be made to shape rather than merely preempt the space of the city.

The February 1963 issue of the *Royal Architectural Institute of Canada Journal*, devoted in its entirety to a presentation and critical appraisal of Place Ville Marie, contained an essay entitled "Some Notes on the Design of Place Ville Marie," in which I set forth my views at the time.

> When we look at Place Ville Marie as a vacant site, denuded of buildings, one fact above all others instantly compels our attention. It is the remarkable polarity that exists between the vast pit on Dorchester Boulevard and the imposing profile of Mount Royal.

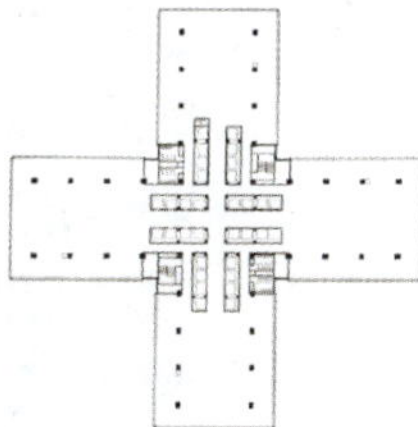

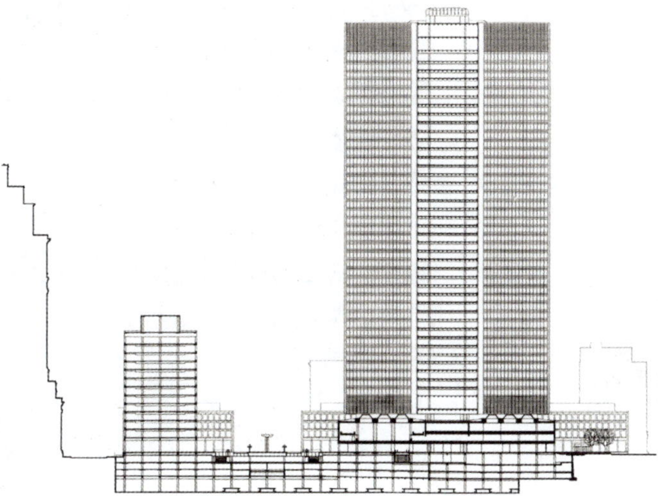

Top Postage stamps featuring cruciform tower and Notre-Dame Basilica, 1976. **Above** Plan and section of cruciform tower. **Overleaf** Tower entry framed by bank quadrants.

1956

1962

For the visual drama and emotive force of this relationship are deeply stirring. The marvelous vista from boulevard to mountain casts a spell that virtually eclipses the clamorous disarray of the immediate surroundings. We feel ourselves momentarily in the presence of a larger, more coherent urban order; the distinctive form of the city becomes articulate here; and the gaping hole, almost in spite of itself, communicates a powerful sense of place.

It is impossible to overstate the significance to Place Ville Marie of this single attribute of our site—its apposite and compelling relationship to the principal topographic feature of Montreal. Clearly, we are dealing here not with an isolated enclave but with a zone of maximum exposure, an intrinsically public place, whose active participation in the mainstream of civic life is irrevocably preordained. This all-important fact has preoccupied our consciousness from first to last, and lies at the root of the design in all its aspects.

The Plaza: By virtue of its situation, our plaza is more than the forecourt to a monumental building and the spatial focus of a private precinct. It is a major protagonist in the dramatic confrontation of city and mountain, and its surface is the principal medium through which Place Ville Marie responds to its environment.

It is fundamental to our conception of the plaza that it should be a plane of strength—a firm "ground"—and that it should limit rather than be limited by the buildings that rise from its surface. We have therefore allowed the plane of the plaza to extend on all sides to the outermost boundaries of the site, so that there is no point on the periphery at which its presence is not clearly felt. On the plaza surface, we have introduced changes of level only at those points where particular concentrations of activity and circulation make them meaningful. Actual incisions in the surface occur only at the most important points of pedestrian access and around the focal center of the site, where they have been handled in such a way as to reaffirm the significance of the surface area that lies between them.

The Office Tower: Out of respect for the intrinsic civic qualities of our site, we were concerned from the beginning that this huge building should serve as well as be served by the space in which it stands. We therefore sought to distribute the building volume in such a way that it would participate actively in the space rather than simply overwhelm it. The four projecting wings of very slender proportion do, I believe, achieve this end; and they have the collateral effect of reducing the apparent bulk of the building as seen from any point in the immediate vicinity. As many Montrealers have observed, however, this does not always hold true for distant views; when sun and shadow are absent, the arms of the cross lose their definition, and the building does indeed loom large on the skyline.

The most difficult of the many architectural problems raised by the cruciform plan was that of achieving a satisfactory resolution of the tower at its base. In order to make the cross shape articulate, it was essential that the base of the building be largely transparent and that the plaza surface be seen to flow through beneath it. In our original solution of 1957, the metal-and-glass volume of the cruciform tower was brought to rest on a massive concrete podium in the shape of a cross, within which were contained the four ground-floor lobbies. The purpose of this podium

Top View from tower of midday performance in plaza. **Above** Tower as seen from plaza, with stairway to shopping promenade in foreground.

1957

1958

was to concentrate the "action" of the building in a sculptural element totally apprehensible at plaza level and in this way to achieve a marriage between the building and the plaza. It was not a completely satisfactory solution, and its weaknesses became ever more apparent as we developed the design in detail.

Fortunately, the entrance of the Royal Bank into the project in spring 1958 provided us with the architectural means to resolve this problem. Many people at that time felt that the integrity of the original plan had been seriously compromised by the introduction of the four bank "quadrants," which play so prominent a role in the executed building. There is no doubt that these monumental blocks interposed between the cruciform tower and the plaza wrought a significant change in the character of both. Nor is there the shadow of a doubt in my mind that both gained immeasurably thereby.

In the half-century that has passed since I offered that judgment, it has been amply confirmed by the test of time.

Opposite Top and Bottom Presentation models of Place Ville Marie. **Overleaf** Lobby of cruciform tower.

TRANSFIGURATION

Conversation with Paolo Conrad Bercah
New York City, February 1998

You have often said that the way a tall building meets the ground is at least as important as the way it meets the sky. Why is that?

The way it meets the sky can be wonderful, but that's something you see only at a distance. You appreciate it as a lively profile, or in the way it glitters, but you are not engaged with a building from afar the way you are engaged with it up close where it meets the ground, where it necessarily declares its relationship with the public realm—a relationship that is either closed or open, engaging or alienating.

The first office tower you designed, the Royal Bank of Canada building at Place Ville Marie, in Montreal, was particularly focused on that relationship.

Yes. In fact, the only original contribution that the Royal Bank building makes to the art of architecture is in the way that it meets the ground. In almost every other respect it is derivative from two well-known sources. The form comes out of the polemic of Le Corbusier and those great cruciform constructs at the Ville Radieuse, and the curtain wall is an interpretation of Miesian ideas about cladding. As a work of architecture, the cruciform tower has a strong but not especially innovative voice. Where it does become innovative is where the tower stops, fifty feet above the ground, and a transfiguration takes place. Imagine a three-hundred-foot square within which there is a cross, each arm eighty feet wide, occupying the center of each side. Now, when that cross comes near the ground, the figure is reversed, transfigured. The cross becomes a void, and the remaining parts of the square become solid.

Why is that transfiguration important?

For two reasons. First, the figural space below displaces the figural volume above, so you feel that the purpose of the tower is not to celebrate itself but to celebrate the space beneath it. And second, the soffit of the tower seems to float above that space; it gives the building a levitational quality. The sense of space created by this act of levitation is enhanced by the fact that the stone blocks that define the square at the base also appear to be floating, unrooted. These effects civilize the building, they make it a good citizen at street level. The transfiguration renders the building permeable and inviting. It gives it a monumental scale that is relevant to the person in the street, whereas the scale of the tower is irrelevant to the person in the street.

The lobby of the Royal Bank building is on a much grander scale than any other you have designed. It recalls the lobbies of certain pre-war office

buildings in New York City, which house an array of activities and enterprises once relegated to the street. The lobby of the Daily News Building, for instance—with its big globe, its café, its newsstand, and so on—is like this; it practically becomes a lobby for the whole of Forty-Second Street.

A significant problem common to all tall office buildings, when considered as citizens, is that the street-level lobby is the only space in such buildings that can pretend to be accessible to the public. To the extent that an office building contributes to public space and public life, that contribution is made largely on the ground floor, or at most by the ground floor in combination with the levels immediately above and below. My preoccupation with the shaping of the ground floor—specifically with the transfiguration of the cross from figural object to figural void—is very much part of my desire to make the most of the civilizing potential of the lower portion of the building.

In any case, you are correct in seeing the articulation of the Royal Bank lobby as probably the most forceful expression of publicness that I have been able to achieve in a tall building. The articulation of the lobby spaces does more than represent the institutional significance of the bank at ground level; it declares the bank's status as a public building—a public building above which floats an enormous, relatively inaccessible private building. At street level, the building at the base is seen as experientially more important than the tower, and because that base is public, it declares that the public realm below is more important than private office space above.

The issue of posture and of the relationship of a tall building to the urban space in which it stands is a profound one. The best and most valuable buildings in a city have the same qualities that important and valuable human beings have: a strong sense of their own identity and at the same time a strong communicative capacity—a will and a capacity to participate in a larger discourse outside themselves. That's why it's appropriate and indeed necessary, in my view, to speak of the skyscraper as citizen.

Above Royal Bank of Canada lobby in cruciform tower, Place Ville Marie.

SHAWMUT PENINSULA, BOSTON

Urban Renewal

My collaboration with I. M. Pei in envisioning Boston's four-hundred-acre Downtown North General Neighborhood Renewal Plan, with the fifty-acre Government Center at its core, brought me as close as I would ever come to fulfilling the hubristic assertion of my youth that we could, we should, and we would remake the world. This is ironic, inasmuch as I had left Boston only a decade earlier precisely because I believed that nothing of interest would happen there in my lifetime. But I had not anticipated the transformations that would soon be wrought by a few skillful politicians and bureaucrats who understood how to make the most of opportunities afforded by the Housing Act of 1949, the federal legislation that authorized and funded urban renewal programs in cities across the country. In January 1961 the newly elected mayor, John Collins, brought Edward J. Logue to head the Boston Redevelopment Authority (BRA), and Logue, who was in a hurry and had no staff of his own at that time, engaged our firm to assist him in jump-starting his ambitious renewal program. The centerpiece of his strategy was a plan to concentrate new facilities serving all three levels of government—city, state, and federal—in a Government Center that would rise on land cleared of what were then deemed "obsolete" buildings and "undesirable" activities in and around Scollay Square.

Two and a half years later, in June 1963, at the behest of Logue, I appeared before the Boston City Council to describe the main features of the **Government Center Urban Renewal Plan** (1961–63, with I. M. Pei). The following excerpts from my testimony on that occasion convey a sense of the thinking that lay behind our plan.

> You will observe that the Government Center plan is organized around a greatly simplified street network.

No less than twenty-two streets within the project area have been vacated and replaced by three major and three minor arteries, exclusive of the boundary streets, which have been widened or realigned.... But traffic is not the only reason for unscrambling the maze of streets that formerly crisscrossed this area. Equally important is the need to create development sites of sufficient size and properly proportioned to meet the requirements of the several governmental agencies that wish to build here, and also to create private development sites that will be attractive to prospective investors for the uses proposed.

A second general characteristic of our plan is that in the configuration of building forms and open spaces, it reflects the peculiar topography of Boston and responds positively to the presence of a number of historic sites and buildings in the immediate environs. Thus the major building groups are distributed radially about the base of Beacon Hill, with the new State Service Center occupying a site on the western flank of the project area, the Federal Office Building in the center following approximately the alignment of existing Hanover Street, and City Hall close to the southern boundary of the project, intimately linked to the downtown business center and occupying a dominant position overlooking Government Center Plaza.

City Hall is in every sense the keystone of our plan. This is as it should be, for among all the public buildings, it is uniquely the seat of local government and ought, in all its aspects, to embody the highest aspirations of the people it serves. It is for this reason that we have selected for City Hall the one site in our plan that may be termed truly pivotal. That is to say, it does not front in one direction only but dominates

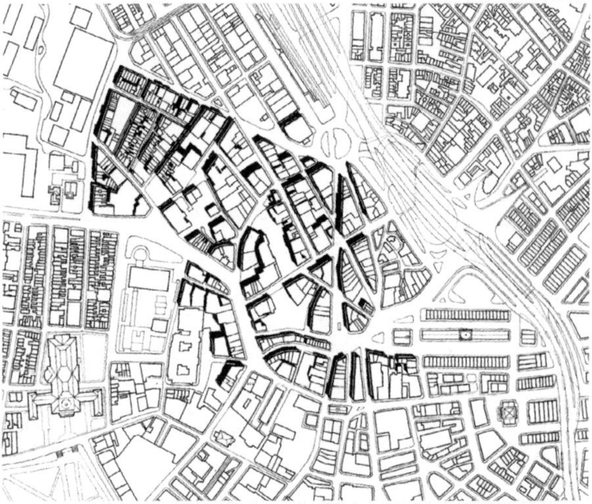

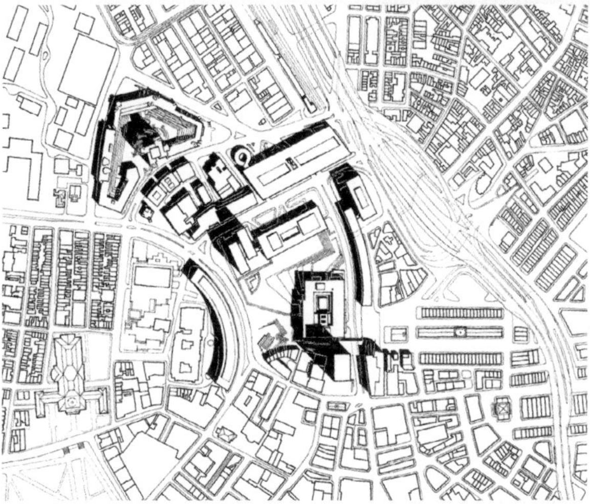

Top Plan of downtown Boston in 1960, showing properties embraced by Government Center plan. **Above** Government Center Urban Renewal Plan, 1963.

the urban scene on all sides, drawing together into one composition all the elements of its surroundings—those representative of the old Boston, the historic sites and buildings dating from the seventeenth and eighteenth and nineteenth centuries, and those also of the new Boston, the massive governmental facilities and large-scale buildings for private enterprise that are characteristic of our time.

In urban design terms, this marriage of old and new in such a way as to reinforce the strength of each has been the crux of our problem, and we have, from the beginning, conceived of City Hall as the one element capable of creating by its presence a viable link between the existing historic and commercial center and the new growth to the north. It is indeed gratifying to find that the winners of the City Hall competition have not only recognized this intent but have brilliantly exploited its full potential in architectural terms, thereby creating a building that we believe will be a source of pride to Bostonians for generations to come.

The council chamber of the new City Hall will look out over Government Center Plaza, which is the major public open space to be created by the plan. This broad paved surface with the City Hall as a centerpiece has been conceived literally and symbolically as a civic gathering point at the heart of the Boston peninsula. As you can see, the plaza is easily accessible from all directions of approach, but it is most fully exposed to the west, where Cambridge and Tremont Streets converge in a sweeping arc at the base of Beacon Hill. This dramatic curvature will be further reinforced by the structure proposed for one of the most important private development parcels—a 600,000-square-foot office building that will occupy

Top Downtown Boston after demolition of buildings in Scollay Square and surrounding area, 1964. **Above** Government Center in 1975.

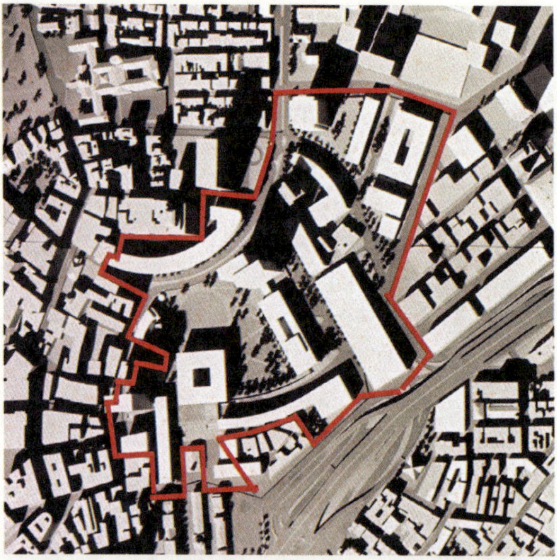

Top Model of downtown Boston, with proposed Government Center outlined in red. **Above** View of model from Boston Harbor, with proposed Downtown North GNRP waterfront development in foreground.

> the entire site fronting on the plaza below Pemberton Square. Incidentally, the ground floor of this and a number of other buildings within the Government Center will be arcaded and lined with shops at street level, so that there will be a continuity of pedestrian-oriented activity running throughout the project area. This feature illustrates one of the most important principles of the plan: that the Government Center should not stand apart as an isolated enclave of public buildings but should instead participate actively in that mixture of life that is the essence of Downtown.

During the half-century that has passed since I addressed the city council, it has become clear in retrospect that the four interdependent features of the Government Center plan that made it politically and economically viable were precisely those that have made its realization in built form so problematic. These were: (1) the substitution of a few streets where there had been many, in order to (2) create a small number of very large building sites, so as to (3) attract government agencies (federal, state, city) to build massive new facilities, and thus to (4) justify the removal of "derelict" buildings in the project area.

Owing principally to Logue's brilliant success in implementing this strategy, Government Center Plaza remains today a space that is overscaled, underpopulated, coldly institutional, and obdurately resistant to the many efforts that have been made to bring it to life. In light of this outcome, it is worth noting that our original Urban Renewal Plan of 1961 envisioned this central open space not as the elaborate paved plaza ultimately built but as a quiet lawn that, had it been realized, would at least have had the virtue of not promising so much more than it could deliver. It is therefore interesting that current efforts to refurbish the plaza are focused on transforming it into a more park-like environment.

Our involvement in the planning of Government Center and the accompanying **Downtown North General Neighborhood Renewal Plan** (1961, with I. M. Pei) drew me inexorably back to Boston and later brought us the commission to design **Harbor Towers** (1964–72) on India Wharf—the site of my Harvard thesis project—where our developer client had already, with BRA permission, created a tabula rasa by demolishing the Bulfinch building. In its pinwheel grouping of three cast-in-place reinforced concrete towers around an arrivals court, Harbor Towers emulated I. M. Pei's earlier Society Hill Towers in Philadelphia and James Ingo Freed's Silver Towers at New York University. As executed, however, the towers in Boston lack both the formal refinement and the material quality of their predecessors. Most devastatingly, the third tower, so essential to the spatial integrity and urbanistic identity of the project, was left unbuilt. A combination of unfavorable circumstances—an unsympathetic client, an unmotivated builder, and weakened BRA leadership after Logue's retirement in 1967—explain but do not alleviate my disappointment in the fate that befell the site on which Bulfinch's great building once stood. Harbor Towers, perhaps more poignantly even than Government Center, brings painfully to mind a remark that my father made to me one day toward the end of his life: "Harry," he said, "you've taken away my Boston."

Top Left and Right Harbor Towers as designed, 1964, and as built, 1972. **Above** From left: author, Ervin Galantay, Richard Beatty, Vincent Ponte, and I. M. Pei touring Boston Harbor, February 1961.

STATE UNIVERSITY OF NEW YORK AT FREDONIA

Academic Center, 1962–69
with Theodore J. Musho, Dan Kiley (landscape)

In the early 1960s, responding to pressures generated by the postwar baby boom, New York launched a vast expansion of its state university system. Governor Nelson Rockefeller, who had a well-developed edifice complex, created a special agency—the State University Construction Fund—to finance and manage the building of new facilities that, by 1970, would accommodate 350,000 students in a university whose student body ten years earlier had numbered less than 100,000. While fifteen major campuses were created de novo in this program, a good deal of the growth was absorbed through expansion of forty-seven preexisting colleges. Our firm was asked to assume responsibility for one of the smallest and most remote of these, the college at Fredonia. It was programmed to grow from a student body of 1,800 in 1963 to one of 5,200 in 1970.

When we first visited this out-of-the-way place, we found the college housed in a group of thoroughly undistinguished buildings set down with only the most militaristically elementary sense of order onto a flat and featureless rural landscape. In the development plan that we proposed and largely carried out over a six-year period, we chose, as a matter of principle, not to turn our backs on these banalities. Instead we attempted, through the interposition of two primary ordering devices, to create a functionally and visually coherent community of new and existing buildings.

The first of these devices is a circular road, 2,200 feet in diameter and a mile in length, that connects the two ends of the central campus while providing access to outlying residential, athletic, and service facilities. Defined by a double row of poplars along its entire circumference, this road embraces the landscape and asserts the presence of the college at a scale commensurate with its new dimensions.

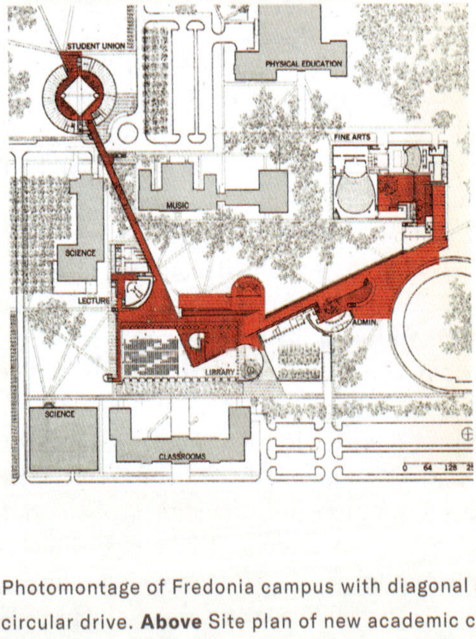

Top Photomontage of Fredonia campus with diagonal spine and circular drive. **Above** Site plan of new academic center. **Overleaf** Administration building, amphitheater, and library.

The second ordering device, interacting with the first, is a diagonally articulated spine defining the main path of pedestrian movement into and through the academic center of the college. We conceived this spine not as a separate, isolated structure but as a continuously modulated element, half-building and half-landscape, integrating and energizing—in a formal as much as a circulatory sense—the programmatically discrete components of the central campus. The design of each of these components is intimately affected by its interaction with the spine. Each bears a contingent relationship to the spine, while the spine itself, however modified by its conjunction with those components, remains by and large the autonomous directive element of the scheme.

Within this building group, there are, however, significant differences in the degree and kind of contingency that they display, and these are carefully calculated to indicate an internal hierarchy of value, to convey a social meaning. The administration building, for example, though its height gives it prominence in announcing the point of entry to the campus, has been positioned and shaped in such a way that it cannot possibly be read as the center of college life, nor as its most significant entity. This is a radically contingent building, with a form that would be incomprehensible if taken in isolation from the circulatory system to which it is attached and the larger community of which it is a part.

The library, on the other hand, appears by virtue of its central position and undisturbed rectangular shape to be almost independent of the spine. Yet when we look beneath its roof, we see immediately that the convergence of the two diagonal paths becomes a major intervention shaping the space and structure of the reading room below. Externally, the library is perceived as the generative

Top Entrance to library. **Above** Administration building and library. **Overleaf** Library and lecture hall, with sculpture by Robert Murray.

center, the virtually autonomous heart of the campus. Internally, the centrality is reaffirmed, but the building's autonomy is forcefully challenged by the invasive diagonals, upon which the character of the internal space is ultimately contingent.

A distinguishing feature of this project is its materiality. This is an architecture composed entirely of one material—cast-in-place reinforced concrete—formed in such a way as to be brought to life by light, a phenomenon for which Louis Kahn coined the poetic phrase "spent light." It is obvious from George Cserna's splendid black-and-white photographs that I was particularly engaged by the capacity of light to define curved surfaces, as well as by the potential for visual drama that is inherent in both the interplay of solids and the juxtaposition of solid with void in a monolithic architecture. These were the means by which we sought to create a perceptible order in this greatly expanded academic center—a distinction of parts within the whole that might animate and give experiential meaning to the rhythm of its life. In our solution, we strove to overcome the institutionally mandated isolation of the several buildings and to engender among them a palpable sense of interdependence and interaction, yet without suppressing the individual identities of their separate roles.

GESTURE

Conversation with Paolo Conrad Bercah
New York City, February 1998

Your second tall building was part of a university campus you planned for Fredonia, New York. This project was a radical departure from your experience in Montreal.

It would be difficult to find two projects more different from each other. Place Ville Marie is a very large commercial complex at the center of a great city; the campus at Fredonia is one of the smallest, most remote, and most rural campuses in the State University of New York system. Transcending these programmatic and contextual differences, though, is an even more significant difference in the language of architecture. Place Ville Marie accepts without question the idea of the orthogonal grid as the pervasive and unchallenged discipline for its architecture. In contrast, the campus at Fredonia transcends the discipline of the orthogonal grid by espousing the more dynamic geometry of its diagonal.

This dramatic shift in sensibility is independent of all the other differences between these projects. You cannot ascribe it to the fact that one project is rural, the other urban; or that one is a campus, the other a commercial project. The shift in the language of architecture reflects my own and my colleagues' efforts to find ourselves as architects and pursue a more adventurous path, or at least a path that questioned the Miesian ethic of formal restraint and strictly orthogonal order that had governed our earlier work. Fredonia perhaps also embodies a subconscious attempt on my part to achieve an identity independent of I. M. Pei's, to make my work distinctive within the work of the firm. The sensibility exposed in Fredonia is distinctly not the sensibility of Pei.

Can you say more about the differences between the projects in Fredonia and Montreal?

They're particularly evident in the one element of Fredonia in which the z-axis predominates, the administration building. It has only nine floors, so it would not qualify as a tall building in an urban context. But it does qualify as a tall building—indeed a boldly tall building—in the flat landscape of the northwest corner of New York State. Fredonia is a village, so there is a landmark aspect to this nine-story building that is as pronounced as the landmark aspect of the Royal Bank building in *its* context. In almost every other respect, however, the projects diverge.

For one thing, the tower at Fredonia embodies an idea that is the opposite of that embodied by the tower at Place Ville Marie. The latter is autonomous, self-referential, and governed entirely by its internal ordering systems. The tower at Fredonia is completely contingent, not at all self-referential, and governed not by its internal system but by an idea about the role it should play in the campus. It was my intention from the beginning that this tower should serve as a landmark at the gateway to the campus—yet by its posture declare that it is not the center of the campus but is playing a supporting role.

Furthermore, the tower at Fredonia is a very gestural building. That is to say, its form is dynamic and extroverted rather than static and introverted. The tower at Place Ville Marie also has a gestural component, but that component is largely confined to the transfiguration that takes place close to the ground; otherwise the building is a huge cruciform object without a gesture. That is because equilateral crosses, though by nature emblematic, are self-referential. One of the reasons (other than liturgical) that the Greek cross was supplanted by the Latin cross in church architecture, for example, is that the Latin cross makes a gesture toward the city. The Greek cross, which addresses all sides equally, is autonomous; it sets itself apart rather than reaching out to its context.

Does a good building invariably have a gestural component?

I would say so. I agree with Wittgenstein's statement that "Architecture is a *gesture*. Not every purposive movement of the human body is a gesture. Just as little as every functional building is architecture." The importance of the transfiguration in the lower levels of the Royal Bank building is precisely that it gives this otherwise nongestural object a gesture. It's true that because of the square geometry, it is a gesture equal on all sides; but it's still a gesture. Is there such a thing as an architecture without gesture? Not a very interesting one, I would say.

Let's take one of Lou Kahn's greatest works, the Kimbell Art Museum. I acknowledge that one doesn't immediately think of that building as gestural. But all you have to do is imagine what the building would be without the porch to realize how important that gesture is. Through the gesture of the porch, Kahn was able to transcend the systemic order of his building without betraying it. You could say that this is precisely what makes the building so wonderful, that the gesture is made within rather than outside the idealized order of the building. Indeed, this is one of the hallmarks by which we recognize the mature work of a great architect.

The campus at Fredonia does not rise to that level. It is undoubtedly a weakness of the tower at Fredonia that it is all gesture. It does not have the dignity you find in the Kimbell, a dignity that derives from the rigorous expression of an underlying systemic order or ideology. The library at Fredonia, however, does have that sort of dignity; and a deliberate contrast is drawn between the pervasive order governing the library and the gesture of the tower, which takes exception to that order.

How did you approach the problem of designing an entire campus?

What is explicit at Fredonia is the effort to give form and focus to what was in effect a limitless field. The very strong geometric discipline is based on the root-five rectangle, a proportional system related to the Golden Mean and inherited from the Greeks. This system governs the layout of buildings in the academic center but was clearly insufficient to give order and identity to the entire 300-acre campus. So we extrapolated from that discipline the *diagonal* of the root-five rectangle, which launches itself from the academic center into the landscape and is complemented and contained by a large circle. The campus thus exhibits three kinds of order: the stable order of the grid, the dynamic order of the grid's diagonal, and the restabilizing order of the circle. The grid is limitless; the circle is containing. The grid says there is no distinction between inside and out; the circle says there is a very strong distinction. And the diagonal is a way of joining those two ideas by means of a third. Only in the library does the discipline of the grid become explicit. All the other components of the campus, in order to assert their contingency, are given less stable forms that depend entirely on their location.

So you were trying to establish a conversation among these different elements.
Absolutely. And the library is the quiet center of that conversation. The gestural buildings are the arts center, administration tower, lecture center, and student union. But the most gestural of these is the tower. In terms of sheer volume it is dominant, and to keep it from being overpowering, we gave it a highly gestural form, one not governed by internal, systemic imperatives and therefore not self-referential. The tower is contingent; it is in the service of the campus, not the other way around. To me this is critically important.

IEOH MING PEI

Toast to I. M. Pei on His Fiftieth Birthday
Knickerbocker Club, New York City, April 26, 1967

There is a proverb, I. M., that has come down to us from the antiquity of your homeland and that seems to me pertinent to this occasion. A wise man said, "Excellence does not remain alone; it is sure to attract neighbors." Your friends around the table here can surely understand the full meaning of this truth, because we have all, over the years of our association with you, enjoyed the splendid adventure of being neighbors to excellence.

Of course, it must be said of you now, as the superbly accomplished practitioner of a universal art, that the world is your neighbor, and that we who salute you here are but surrogates to a vast throng of friends and admirers whose good wishes are always with you. Nonetheless, because we were among your earliest neighbors, and more important because we have for you that special affection that is the reward of having worked together toward high goals, we would like to claim the privilege now of drinking a toast to the continued health and prosperity of our mutual friend, Mr. I. M. Pei.

This toast was repeated on April 30, 2017, at a dinner at the Rainbow Room celebrating I. M. Pei's 100th birthday.

PARTNERSHIP

Conversation with Cynthia Davidson
New York City, April 2015

You have often expressed disappointment in the quality of teaching at the Harvard Graduate School of Design during your years as a student there. Were there no good studio critics?
Yes. Luckily for me, there was one really good critic during those years, and his name was I. M. Pei.

Who wasn't that much your senior.
Nine years—not much now, but a lot when you're in your early twenties. Pei had been hired as an instructor immediately after completing Gropius's master class in '46. His thesis project, a museum for Chinese art in Shanghai, was regarded by Gropius as the finest piece of student work done under his tutelage. I was lucky to have Pei as a studio critic in '47 and again in '48. That's where our friendship began, and it continued after he moved to New York in the summer of '48 to work for the developer William Zeckendorf, Sr. Zeckendorf hired Pei to help

him dream big dreams, and at a certain moment the big dreams turned into the Helix, a spiral apartment tower that caused quite a splash at the time but never got built. Pei had no staff whatsoever, and he needed a model and some drawings. He asked me to organize a team of former students in Cambridge to help with this. I had just graduated and was working for Hugh Stubbins in the fall of '49. When the project was published—it was featured in a special section of *Architectural Forum* in 1950—I. M. was kind enough to put a credit, "Harry Cobb, collaborator," on the page, but the Helix was completely Pei's work.

In midwinter of '50 Pei had his first real construction project, the Webb & Knapp office in the penthouse of 383 Madison Avenue. That's when he began to assemble people, mostly from the GSD, and that's when he invited me to join him. So on April 1, 1950, I arrived in New York City.

It seems that Zeckendorf enjoyed having architects at his elbow.
Yes, he loved the idea that he had his own architects.

What was it like working with Zeckendorf on Place Ville Marie in Montreal?
In a word, thrilling.

Why was this project in your hands and not I. M.'s?
The Canadian National Railway had created this twenty-two-acre, center-city site, several blocks long, in 1915 or '16, when the railroad tunnel was built under Mount Royal. They had filled up the pit on one block with the railway station, and they had visions of a Rockefeller Center for the adjoining seven-acre site. They wanted a developer who was willing take on

the whole site, not just a piece of it, and they couldn't find one in Canada. So they came to Zeckendorf as a last resort. Zeckendorf immediately saw that this was a dream come true for him. He seized the opportunity, but then he had a dilemma. This was a huge project, and whoever was going to lead the design team would be occupied full time. Pei was traveling with him all around the country looking at urban renewal opportunities, so Zeckendorf couldn't allow Pei to focus on just one project. That's how it came to me. And indeed it did occupy me almost full time for seven years.

We've been talking about Place Ville Marie, but I want to go back. How did the formation of I. M. Pei & Associates occur in 1955? I'm assuming it was a breakaway of sorts from Zeckendorf.

Not really. It was just that the significance of the work we were doing clearly required that we have a separate identity as architects. I think Zeckendorf was completely happy with it, because he saw Pei's rising star as confirmation that he had bet on the right horse. The Helix apartment project, the Webb & Knapp office, and Mile High Center in Denver had put Pei on the map, so to speak, and then the subsequent built works for Zeckendorf—major urban renewal projects in New York, Philadelphia, Pittsburgh, Washington, and Chicago—attracted a good deal of attention in the decade of the fifties.

All those projects were done under Webb & Knapp?

Yes, as was Place Ville Marie. But because I. M. was getting so much attention, he was being told by friends in the profession, "Look, you better have an identity separate from Webb & Knapp." So we registered the name I. M. Pei & Associates with the State of New York in

1955, but we continued to be employees of Webb & Knapp until August 1960.

During the late '50s, Pei started accepting commissions that weren't for Webb & Knapp projects: for example, the Center for Earth Sciences at MIT, in '58. The contract was with I. M. Pei & Associates, not Webb & Knapp. So having our own identity was important to our practice professionally on several levels. And it was also useful to Zeckendorf because, while he loved having his own architects, he even more loved having them achieve recognition from an institution like MIT.

It was good for him.

Yes, it was good for him. He and Pei were both seen as exotics, and the combination of the two them was tremendously exotic—catnip for the press. For example, the Webb & Knapp office, which was finished in '52, got a big spread of Ezra Stoller color photographs in *Fortune*. Pei and Zeckendorf both had this instinct for what was going to grab attention. Pei proposed, and Zeckendorf agreed, to populate the office with major artwork.

The project was the addition of a penthouse on top of a very ordinary office building on Madison Avenue at Forty-Sixth Street, but it had an outdoor terrace because it was on the setback. Pei took advantage of that to make a pool enclosed by a marble wall, and in that enclosure he placed this wonderful Lachaise sculpture. At that time—long before the era of high-style corporate headquarters—it was still a little shocking to walk off the elevator into a real estate office and see this delightful garden. In his office Zeckendorf also had a small Matisse bronze and an exquisite blue and white Chinese vase that Pei picked out for him. And in the semicircular aerie above, where Zeckendorf entertained movers and shakers, there was a large still life by Le Corbusier, on loan from MoMA. Otherwise, everything in the office was designed by our group, from the ashtrays on up: the lamps, the uncomfortable chairs, and Zeckendorf's desk with two built-in telephones. I myself spent several months detailing and supervising construction of a cylindrical thuja-burl wine cabinet.

But other clients didn't, or couldn't, come calling because you worked with Zeckendorf, right?
Commercial clients couldn't come calling, but universities and other institutional clients could. Zeckendorf was having his ups and downs financially. By the time Place Ville Marie was finished, he only owned 3 percent of it. In order to get it built, he had to give it all away to insurance companies and bankers. And by 1960, it was convenient on both sides for us to separate completely so that we would no longer be employees of Webb & Knapp. That entirely amicable separation occurred on August 1, 1960. We had about seventy people, so we started with a significant staff, but without ever having balanced a book. We didn't even have an accountant. We had never had a profit-and-loss statement. We didn't know much about the business side of architecture.

You must have been licensed?
Yes, in fact I was licensed in '52, several years before I. M., who didn't become a U.S. citizen until 1955. Fortunately, there was an essential third leg to the stool of I. M. Pei & Associates, and that was our managing partner, Eason Leonard. When you look at our firm's letterhead, you'll see the founders are Pei, Leonard, and Cobb. Eason Leonard, who had previously been a project manager in the office of William Lescaze, was our managing partner until both he and Pei retired at the end of 1990.

So why were you called associates at the outset and not partners?

It was "associates" because Pei was the rising star and I was still very much his junior. But the three of us were registered as partners from the beginning. And all three of us had significant shares. I. M. was very fair, even generous in that regard. When our group became a separate firm, Pei had to make a decision about who the partners were going to be. He asked his attorney how he should structure the partnership, and the attorney said, "You should limit the partnership to the people you can't do without." So that's how it ended up being Pei, Leonard, and Cobb.

We were fiercely committed to being on what we saw as the cutting edge of things, in two ways in particular: architecture at an urban scale—big things—and architecture as a craft. Detail was extremely important. Pei and I, and later Jim Freed, who became a partner in 1980, shared those aspirations. Our commitment to detail and craft was, from the managing partner's point of view, what made the practice so difficult, because we never stopped designing; we did things over and over and over again, especially in our pursuit of perfection in board-formed reinforced concrete.

Our practice was as precarious as it was successful. The reason we survived was because Pei's star was rising so rapidly that we could somehow get past the fact that we were often losing money.

You were asking me about the tensions that existed within our practice, particularly between me and Pei. What you have to understand is that our partnership was rooted in a very solid foundation of friendship, which generated a certain trust that somehow was able to survive multiple stresses across four decades of working together.

Trust is what you need in any relationship.

Yes, and another reason it survived is because Pei and I are so different. He's a natural rainmaker, which could never be said of me. When he appeared on the cover of the *New York Times Magazine* back in '79, the headline read, "Winning Ways of I. M. Pei." He positioned himself very cleverly, I would say, whether it was intentional, instinctive, intuitive, or all of the above. Pei was always very focused on his path. Zeckendorf gave him a leg up in the beginning, but I. M. was eager to get past that and go on to things that interested him more. If you asked him about his time with Zeckendorf, I. M. would tell you that there was just too much of it, and that he would have liked to have moved on from that much sooner.

But for me, the ten years with Zeckendorf were absolutely splendid. Even though my own professional identity was completely subsumed within the rising star of I. M. Pei, I didn't feel myself to be eclipsed by that star during the first decade or more of our work together. After all, Place Ville Marie was my project. I was wholly responsible for the design of this enormous mixed-use development, working with Zeckendorf, and I had a wonderful time doing it. But in the mid-sixties, when Pei began to get a lot of attention, there were articles in *Time* magazine and elsewhere that attributed the design of Place Ville Marie to I. M. Pei personally. It really didn't bother me a lot—maybe I was born with a defective ego!—but it bothered some of the people I had worked with on the client side who thought that I should be getting credit. And they wrote letters to the editor.

So there began to be this tension, which almost reached a breaking point in '65, because by then I really did want my name on the door. Pei wouldn't go along with that. He was being advised that any dilution of the singular identity of our firm would seriously hurt his candidacy for projects he was most interested in—not commercial projects but cultural projects. And he was right. For example, it's unlikely that either the Kennedy Library or the National Gallery East Building would have come to our firm if its singular identity had been diluted by names other than Pei.

Well, in '66, it changed from associates to partners, which acknowledged that he had partners by putting that word on the door.

Yes, but then fifteen years later there was another crisis. I. M. and I had agreed that with the expansion of the partnership in 1980 to include Jim Freed and others, the firm name would be changed. But conflicting agendas within the group of new partners created a stalemate that once again precluded the name change. At that point, I had a choice either to live with the name as it was or to leave. My solution, which I've always been perfectly open about, was to stay but also to go. As a corollary of staying with the firm—a corollary that I thought essential both to my own professional survival and ultimately to the survival of the firm—I decided to go to Harvard [in response to Jerry McCue's invitation to chair the department of architecture at the GSD].

I. M. went along with my plan, although I'm sure he thought it a waste of my time, an unnecessary diversion from the primary goal of being an architect, which is to build. But I said to him, "Look, someday you're going to retire, and if I remain with this firm, the responsibility for extending the practice will fall largely on me. It will only work if I have somehow been able to establish my own identity as an architect. And how can I do that? I can't do it just by continuing as a design partner in this firm—as a planet orbiting the Pei star. I have to do something more, something outside that orbit." I had been teaching since the early sixties, mostly at Yale, but also at Penn and other schools, so I had established my credentials as a design critic. And by the mid-seventies, largely because of the Hancock debacle, I had achieved some recognition, if not to say notoriety, within the profession.

The Hancock brought you a certain recognition, yes.
And I had brought in a few projects on my own, like the Portland Museum. But I felt strongly that none of that would be enough if I didn't do something that would give me credibility as a leader, so that it wouldn't seem that the practice was coming to an end when Pei retired. Nobody understood this. Everybody saw my going to Harvard as a first step toward leaving Pei. Even he may have seen it that way, although he never said so to me. But my purpose was exactly the opposite. I needed to go in order to be able to stay and ultimately lead the practice to which I had committed my life.

I. M. remained perplexed by my activities as chair at Harvard. For example—and this will show you where his mindset was—he was totally nonplussed by my Gropius Lecture on "Architecture and the University," and quite openly critical. He actually said to me, "How could you have done this? You missed a great opportunity to present your work." He just couldn't believe that I had wasted this platform by talking about education.

So you can see that both the friendship and the tension between me and Pei took my professional life in directions that it otherwise might not have gone, which you can look at negatively or positively. I prefer to look at it positively.

How did the office work between you, I. M., and the other partners? Did you run separate teams, since you were doing more developer-type work and I. M. was doing more institutional work?
Well, it depended on the project. Over the years there were a number of projects where I worked with I. M., helped him in various ways, if and when needed. I always enjoyed that. But for the most part, starting in the mid-fifties, we worked separately.

Did you critique each other's projects?
Not a lot of critiques, because I. M. wasn't into that sort of thing either. Also, we were busy, so there were not as many internal critiques as there should have been.

Did you have design teams?
Yes. But we didn't have separate studios under different partners as some firms do. People moved as needed. Some people worked with me more than with others, but generally speaking, people did not get stuck in one place. We shared staff, even though we didn't engage each other a lot in the work we were doing. But as I said, you must understand that I. M. and I drew on a deep well of trust that somehow kept things together in times of stress. Despite our separate tracks in the practice, there were a number of occasions where I played a supporting role in his work, like the early phases of the National Center for Atmospheric Research or the first Hancock project. The Hancock commission didn't come to me; it came to Pei. I helped with the first project, but it was really I. M.'s project.

So that was before the tower we all know?
Well, Pei's project included a tower, but it was totally different—not a single building but two separate buildings

on two blocks framing an open space. We finished the project in fall of '66. Ed Logue loved it; everybody loved it. But then the client called up and said, "Stop, we're going to think about this." They thought about it for a whole year, and consulted real estate people who convinced them that the design was unaffordable and inefficient. So they came back in the summer of '67, almost a year later, and said, "We're going to start over, and here are the conditions. There is going to be one building on one block, and it has to have at least two million square feet and at least 30,000 square feet per floor, and it has to cost no more than thirty-three dollars a square foot."

We had just landed a big job in Toronto, the headquarters of the Canadian Imperial Bank of Commerce, which Pei was doing. He was quite excited about that project and was completely turned off by Hancock's behavior. So the question was, "Well, what do we do now?" It was a big decision for the partnership. I. M. said, "I'm not doing it. But this is your city. If you want to, you should do it." I can't tell you exactly what went through my mind, but I took the bit in my teeth, and the Hancock Tower was designed, literally, within two weeks in mid-September of 1967.

Two weeks?

Conceptually, it was all there within two weeks. There was a lot of pressure to move fast because of an upcoming mayoral election. After being accepted by Hancock, the new design was announced publicly in November of '67. Everybody hated it, and none more vociferously than Ed Logue. He lobbied strongly against it during the nine months of very acrimonious debate that followed, before a building permit was finally issued in August of '68.

And then?

The Hancock Tower, which was the center of my life from '67 to '76, almost destroyed our practice because of the controversy it provoked and the highly publicized problems during its construction. What undoubtedly saved our practice during that period was the National Gallery East Building, which was the center of Pei's life from '68 to '78. The almost universal acclaim that greeted the East Building gave us the momentum to get past the Hancock debacle. So it's interesting that our firm's two AIA Twenty-five Year Awards are for those two buildings that have such very different histories and serve such very different purposes.[1] Pei's building is a cultural monument, and mine is an aggregation of offices—perfect embodiments of our divergent life stories. Nonetheless, they are similar in one important respect: they are both fundamentally contingent works. The East Building is totally contingent on its place within the geometry of L'Enfant's plan, and the Hancock Tower is totally contingent on its adjacency to Trinity Church. And there's another similarity: for both of us, these may be arguably our most significant built works.

1 In 2017 the firm received a third Twenty-five Year Award, for the Grand Louvre.

COPLEY SQUARE, BOSTON

John Hancock Tower, 1967–76
with Harold Fredenburgh, Michael D. Flynn

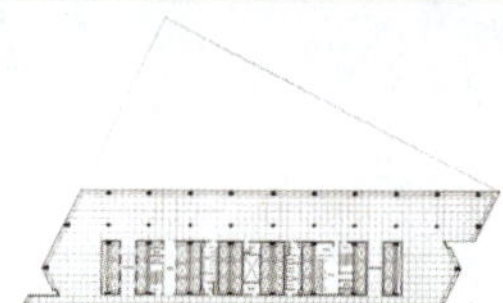

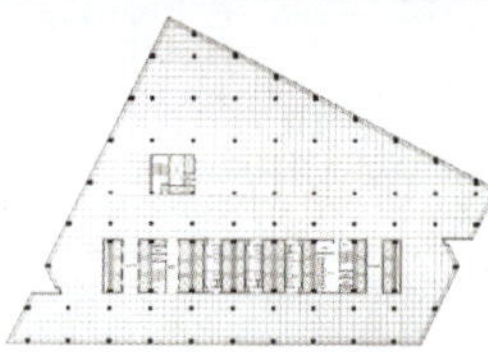

The floor plan of the John Hancock Tower exhibits for the most part a rigorous adherence to the discipline imposed by those characteristic internal systems—structural, mechanical, circulatory, operational—that largely determine the design of every tall office building. But we may observe the presence of one feature that seems to challenge the hegemony of internal systems: namely, the skewing of the end walls so as to produce a notched rhomboid rather than a rectangular plan-form. While this deviation has been accomplished in a way that is coherent with systemic elements of the plan, it nonetheless cannot be explained by reference to any identifiable internal need. A yet more pronounced aberration occurs in the plans of the lower eight floors, where one long side of the rhomboid has been rotated outward to form a trapezoid within which the structural grid is extended to a not entirely comfortable intersection with the enclosing walls. This peculiar form—so radically different from the undisturbed autonomy of the cruciform tower in Montreal—becomes explicable only when one turns finally to the site plan and sees the building in its urban setting. The rhomboid tower rising from its trapezoidal base is then immediately perceived as a response to the particular *external* situation of the building, most notably its adjacency to Copley Square and H. H. Richardson's Trinity Church.

But just what was that situation? This is the question to which my answer engendered so much fear and loathing in the city of my birth. I began with the observation, not in itself controversial, that while Copley Square and the monuments populating it clearly embodied the vision of an ideal city, the experiential reality at street level was something very different and very troubling—a public space desecrated by the rupturing of its enclosure and the intrusion of massive commercial buildings that seemed to render the space itself irrelevant and meaningless. Indeed, so chaotic was the urban scene surrounding Copley Square that it appeared at first to defy rational analysis. By this time, however, I had at last come to appreciate the city as a living organism in a constant state of change—a dynamic process that can never be understood by looking at a single image. I therefore argued that the only way to understand what ought to be done *now* was to understand how Copley Square had reached this impasse—to place it, so to speak, in the stream of history. Although that history, with the extraordinary topographical transformation it embodies, has its origins early in the seventeenth century, its immediately relevant episodes date back to the 1830s, when two railroad lines were built to link Boston to its western hinterlands. These rail lines crossed in the middle of what was called the Back Bay, blocking its tidal flow and causing it to become stagnant. The health hazard, combined with pressures for growth, led to the filling of the bay—a vast project that provoked numerous proposals for laying out this newfound territory. With the single exception of one delightfully imaginative plan, which was unfashionably baroque

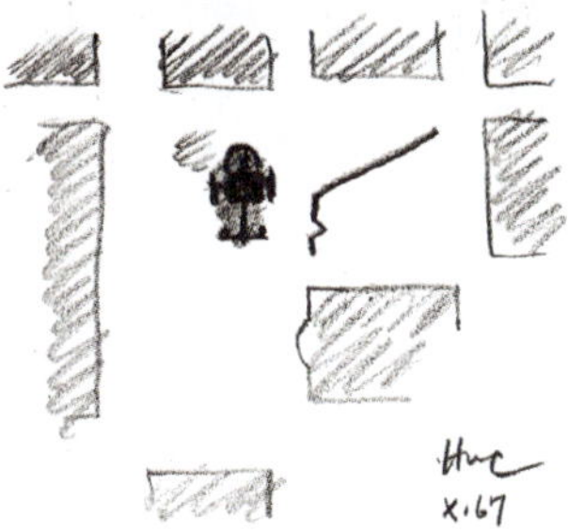

Top Copley Square, with Prudential Center behind Boston Public Library, 1966. **Above Left** Author's site-plan sketch. **Above Right** John Hancock Tower in Copley Square. **Opposite** Robert F. Gourlay, plan for Boston, 1844.

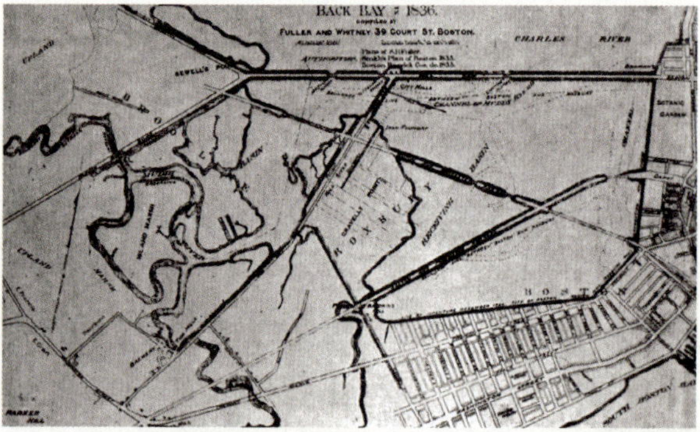

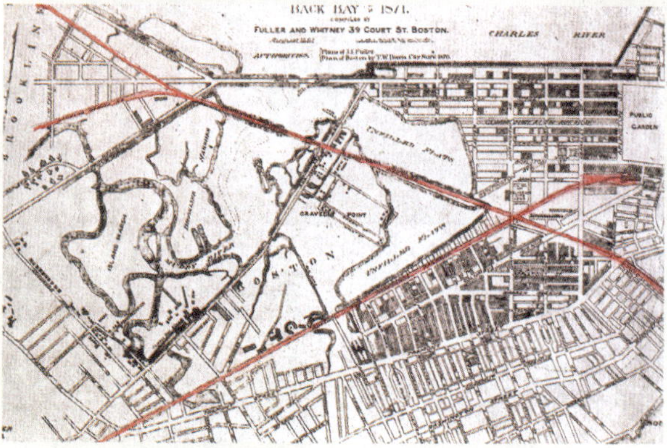

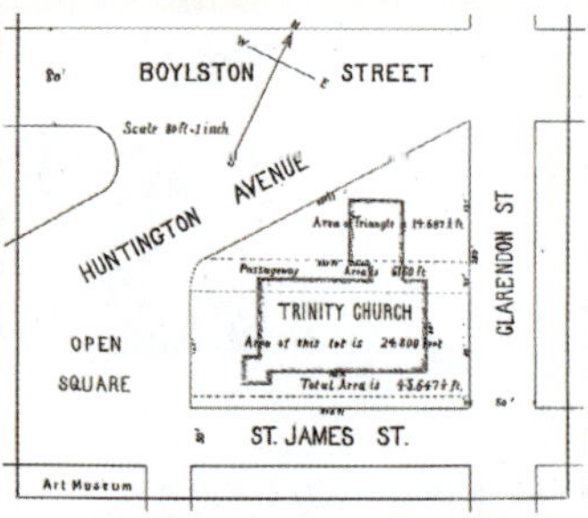

Top Map of Back Bay, 1836. **Middle** Map of Back Bay, 1871 (color added). **Bottom** Trinity Church early site plan, 1872.

in its inspiration and was immediately rejected in Puritan Boston, all these plans, while exhibiting a confident clarity in handling the area between what is now Boylston Street and the Charles River, displayed an equally marked ambivalence, reflecting deep puzzlement, about how to handle the area just to the south, where the rail lines crossed. This ambivalence remained unresolved as the filling advanced, and consequently what was to become Copley Square was never really planned but simply stumbled into shape, as Walter Whitehill succinctly remarked, between the arms of the St. Andrew's cross formed by the rail lines. A decisive moment in this story occurred in 1871, when Boston's leading Episcopal parish announced its intention to build a new church on a trapezoidal lot in what its rector recalled was then "a desert of dirt, dust, mud and wind."[1]

Here we must pause to ask a question: Why, when they could have had their pick of any number of splendid corner lots in the well-ordered blocks of the Back Bay, did the vestrymen of Trinity Church decide to go way out in left field, so to speak, to the remoteness of the then-nonexistent Copley Square? The answer, explicitly stated in parish records, is that they wanted their new church to be surrounded by streets on all sides, so that as a freestanding edifice it would proclaim Trinity's autonomy—and, by implication, its primacy—as *the* church in a burgeoning city that saw itself, not without reason, as the "Athens of America." In the pursuit of this goal, they invited designs from six of the country's leading architects, five of whom submitted competent if uninspired exercises in the then-fashionable Gothic Revival style. And then there was the scheme submitted by H. H. Richardson.

1 Walter Muir Whitehill, *Boston: A Topographical History*, 2nd edition (Cambridge: Harvard University Press, 1968), 168, 171.

It has often been noticed by critics and historians that Richardson's competition design, as represented in his perspective drawing, was compositionally awkward and stylistically confused. As James O'Gorman writes, "Certainly his project was not measurably better than several of those who lost. We do not know," he adds, "specifically what swung the committee in his favor."[2] It is true that we cannot *know*, inasmuch as there are no surviving records of the jury deliberations. Yet with Richardson's drawing in hand, together with parish records documenting the vestry's reasons for acquiring the Copley Square site, we can surely *surmise* why Richardson won. He won because he alone conceived and presented his project as a bold and absolutely unambiguous symbol of the aspirations, both explicit and implicit, that motivated his prospective client's building enterprise. When we consider his drawing, gawky and even absurd as it may appear to a critical eye, we cannot fail to marvel that an architect who was not yet entirely the master of his art had nonetheless so thoroughly mastered the companion art of seduction—an art practiced with such consummate skill that even the shape of the drawing, a roundel, emphasizes the strength of his conception while concealing its weaknesses, and by its cosmic connotations subtly reinforces his claim to be, without question, *the man for the job*.

Although Trinity Church, as built, is vastly superior to the design represented in Richardson's competition drawing, the strengths and weaknesses of both are remarkably similar in kind—so much so that the "official" Richardson-authorized photograph of the completed building shows it from the same angle, albeit from the opposite side. Clearly, the architect's aim was to display to best

2 James F. O'Gorman, *Living Architecture: A Biography of H. H. Richardson* (New York: Simon & Schuster, 1997), 102.

Top H. H. Richardson, Trinity Church competition drawing, 1872. **Above** Trinity Church in late 1870s.

Above Copley Square in 1900. From left: Trinity Church, 1877; Museum of Fine Arts, 1876; Boston Public Library, 1895.

BOSTON POST, FRIDAY, SEPTEMBER 24, 1897.

CITIZENS OF ARTISTIC TASTE RISE IN PROTEST.

VIEW FROM COPLEY SQUARE AS IT WILL LOOK WHEN THE NEW MAMMOTH APARTMENT HOUSE BECOMES A NEAR NEIGHBOR OF TRINITY CHURCH AND THE ART MUSEUM.

Determined Opposition to the Proposed Ten-Story Apartment House in Copley Square.

F. O. PRINCE EXPRESSES HIS INDIGNATION.

Top *Boston Post* headlines, September 24, 1897.
Above Copley Square, with large parcels of land behind being prepared for development, circa 1900.

advantage the powerful composition of apse and transept surmounted by a central tower, while concealing the unfinished west front, which the architect struggled with for more than a decade but never resolved in a form that his client could afford. Unhappily, and ironically, Trinity's disappointing west front, feebly embellished by towers and a porch after Richardson's death, was soon made to appear even more conspicuously wanting by its forced confrontation with the magisterial facade of the Boston Public Library, built to the design of Charles Follen McKim, who as Richardson's assistant had himself drawn the Trinity competition plans.

With Trinity Church, the Public Library, and the Museum of Fine Arts framing Copley Square, Bostonians entered into what would become a century-long and still ongoing debate about the character and purpose of the city's most important civic space. This debate, as evidenced in an amazing variety of unfulfilled dreams and unsatisfactory fulfillments, has been accompanied by two opposing phenomena: the unceasing vigilance of Bostonians in protecting the integrity of the square from what they perceive to be inappropriate incursions, and the even more relentless pressures for change to which the square is rendered vulnerable by virtue of its peculiar topographical setting. In the perspective of history, it is clear that the outcome was never in doubt. "Citizens of artistic taste" might rise in protest, as recorded by a *Boston Post* headline, but their efforts must in the end prove fruitless against the onslaught of change that, ironically, was concentrated in the Copley Square district precisely because it was so firmly excluded from the residential enclave of the adjacent Back Bay. As Boston outgrew its historic downtown, the largest commercial-space users, including the John Hancock Mutual Life Insurance Company, found that only in the vicinity of Copley Square could they acquire sites large enough to meet their needs. The final coup de grâce came in the early 1960s, when the rail yards became the Prudential Center, with its centerpiece skyscraper looming behind the Boston Public Library, and an expressway interchange at Dartmouth Street destroyed the enclosure of the square. After suffering those indignities, Copley Square—a distillation of memory extending cusp-like into the territory of invention—had been so desecrated that it had lost all credibility as a meaningful public space. To recover its meaning, or more accurately to find new meaning, the square, so we believed, must welcome rather than reject a dialogue with the new scale of urbanization that had engulfed it. We saw the Hancock company's need for two million square feet of additional office space as the appropriate occasion to launch that dialogue, with the aim of, at last, joining memory to invention for the benefit of both. Seizing this opportunity, we proposed that Copley Square should have its own tower.

Our proposal was not well received. Indeed, the response in Boston was one of shock and horror. What we saw as the right building in the right place at the right time was seen by almost everyone else, and above all by our fellow architects in Boston, as the wrong building in the wrong place at the wrong time. But after nine months of acrimonious public debate, the necessary permits were obtained, and in the fall of 1968 construction began. Permission was granted not because I had succeeded in converting people to our way of thinking—for with only a few exceptions I had not—but because had a building permit been denied, the Hancock company might well have carried out its threat to move its headquarters with its 12,000 employees to Chicago. This brazen exercise of

Top Copley Square with John Hancock Tower, looking east from Boston Public Library, 1976. **Above** Newspaper clippings, January 1968.

corporate arm-twisting on the part of our client naturally contributed to the widespread opinion, often explicitly conveyed to me in person, that my colleagues and I had prostituted ourselves professionally in accepting and carrying out this commission. To compound the agony, during construction the building endured a series of mishaps that caused us and our client to experience the rare privilege of being, for almost half a decade, simultaneously despised and ridiculed. The most notorious of these problems, publicized worldwide, was the failure of insulating glass units that necessitated removal and replacement of all 10,334 panels in the curtain wall. Many in Boston saw all this as entirely just retribution for the egregious overreaching of the city's largest corporation. Mercifully, however, an entrepreneurial T-shirt artist didn't lose his opportunity to find a lighter side, with which I was able to outfit all three of my daughters in the otherwise miserable summer of 1973.

Although the deceptive mutability of its image may suggest otherwise, there is nothing mysterious about the design of the Hancock Tower. It perfectly illustrates my view that the architecture of a tall building is 99 percent logic and 1 percent art—but don't you dare take away that 1 percent! The extreme disparity in size between the tower and the church was the central predicament we faced. We chose to deal with it not by creating a gratuitous distance between the two—this would only have exacerbated the problem—but by bringing them into close proximity while positioning and shaping the tower in such a way that it becomes the contingent satellite and the church the autonomous center in the composition.

To accomplish this, several aspects of the tower's design may be cited as essential. First, the attenuated rhomboid plan-form, placed diagonally on its site, emphasizes the planar while minimizing the volumetric presence of the building, so as to effectively disembody the tower as seen from the square. Second, a bullnose corner detail facilitates the crucially important transition from trapezoidal base to rhomboid tower. Third, notches bisecting the end walls accentuate the weightless verticality of these planes and make legible the tower's nonrectangular geometry. Fourth, the tower's uniformly gridded and reflective surface, stripped of all elements that could suggest a third dimension, mutes the obtrusiveness of its enormous bulk and defers in all respects to the rich sculptural qualities of its much smaller neighbor. Fifth, rather than standing on the ground, the tower's rhomboid volume slips weightlessly up out of the surrounding granite pavement, from which it is separated by a one-inch-wide perimeter slot. Finally, the triangular space created between the church and the broad face of the tower pays homage to the apsidal view of Richardson's building, reinforcing its intended role as the architectural cynosure of Copley Square.

With regard to this latter aspect, it should be noted that the three-story lobby at the base of the tower is sheathed in precisely the same manner as all other floors; had the monumental scale of this space been directly exposed to view, it would surely have destroyed the delicate balance in the dialogue between church and tower. This concern also accounts for the modest scale of the three entries, originally sheltered by clear plastic domes, which were subsequently replaced by an attenuated stainless steel canopy. Truth be told, the tower's reflective surface and reticent posture do not invite entry. I used to joke with my colleagues—but not with our client!—that the proper means of gaining access to this impenetrable monolith would be through the porch of Trinity Church and along the nave to the crossing, where one would turn and descend by escalator into a tunnel below the street and emerge, finally, in the tower's elevator lobby.

On October 28, 1980, more than four years after the building's completion, in my inaugural lecture as chairman of the architecture department at Harvard, I summed up my view of the matter as follows:

> We adopted a strategy of minimalism in the design of the Hancock Tower not for ideological reasons, but because the *situation* of the building demanded it. In the determined pursuit of our goal—to achieve a symbiosis between the church, the tower, and the square—we excluded everything that did not contribute directly to this end. For we believed that only thus could we temper the inherent arrogance of so large a building and endow it with a presence that might animate rather than oppress the urban scene.

Top Detail of tower exterior, reflecting Trinity Church. **Above** Tower, with original domed entrance canopies, and Trinity Church.

Today, more than three decades after writing these words, I find that I can still subscribe to them. Yet I also find myself still confronting a few questions that just won't go away:

Can this accommodation justify that transgression?

Is this performance appropriate to that occasion?

Does this tower belong in that city?

To each of these questions the answer, it seems to me, must finally be both yes and no. This persistently disturbing ambiguity, in which the building discloses the anxiety of its predicament, perhaps explains why, among all my built works, the Hancock Tower is as close as I have ever come to poetry.

It is also as close as I have ever come to silence. The building's restraint to the point of muteness, its refusal to reveal anything other than its obsession with its urban context, is surely its greatest strength but also its ultimate limitation as a work of architecture. Despite the forcefulness of its gesture, the tower remains virtually speechless, and this resolute self-denial is, in the end, both its triumph and its tragedy.

Above Boston Common reflected in facade.

Opposite Axonometric drawing of curtain-wall components.

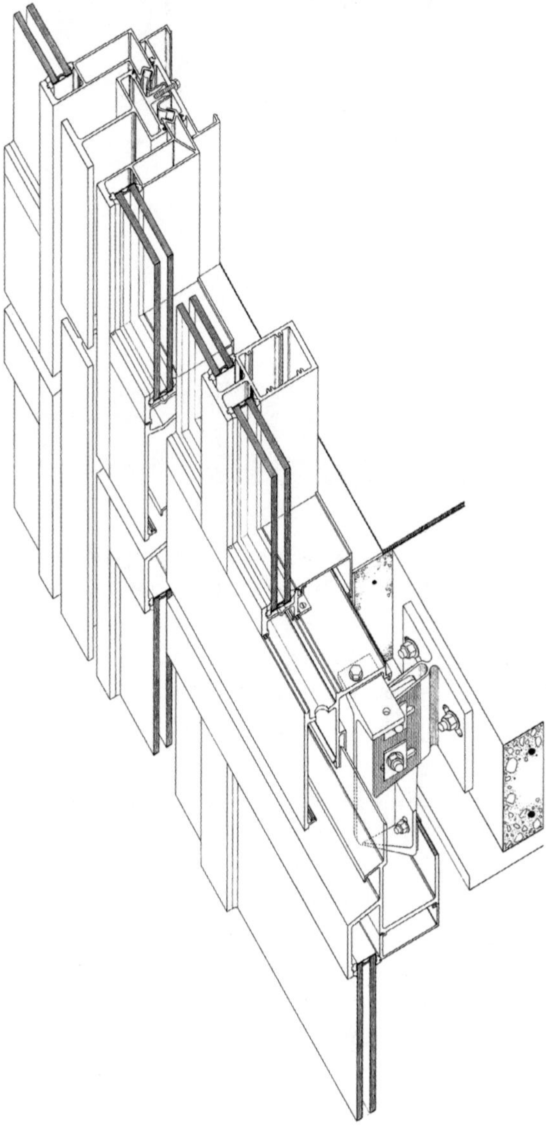

THE EXCEPTION

Conversation with Paolo Conrad Bercah
New York City, February 1998

You have said that the Hancock Tower expresses the anxiety of its predicament. What do you mean by that?
In *The Dynamics of Architectural Form*, Rudolf Arnheim cites the Hancock Tower as an example of catastrophic disorder and declares that the building "betrays its guilty conscience." I prefer to acknowledge, as you say, that it betrays the anxiety of its predicament. And that is precisely the sense in which the building is poetic: I mean simply that the tower makes evident with exceptional clarity the predicament afflicting all works of architecture. It is the predicament of architecture's dual nature. How we evaluate a work of architecture depends on which element of this duality we are considering. If we think of the building as a work of art, then everything is in the work, and attempting to evaluate it in terms of generalized ideas of right and wrong tends to be a meaningless exercise. But a work of architecture also has a societal function, and in evaluating its performance as a citizen,

general ideas of right and wrong—that is to say, ethical principles—arguably do apply. And architects cannot casually excuse themselves from the obligation to respect these principles by assuming the mantle of art, saying, "I do not have to worry about the principles of human duty because I am making a work of art."

Architecture is thus caught in a conflict. On the one hand, it is impossible for architecture to ignore the ethical obligation that stems from the fact that buildings are intended to be useful. On the other hand, it is fatal for architecture to become trapped in the condition of being merely useful. This makes architecture a very complicated and contaminated field. If you look at it from the ethical perspective, it is contaminated by its art status, and if you look at it from the artistic perspective, it is contaminated by its use status. Yet that is precisely what makes architecture so important in the culture: it is the art form most inescapably contaminated by the systems of power and standards of ethical conduct that govern society.

How does the architect reconcile these competing claims and conflicts?

Every architect in every situation is constantly having to balance the obligation of the building to conform to certain norms in order to make itself useful with the obligation to ignore those norms if necessary in order for the building to fulfill its equal obligation to be a work of art. Now, we see everywhere the resolution or the nonresolution of these inherently conflicting values, but there are very few instances in which the conflict is as explicit and as seemingly irreconcilable as in the case of the John Hancock Tower. In terms of every general rule that one could apply, the project is at best ill-considered and at worst almost criminally flouting of societal norms. I'd argue that despite the seeming validity of those generalities, their violation in this particular case was essential to achieving the building's function as a work of art. Does one justify the other? It is hard to say. Were it not possible to undertake this project and execute it as a work of art, that would be totally unjustifiable. It may be that even as a work of art, it is still unjustifiable as a violation of societal norms. But because it has earned its status as a work of art, it brings into focus the dual condition of architecture, which is, after all, nothing more than a very exaggerated case of the dual condition we face every moment of every day of our lives. The role of the work of art is precisely to illuminate and give meaning to the human condition, and you do not illuminate and give meaning to the human condition if all you are doing is conforming to prescribed societal norms. Hence, what you are doing may justifiably take exception to established norms, because people's lives are illuminated and enriched by that.

It is nonetheless a profound ethical question whether one should accept a commission that is going to involve such a radical exception. Many people, especially architects, felt—indeed, some still feel—that you should never have undertaken the Hancock project. How did you make the decision to do so?
That is a good question; in a sense it is *the* question about the Hancock Tower. If you talk to architects who were practicing in Boston when our design was first announced, I think most of them would say it was not the skill or correctness of the design they were principally concerned about but the morality of accepting the commission. Their opposition was based on a very simple but strongly held idea: namely, that it would be morally

wrong to put a tall building in that location. There was some acknowledgment that the formal strategy was clever, but the feeling was that no matter how clever it was, it could not possibly make up for the egregious intrusion of closed commercial offices at a vast scale into the public space and public life of the city.

Furthermore, the public space in question was not just any public space, but Copley Square. With Trinity Church, the Boston Public Library, and other major monuments in and around it, Copley Square is Boston's great civic space. In the nineteenth century it embodied the idea of Boston as a bastion of Eurocentric culture and values. For twentieth-century Bostonians it has remained a sacred space, and its proposed violation by a skyscraper was regarded as a kind of sacrilege. Yet it was precisely my awareness of that historical situation that compelled me to pursue the project. The decision also had to do with the nature of our practice and its engagement with the city, the nature of my relationship with my partners, and my personal background.

In fact, you did quite a lot of work in Boston before the Hancock project.

Yes. Because of our work first for Boston Redevelopment Authority director Ed Logue in the planning of Government Center and subsequently for the Christian Science Church in the Back Bay, our practice had been thinking hard about Boston for at least five years before Hancock came along. In a way, our work for Logue made Hancock possible; it never would have happened if Government Center hadn't happened. The site on which Hancock was built had been owned by the federal government, which had intended to put a federal office building on it. But Logue's perception was that you would never get Boston out of its doldrums if you didn't "bunch your hits," as he put it. So he picked up any initiative that was under way in the city and moved it into what would become Government Center, thereby creating the critical mass necessary to accomplish that project. The result was that the site originally intended for a federal building in Copley Square became available.

But there also would have been no John Hancock Tower without the Prudential Center. While the big players of Boston were dormant and not investing in the city, outsiders like Prudential were finding opportunities there. The company had acquired a large parcel of railroad land just west of Copley Square and, in 1964, erected a fifty-two-story tower, the tallest in the city. The Prudential Center was seen as a gratuitous slap in the face of Hancock, the hometown company, and that challenge inspired the chairman of Hancock to want its tower to be the tallest building in Boston. In fact, you could say that it was the Prudential Center that finally dragged Hancock, kicking and screaming, into the twentieth century. It made the Hancock Tower possible by challenging the Hancock company to think entrepreneurially, in terms of big buildings, and to get out of its very conservative ways.

How did the company represent its intentions to you?
In the early stages of the project, during the summer of 1966, Hancock was very open with us. There were lots of conversations and questions: What shall we do here? How do we make this really sing? How do we make this a project that will really be good for Copley Square, that will add a mix of uses as well as being sympathetic to its scale? In other words, the company's executives were very responsive clients, and the resulting design concept, for which I. M. Pei was principally responsible,

called for a slender concrete tower framed by a pair of low-rise buildings that shaped a small plaza embracing Clarendon Street. The proposal was well received, and in the fall of 1966, with Ed Logue's enthusiastic support, our clients went so far as to make it public. Then suddenly they closed up. For what reason, they did not reveal; they simply stopped. They said, "Wait a minute, we'll call you later."

They called us eight months later. During those eight months, they had consulted real estate experts and construction people and so on. When they came back, they had transformed themselves from a wonderful client into a monster. That monster manifested itself in a set of very crisp, unequivocal directives, and we were asked if we would care to respond to them. If not, the company would look elsewhere. The directives were as follows: we need two million square feet; all of it has to be in one building; it has to be on that one site, next to Trinity Church; it has to have at least 30,000 square feet per floor; and it can't cost more than thirty-three dollars per square foot. And by the way, here's the fee, here are the consultants, everything is laid out. No discussion—take it or leave it.

That was the manner in which Hancock presented its revised program. The conditions had changed so radically that there would have been no real embarrassment in declining. Every opportunity was offered to withdraw, to say, "No, thank you," and it wouldn't have been difficult to do so.

Under those circumstances, why did you go ahead?
The only way it can be explained is that despite these conditions, I saw an opportunity. It had to do with my love of Boston and my sense of what was necessary and

important for the city. I felt it was necessary for Copley Square and necessary for Boston to embrace the disjunction of scale that had been manifested in the crudest possible way by the Prudential Tower. In my mind the main justification for the Hancock Tower was that the overbearing presence of the Prudential Tower had pushed Copley Square into obsolescence and meaninglessness. In its posture, the Prudential Tower was self-centered, self-referential, autonomous, squared. What it said to Bostonians was: You are out of it, you have had it. I am the future, Copley Square is the past. It belongs to another age, it is a museum piece, it has nothing to do with modern life, it is of no significance anymore.

What I believed then and I still believe is that the only way to restore Copley Square to its intended role in the city was to give the square its own tower. I believed that it was essential to achieve the transition in scale, the juxtaposition of big and small, new and old, memory and invention, and to achieve it right there on that spot, right next to the great historic monuments of the city, in its most sacred space. Counterintuitively, the very banality of Hancock's program—with its two million square feet, its infinity of cubicles, and so on—had opened up this opportunity to strengthen the role of Copley Square and remake it as a key element in the city.

My conviction about this, incidentally, reflected the radical change in my own belief system that had occurred during the 1960s. The cultural mood of the time, the general loss of confidence in the structures of power, had reverberated in architecture as a loss of confidence in the modern movement, in urban planning, and in urban renewal. For me it meant a loss of confidence in large-scale interventions, accompanied by a growing interest in conceiving of the city as a collection of interactive fragments. So while I had once been attracted to the idea of the city as a system and the idea of remaking the world on a grand scale, by the time I got back to Copley Square, my thinking about the city and about the way that architecture could or should intervene in it had undergone a profound transformation. The Hancock commission, for all its apparent shortcomings, seemed to lend itself to the kind of intervention that I now thought architecture ought to make, an intervention that would be an act of affirmation rather than an act of denial.

In this I was at odds with my colleagues in Boston, who felt it was important to deny or fend off the change of scale, at least in Copley Square. But the city is not about being frozen in time; it is about constantly embracing and responding to the changes of a particular place. I thought it was important to do something for Copley Square that would make it once again relevant, not only as part of the city's history but as part of its ongoing life—something that would make it embody that link between the traditions of Boston and the idea of the future.

In all this your native understanding of Boston seems to have been very important.

It was. We would never have proceeded with the Hancock Tower if I hadn't been born in Boston. My partners more or less took the position that the decision was up to me: this was my town, and since this was going to be a very difficult, controversial, high-risk project, it was something I needed to be comfortable with. For my part, it is inconceivable that I would have undertaken the project if I hadn't had the confidence that comes from being a native. There is no other city in the world in which I would have presumed to intervene in the way the Hancock Tower intervenes in Boston. There is something about places you feel you really know, or people that you feel you really know, or institutions that you feel you really know. If you really love those places and people and institutions, that love is manifest—or ideally ought to be manifest—in a critical way. It's precisely because you love and know something that you can change it; otherwise you are reticent. I've built big buildings in dozens of cities, and I know in my gut that the kind of move that I dared to make in Boston I would not presume to make anywhere else.

I am by nature a cautious person, understated to a fault. It takes a particular set of circumstances to make me bold. In the case of the Hancock Tower, these were the circumstances: I grew up in Boston, and I know it very well; I spent many years learning about tall office buildings, and I know the problem inside out. Now I come to a project that employs all that I know in a situation that requires me to be an artist or to be nothing. To have the building there and not to have it seen as a work of art would be really unforgivable, the worst thing I could do to my hometown. So I was forced into being bold because to have been cautious would have been fatal.

This, then, is the ethical dilemma: is an artist—and in this case I have to cast myself as an artist, since that is the only way the project can be justified—entitled to risk so much of the public interest, to take such radical exception to societal norms, in the enterprise of making a work of art? The Hancock Tower is one of those events for which you cannot construct a scenario; you cannot imagine it happening. In theory it cannot be justified. What can you say about it? The only thing you can say is that it happened. So...*it happened!*

Considering the degree of opposition to the Hancock Tower, it is amazing that it ever got built.

I spent the better part of a year going to meetings of every conceivable group in town, making my case for why I thought it was the right thing to do, but the Hancock Tower was built not because I convinced anybody that it was the right thing to do. It was built because the political leadership of Boston could not afford to lose the Hancock company, the largest employer in the city. The company had made a very explicit threat—which it could easily have carried out—to move its headquarters to the John Hancock Center in Chicago, a building considerably taller than the Hancock Tower. Since everyone knew they had that option available, the company was able to obtain zoning variances, get approvals at the political level, and overrule the advice of every possible watchdog body interested in planning and building and architecture, including the Design Advisory Committee of the Boston Redevelopment Authority. The committee included the deans of the Harvard and MIT schools of architecture together with three of the leading senior architects in Boston, and it voted unanimously to reject the proposed design.[1] In fact, many people—the people concerned about the zoning variance and its implications, the Boston Society of Architects and its blue-ribbon panel—correctly saw that for Hancock to do what we had proposed on that site would amount to an egregiously blatant evasion of the spirit if not the letter of the zoning law.

1 In addition to its chair, Hugh Stubbins, the committee comprised Harvard dean Josep Lluís Sert, MIT dean Lawrence B. Anderson, MIT dean emeritus Pietro Belluschi, and Nelson W. Aldrich. Its report concluded by stating that "the architects have been given a task to which no reasonable solution can be found under the presently imposed physical conditions."

And you were implicated in that.

Yes; we were seen as accomplices in something that was thought to be brutal, uncivilized, and inappropriate. My colleagues in Boston could not accept the notion that something that violates societal norms could be transformed into something good by way of architecture. It's part of modernist morality that good architecture comes out of good social intentions. But I do not believe that architecture can or even should aspire to cure the ills of society; that's not what I mean when I talk about the architect taking moral initiative. It has to do rather with finding opportunities for architecture in the cracks between competing interests in the systems of power.

Can you give an example of how conflict within that power structure created opportunities for you?

The most important as well as the most obvious example is the irreducible minimalism of the tower—its radical understatement. Once we had satisfied our client's programmatic and budgetary requirements—for two million square feet of floor area, for 30,000 square feet per floor, for a cost not exceeding thirty-three dollars per square foot—we were able to insist that the building had to be done our way. The leverage arose directly from Hancock's awareness of the unpopularity of the enterprise—their "guilty conscience," if you will, about having imposed the project on an unwilling city. The conflict between the client's wish and the force of public indignation left an opening for us to exercise some kind of moral authority. A trivial but amusing case in point is the matter of signage. The chairman wanted to put the famous John Hancock signature across the top of the building. We said: "No. The tower must remain silent. It cannot be made into a billboard." He was frustrated and angry, but he gave up on the sign.

When it became necessary to replace the glass, didn't another conflict arise over the size of the glazing?
Yes, and that conflict posed a much more serious threat to the architectural integrity of the building. Fortunately for me and for the tower, by the time the glass began to fail, in the fall of 1972, there had been a change of leadership at Hancock. The chairman who had initiated this project—the one who had threatened to move the company to Chicago, who had insisted on a tower taller than Prudential's, and who had wanted to emblazon John Hancock's signature across the top—resigned abruptly, in the middle of construction. We never knew why, but something happened internally, and he was gone. The chairmanship was then assumed by a person much more typical of Hancock's corporate culture, a rather conservative lawyer who, in my opinion, never would have built the tower on his own initiative. In early 1973 the new chairman found himself saddled with a horrendous problem: a glass skyscraper that was beginning to disintegrate before his eyes. But he turned out to be a person of great intelligence, unfailing moral integrity, and exceptional leadership qualities. Throughout the entire three-year agony of dealing with the glass and other problems, he never panicked, even though people were panicking all around him.

The investigation of the Hancock glass problem took years, but the decision on the matter of how the glass would be replaced came at a single meeting of the building committee of the board. I had been warned beforehand that the executives who were running the project were going to present a unanimous recommendation that each of the large, 5-by-11-foot glass panels should be replaced with three smaller pieces. In fact, I had been told by Hancock executives at all levels that the glass would be subdivided, period. “You’d better make up your mind to it,” they had said, “because that’s what’s going to happen.” The meeting would be my one and only opportunity to forestall that outcome, and in preparation I made a large photomontage showing the effect of subdivided glass on the broad face of the tower.

I went to the meeting and said: “If you reglaze the tower as it was designed, there is a chance that this building will eventually be accepted as a good citizen. If you reglaze it with subdivided glass, you, the John Hancock Company, will never be forgiven.” I showed them the picture of what the building would look like with the subdivided glass, and I got no response whatsoever from anyone except one person, the chairman, Gerhard Bleicken. He said, “We are going to proceed with the building as designed.” He personally overruled his entire staff and all the other members of the board and decided to do it that way. The chairman’s decision was the single most important event in my life as an architect.

What would have happened if they had proceeded to subdivide the glass?

It would have been a disaster of a magnitude that is possible only in minimalist art, where every detail counts. The Hancock Tower by definition is a minimalist object; that is the aesthetic premise. The effect of the subdivided glass would have been totally devastating, yet I could not have prevented it. At that point too much had happened. I couldn’t even resign from the project; there was virtually nothing I could have done. That’s why for me the chairman is the hero of the story. This middle-aged gentleman, a lawyer with, as far as I know, little prior interest in architecture, understood what was at stake. He and he alone made the decision.

Were there aspects of the project over which you lost the battle?

Yes, there was one major disappointment. The Hancock company had made a commitment to convert its original headquarters building, across Clarendon Street, to cultural use, and we had designed a quite extraordinary adaptive reuse of that building in which it was to house the Children's Museum, the Boston Center for Adult Education, and the Massachusetts Horticultural Society. During the brouhaha about the glass, Hancock quietly abandoned the project. What really upset me was that I had made many public commitments to the project on behalf of our client. I had argued very strongly that quite aside from the architectural merits of the tower, the economic leverage it provided was going to allow something to happen that would be very important for Copley Square: it would make it possible to bring cultural life back into the area, reaffirming Copley Square as a cultural center. The adaptive reuse of the Clarendon building

Above Interior view of unbuilt Hancock Place proposal, 1972.

to house three important cultural institutions was to have been the fulfillment of that promise. Hancock's abandonment of this part of the project was a great though little-noticed tragedy, but I was powerless to prevent it.

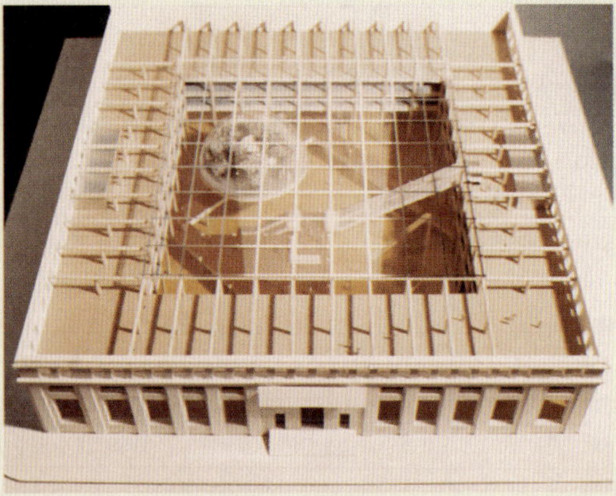

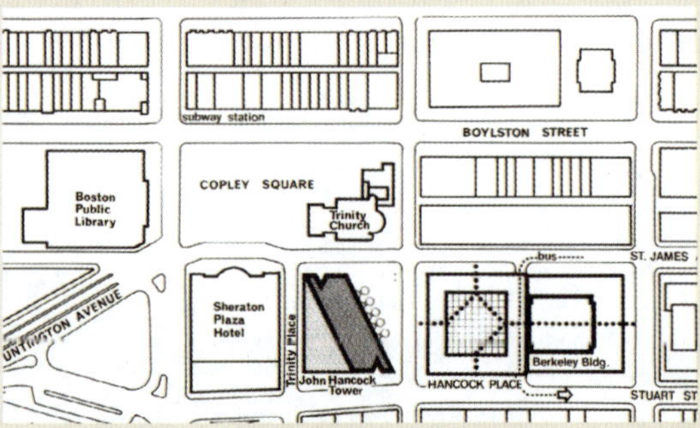

I would say, though, that the Hancock Tower plays something of a heroic role in Boston.

If so, it's because it took a heroic act to put Copley Square back in the game. Nobody agreed with me at the time, and some still don't. But I maintain that I am right, and every time I go to Boston I am sure that I am right. And the world tells me that I am right because picture books about Boston put the Hancock Tower and not the Prudential Center on their covers. They do so not because Hancock is a few inches taller but because it is connected to Boston, it says something about Boston. Prudential says nothing about Boston. It could be anywhere. But the Hancock Tower is emblematic of Boston in all respects, even, for example, in its "guilty conscience." Bostonians are by nature full of guilt; it is the residue of Puritanism. Arnheim's remark is, I think, a perfectly valid interpretation. One can and should have a guilty conscience about doing something so egregious. That does not mean that one should not do it, but one has a guilty conscience about it because it is so problematic.

If there's one thing that I believe strongly—to return to what we were saying earlier in this conversation—it is that generalized rules are of little use when we speak of cities. There is no way that I could ever write a rule, a guideline, that would allow something like the Hancock Tower to happen. It's almost unimaginable. And yet in that place, it says something about the predicament of our culture. It's not warm and fuzzy; it's uncomfortable. But then the predicament of our culture is uncomfortable. The juxtaposition of scales is uncomfortable. The expansion of commerce is uncomfortable. All these things are uncomfortable. Architecture is not necessarily about making them seem comfortable, although it can sometimes be. But in this particular case it couldn't be. The building could only rise to a level where it can be called architecture rather than a crime against humanity.

Opposite Model and site plan of Hancock Place proposal.

ON BUILDING IN CITIES

Lecture at Harvard Graduate School of Design
November 20, 1974

I am delighted to participate in this series of talks by Harvard Graduate School of Design alumni: talks that I hope will become a tradition, not because we alumni are a fount of pure wisdom—that proposition might be difficult to prove!—but because a continuing dialogue between the school and its professional offspring seems to me clearly beneficial to the well-being of both.

Honored as I am by your invitation, I nonetheless feel that in some respects this lecture is scarcely needed to keep you informed of my current work. I imagine that no building project in history has been more lavishly reported by the media than my recent pioneering work in plywood over at Copley Square. So I'm sure you'll be relieved to know that I will dwell no further on that overworked subject this evening, except to mention that some people seem to like my beleaguered tower in its present black-on-black incarnation. This has led me to consider whether I shouldn't celebrate the event by issuing some sort of manifesto—a counter-polemic, if you will, to the Whites, the Grays, and the Silvers. My group, which would be composed exclusively of fellow disaster victims, might as well call itself the Black-and-Blues. Given the profession's appetite for scurrilous gossip, we would surely qualify for a special issue of Peter Blake's *Architecture Plus*.

Since I am a stranger to many of you here, I should inform you at the outset that virtually my entire professional life has been devoted to urban projects of large scale. Among the participants in this series, I suppose I am the only one who has never built a private house. More by accident than by design, I was thrust at the beginning of my career into the arena of big development—an arena clamorous with the competing cries of politicians, public servants, corporate bureaucrats, money managers, and real estate entrepreneurs—empire builders all.

I have therefore been deeply immersed in what Lewis Mumford has scathingly termed "the power system with its dynamic—or should one say demonic—expansion of power, productivity, profit and publicity." After almost twenty-five years of contending with this system, I suppose I am nothing if not a pragmatist. But I am an optimist also. For though I do not deny the actuality of Mumford's ominously alliterative quartet—power, productivity, profit, and publicity—neither do I accept the premise that our cities are doomed so long as these very ancient motives persist in society. Indeed, if anything is likely to obstruct the improvement of cities, it is the insistence that they cannot be improved until the very impulses that brought them into being have been exorcised from the human psyche.

Mumford's view is in fact a latter-day reaffirmation of the resolutely anti-urban bias that has characterized American intellectuals since Colonial times. The metaphor of the city as a cancer on the body politic has, after all, been a leitmotif of American thought since it was first enunciated by Thomas Jefferson almost two centuries ago, and it remains today deeply embedded in our national consciousness, blurring our perception of the city even as we face the reality of urbanization on a scale inconceivable to the founding fathers. But despite this deeply rooted residual negativism, the attitude of American society toward its cities is measurably more positive today than it was a quarter-century ago. It is a truism that during this period, all of our major cities have faced a crisis of explosive growth at the perimeter accompanied by decay at the center. Our response as a nation to this crisis took the form of two self-inflicted traumas. The first was Title I of the Housing Act of 1949 as amended, commonly known as urban renewal, and the second was the

Federal Aid Highway Act of 1956, better known as the Interstate Highway Program. If we are honest with ourselves, I think we must admit that the errors and excesses spawned by these legislative acts, rather than their merits, finally brought home to us both the value and the fragility of our cities. The destructive force as well as the gargantuan offspring of these programs astonished us. And while we licked our wounds and pondered our folly, a new awareness seized the American mind. We began to understand that the city is *the* indispensable agent through which a society enriches its present life by simultaneously remembering its past and inventing its future.

For a nation still bemused by the philosophy of Emerson and the myth of the frontier, the growth of this new consciousness was a major awakening. But lest I be misunderstood, I must quickly add that however bleak some of its products may be, urban renewal as a process has enormously strengthened our capacity to guide the future growth of cities. It has fostered, indeed compelled, a constructive dialogue between agents of government and those elements of the private sector that are the principal builders of cities. It has also created new and effective mechanisms for implementing public policy in urban development. Among the most notable of these are the concepts of incentive and special district zoning, two ideas that bore fruit in several major cities during the last decade. And perhaps most important of all, urban renewal engaged the attention of many bright young professionals: lawyers, economists, and social scientists as well as architects and planners, who were concerned about the deteriorating urban environment, and who found in this program a vehicle for action.

In retrospect, I think it can be seen that the emerging positivist view of the American city has been reflected in, or perhaps more accurately foreshadowed by, the arts—music, painting, sculpture, literature, and even, to a limited degree, architecture. It is indeed ironic that architecture should be the last and the least to comprehend and make eloquent the new urbanism; but it is nonetheless readily explainable.[1] For by virtue of the investment of materials and labor required to bring it into being, architecture is generally the product—and too often the unquestioning servant—of established institutional value systems. And to compound the retrogressive consequences of this dependence, the modern movement in architecture was itself built on a largely anti-urban theoretical base—rejecting the city entirely, as with Wright and his followers; or losing sight of its highest civilizing functions in an obsession with the systematic and totalitarian reordering of human settlements, as with the early European modernists. My generation in architecture was exposed to these conflicting theories in school and was profoundly confused by them: first by their evident mutual incompatibility, and subsequently by our inability to reconcile them with the reality confronting us. This confusion certainly accounts in large part for many of the follies of urban renewal, as well as for the fact that with few exceptions, our profession has been more the follower than the leader in the evolution of a new attitude toward the city.

One does not have to accept all of Robert Venturi's notions about the American scene in order to acknowledge that his is the *only* significant contribution to architectural theory that is essentially coherent with the nature of the modern city. Pluralism, complexity, ambiguity,

1 My use of the term "new urbanism" predated by at least a decade its later use by the New Urbanists to convey a very different meaning.

contradiction, paradox: these are the qualities in architecture that Venturi has brought into focus and placed in historical perspective. In so doing, he built a bridge between architecture and urbanism across which armies of architects have since tramped—among them some to whom Venturi himself is virtually anathema. But I do not wish to pursue further the question of who did what to whom. That should be left to historians more competent than I. I would only point out that whatever the sources, a new spirit has emerged in architecture within the last decade—a spirit whose major themes are contextual analysis and the notion of architecture as primarily a situational rather than an abstract art. Since I have had cause to deal with these ideas in practice, I will take this occasion to make a few observations about them.

There are two very distinct classes of context or situation within which a building takes form. The first is its *physical* or *environmental* context, which scarcely needs further definition. The interpretation of this context may be easy or difficult, and there may be doubt about what constitutes a suitable response to it. But the facts are unarguable. They are clearly perceptible and at least momentarily immutable. An astute architect can readily comprehend and interpret the physical context. The second class of contexts, which I shall call *societal*, defines the programmatic and institutional situation of the building. The societal context is often obscure, complex, and highly unstable. It is vulnerable not only to misinterpretation but equally to misperception. Furthermore, the societal context can never be fully comprehended or adequately interpreted by the architect alone. An architect needs a client—and I mean by this term not merely the individual or group that has commissioned the building but the entire constituency of interests that use or are affected by it. And here we come to what is for me at once the most exciting and the most difficult challenge of building in cities—the accommodation of interests. I confess that this seems a lifeless phrase: *the accommodation of interests*. But perhaps I can animate it by going to the source that inspired it, Edmund Burke's *Reflections on the Revolution in France*. Discussing that nation in the last decades of its monarchy, he wrote:

> You possessed that variety of parts corresponding with the various descriptions of which your community was happily composed; you had all that combination and all that opposition of interests, you had that action and counteraction, which, in the natural and in the political world, from the reciprocal struggle of discordant powers draws out the harmony of the universe. These opposed and conflicting interests, which you considered as so great a blemish in your old and in our present Constitution, interpose a salutary check to all precipitate resolutions. They render deliberation a matter, not of choice, but of necessity; they make all change a subject of *compromise*, which naturally begets moderation; they produce *temperaments*, preventing the sore evil of harsh, crude, unqualified reformations, and rendering all the headlong exertions of arbitrary power, in the few or in the many, forever impracticable. Through that diversity of members and interests, general liberty had as many securities as there were separate views.[2]

I do not doubt that scholars would take issue with that passage as a portrayal of conditions in France before the

2 Edmund Burke, *Selected Writings and Speeches*, ed. Peter J. Stanlis (New York: Doubleday Anchor, 1963), 530.

revolution. But I regard it as a very adequate manifesto for the building of a humane city.

Returning to my theme, building in cities requires the accommodation of interests. And this is where the client is crucial. Most large building projects today have multiple clients. Typically, for example, there may be a developer, one or more major institutions as tenants, an insurance company as mortgagor, a planning commission, a design review board, interested community groups, and the local public agencies. Through contact with these clients and with their respective programs, the architect gains such access as possible to the various *interests* that need to be considered. But the problem is that while the physical context of the building is clearly defined by what exists around it, the societal context may be quite inaccurately or incompletely defined by the client groups involved. This may come about because some real interests are not represented among the several clients; or, as more commonly occurs, the interests of one of them overrides most or all of the others. Naturally the most important member of the client constituency is the immediate sponsor, individual or corporate, whose programmatic needs the building must fulfill. But in an urban situation, the concerns of clients other than the sponsor are so essential to an understanding of the interests involved that we are justified in evaluating the sponsoring client by the extent to which that client permits or encourages access to the others.

In my experience, such an evaluation produces some surprising results. For example, an enterprising developer, though conventionally regarded as the purest embodiment of venality and greed, can sometimes be an excellent client for building in cities. The reason for this is very simple. Developers are usually not in a position to override all interests other than their own; and if they have brains in their heads, they know that the long-term success of a venture will be assured by satisfying as many of those interests as possible. Furthermore, good developers are sensitive to the life and internal structure of the city. They know how it works, and it is to their advantage to make it work better. For such clients the profit motive, though no less strong, can act as an incentive to the accommodation of diverse interests within their entrepreneurial programs.

Corporate and institutional clients, though usually considered by architects to be more "enlightened"—if that word has any meaning—are sometimes less so in this critical respect. And it is understandable that this should be so, for the pressures generated by their own internal demands are often so great as to override the counterforce of interests beyond their walls. But whatever the balance of forces impinging on a given project, as architects we are apt to find, when we build in the city, that our conception of our constituency embraces interests beyond those recognized by our immediate client. And the resulting conflict of intentions has predictably aroused deep feelings of frustration in the architectural profession.

In the current issue of *Boston* magazine, Jane Holtz Kay makes this frustration the central theme of an article that might, if taken to heart, force this school to close its doors for lack of applicants.[3] The "servant architect," the "middleman architect," the "architect caught in society's vise"—V-I-S-E, that is: these are the vivid terms with which Ms. Kay depicts the purported misery of our lives. Well, I don't disagree with those terms—we are servants, we are middlemen, and we are caught in society's

3 Jane Holtz Kay, "Sizing Up Boston Architects: The Gentlemen Learn to Hustle," *Boston*, November 1974, 64.

vise—but contrary to her implication, that is in my opinion exactly where we belong. To be in society's vise is the very essence of being an architect. And because I hold this view, I have never been enthusiastic about the notion that architects can or should try to escape to a better world by becoming their own clients. Since, as I have pointed out, my conception of the word *client* embraces a multiple and not a singular constituency, I don't think architects can materially alter their "servant" position by simply merging themselves and their interests with the nearest warm body—the sponsoring entrepreneur. But I do fear that through such a merger architects may substantially weaken what I know from experience to be the real source of whatever strength they possess: their independent judgment as professionals. My skepticism about the architect as developer is therefore based not on ethical but on practical considerations—and I regard John Portman as simply the remarkable exception that proves the rule.

One of the most encouraging by-products of the often unhappy history of urban renewal has been the evolution of conglomerate clients, particularly for projects in housing and community development. These client groups, which usually include representatives of city government, local financial institutions, and the community involved—have the great advantage of making directly available to the architect all or most of the major interests that must be accommodated to assure that the project is both achievable and responsive to user needs. There is no doubt that this broadening of the sponsoring client's constituency greatly strengthens and enriches the programmatic frame within which the architect necessarily works. If we understand this new resource and know how to use it, a better city is bound to result.

Still another important by-product of urban renewal is the emergence of clients other than the sponsor as key determinants of the building program and built form. For example, many local redevelopment agencies have learned how to compel conformance with the public interest as they conceive it, through such mechanisms as land disposition agreements and design review boards. The importance of the incentive and special district zoning strategies that I mentioned earlier lies in their peculiar effectiveness both in defining public interests and in assuring their accommodation. Although we may sometimes be inconvenienced by such secondary clients and the interests they advocate, I give my full support to the principle involved. For the intervention of these agencies signifies the struggle of our society to improve its cities, not by imposing vast preordained building programs, but rather by the humane accommodation of interests in the perpetually fragmentary process of growth natural to a free people.

I'm afraid that last thought was rather turgidly expressed, but before consigning it to oblivion, I want to extract one key word. It is *fragmentary*—a word that brings to mind a paradox central to the problem of building in cities. Viewed in its urban context—and I refer to both the physical and the societal context—every building or building group, no matter how extensive, is but a fragment, a piece of the city, as it were. And yet in an equally real sense, many buildings, especially big buildings, are of necessity whole entities—freestanding, autonomous, self-sufficient. As the institutions of our society, both public and private, grow ever larger and more complex, the resolution of this paradox—reconciling the idea of the fragment with the idea of the whole—becomes correspondingly more crucial to the quality of urban life. Whether we speak of corporations, universities, hospitals, or agencies of government, the problem is the same: it has become increasingly difficult for a major institution expanding in response to complex, internally generated needs to build in the city without despoiling it—to become, despite its size, a successful fragment of a larger whole. This is clearly a problem that cannot be solved by architectural means alone. It requires adjustment in program as well. But whatever the specific means employed, I believe the solution is to be found in the deliberate accommodation of those interests that constitute the urban context, permitting them to distort the otherwise self-determined form or function of a building and thus to demonstrate its fragmentary character.

To me it seems entirely appropriate that the *situational* aspect of building in cities has become a major preoccupation of architecture in our time. We have learned—is it possible that we had forgotten?—that the proliferation of perfect prototypes within a perfect order does not make a city. To make a city we must temper and perhaps abandon preconceptions of ideal form; we must welcome the natural diversity of interests inherent in the idea of the city; we must accept this diversity—this combination and opposition of interests—as constituting the essential programmatic substance to be accommodated in building and celebrated in architecture; we must, in sum, practice the humane civic art of place and occasion.

Retrospect, 2018

In this talk I acknowledged, indeed celebrated, the fundamental changes in my sensibility and aspirations that had been brought about by my first quarter-century in practice—most notably by the experience of designing three major built works of that period: Place Ville Marie, the college at Fredonia, and the John Hancock Tower.

Above Model of Lafayette Place proposal for Washington Street in downtown Boston, 1973.

Gone was my earlier enthusiasm for remaking the world through comprehensive urban planning; in its place I embraced the contingent, the speculative, the fragmentary, together with the interplay of "opposed and conflicting interests" that I now saw as constituting the essence of urban life and urban culture.

Exemplary of this shift is the concept plan for Lafayette Place (with Harold Fredenburgh), an urban development project in downtown Boston that my colleagues and I were working on at the time of the lecture. Though unbuilt, this twelve-acre mixed-use project is worthy of note for its attempt to bring the benefits of large-scale redevelopment without violating the grain and pattern of its host city. Instead of an alienating monolith, we proposed a cluster of stepped building volumes that respect the established scale of Boston's downtown, address the surrounding streets, and create in their interstices a network of intimately scaled alleyways lined with shops.

Unfortunately, in his efforts to obtain the necessary financing, our client lost control of the project, which was ultimately built by another developer to the design of a different architect and precisely in accord with the inward-focused shopping-mall formula from which we had sought to escape. Bostonians stayed away in droves, and the project failed.

Subsequent experience, while confirming me in my preference for the fragmentary and the contingent, has also reminded me that a city cannot live on such episodes alone. However thrilling they may be, these interventions will fail if not served and joined by a comprehensively planned urban infrastructure.

THE STREETS OF FALMOUTH NECK

Conversation with Peg Brown
Portland, Maine, August 2006

Ancestors on both sides of your family lived in Portland—in fact, on the very site of the Portland Museum of Art. What can you tell us about them?

My father's great-great-grandfather, Matthew Cobb, was a successful sea captain in the West Indies trade, and in 1801 he commissioned Alexander Parris, who was the leading architect of his time in Boston, to build the house that stood on the Congress Square site now occupied by the Payson Building. In 1807 President Jefferson placed an embargo on trade with the West Indies, and many in Portland were bankrupted, including my ancestor. I'm not sure how much longer he stayed in the house, but it eventually passed to others and was still standing in 1897, when it was replaced by an office block known as the Libby Building. It, in turn, was demolished for the Payson Building. I always harbored a hope, when we were excavating for the basement of the Payson Building, that we would find some spoon or other object from my ancestor's house, but nothing showed up.

Top Alexander Parris, Matthew Cobb House, 1801 (photograph circa 1880). **Above Left** Rev. Ichabod Nichols (1784–1859). **Above Right** First Parish Church, 1825.

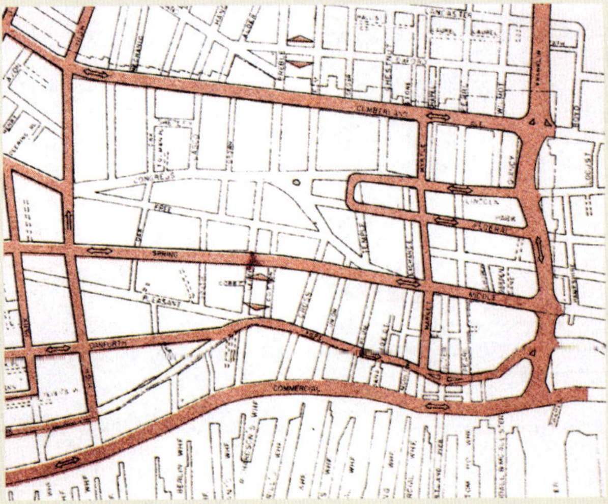

Top Downtown Portland street plan, 1966.
Above Victor Gruen Associates, proposed circulation system for Portland, 1967.

On my mother's side, my great-great-grandfather, Ichabod Nichols, was for half a century—1809 to 1859—the minister of the First Parish Church on Congress Street at the head of Temple, and he built the present church in 1826. In fact, he's buried in the churchyard.

Your ancestors are obviously a very important part of Portland history. How did your own involvement with the city begin?
I have spent part of virtually every summer since 1937 on an island in Penobscot Bay, about seventy-five miles down east from Portland. The curious fact is that for almost thirty years I simply drove by Portland. I didn't look seriously at the city until 1966, when I was invited by the Portland Museum of Art to give a lecture on the subject of urban design. I felt that it wasn't right to give a lecture in Portland without knowing something about the city, so I made a special trip there, and it was sort of love at first sight. I became completely enchanted: by its history, its architecture, and above all its streets. I discovered that Portland had one of the most beautiful street systems in North America. I completely changed my plans for my lecture, which became a kind of love letter to Portland, illustrated with historic photographs and diagrams that I made myself, showing how the street system had evolved over three centuries. In the course of my research, I also discovered that the architect-planner Victor Gruen had been engaged to do an urban renewal plan for downtown. I believed that his proposed plan was exactly the wrong thing to do to Portland, and I started agitating against it during that first lecture.

Because of my own involvement in urban renewal in Boston and elsewhere, I was very much concerned about the way this vast federally financed program was erasing the history of cities. I had a growing awareness that things were going on that would later be regretted. I was also very much aware that the reason Victor Gruen had been hired to make this plan was that the city fathers were desperate to do something about the continuing decline of the downtown. Portland had been in recession for almost a century, ever since a big fire destroyed its waterfront wharves and warehouses shortly after the Civil War. The urban renewal program was seen as a lifesaver for cities like Portland where, if you could show that the city was a slum, you could get money from the federal government to make big changes. Unfortunately, the changes proposed by Gruen for Portland would have converted the center of the downtown into an enormous cookie-cutter shopping mall. In order to make Congress Street into a pedestrian zone, the two streets flanking it on the north and south, Cumberland and Spring, were going to be widened and made into thoroughfares with parking garages on both sides. It was a classic shopping-center strategy that completely ignored, and indeed proposed to erase, Portland's unique topographical and architectural qualities.

I made my case for stopping this plan during my 1966 lecture, and I continued to do so for half a decade after that. And I was listened to. Portland's city planners came to our office in New York and asked us to devise a new plan that would reconsider the effect of the urban renewal strategy. I wanted very much to do that, but I put one condition on it: namely, that the city would not proceed with the widening and extension of Spring Street, which I viewed as a devastating surgical operation that would wipe out the most important elements of the street system of Portland. I felt that if they could defer this part of the plan and give us a chance to produce another vision, there was a real possibility, but if they didn't defer it, the horse would already be out of the barn and there was no point.

As it turned out, the City Council did not agree to my condition. They had recently negotiated a deal with Holiday Inn to build a new hotel on Spring Street. They desperately wanted that hotel, and the agreement with Holiday Inn specified that it would be built only if the Spring Street arterial went forward as planned. As a result, we didn't make a plan for Portland, and a greatly widened Spring Street was extended to a catastrophic collision with Middle Street. It's a classic example of urban renewal gone wrong. It's a tragedy because it's unrecoverable. It destroyed the most beautiful part of the street system of Portland—the wonderful S-curve of Middle Street.

Above Views of Middle Street in 1863, looking west and east from Temple Street, in contemporary lithographs.

CONGRESS SQUARE, PORTLAND, MAINE

Charles Shipman Payson Building
Portland Museum of Art, 1978–83
with Paul Marantz (lighting), Laurie D. Olin (landscape), John Holverson (museum director)

When, in the summer of 1976, Charles Shipman Payson decided to donate to the Portland Museum of Art his collection of four oil paintings and thirteen watercolors by Winslow Homer, he made it a condition of his gift that the museum would build a new wing to house these and other works in its growing collection. In response, the museum purchased several properties adjoining its existing galleries, which had been built in 1911 to the design of John Calvin Stevens. The properties thus acquired included a nondescript brick-clad office block fronting on Congress Square that had, at the end of the nineteenth century, displaced Matthew Cobb's handsome Federal-style house. This ancestral connection to the site, though marginally interesting, had nothing to do with my eagerness to be selected as architect of the museum's new wing. What seized my imagination was the opportunity to design a building for an important cultural institution fronting on a major public square in the city with which I had fallen in love a decade earlier. This opportunity was especially appealing to me because I felt an urgent need at that time to take a break from the large-scale commercial building projects to which, with the sole exception of the Fredonia campus, I had devoted the first three decades of my professional life. Having only recently emerged from the ordeal of the Hancock Tower, which indeed had threatened to destroy our practice, I was thrilled to be awarded the Portland commission, and I proceeded to immerse myself in it as in no other.

In the fall of 1981, while the Payson Building was under construction, the Payson Homers were exhibited at the Coe-Kerr Gallery in New York. In an essay written for the accompanying catalogue, I described the design and summarized its intentions as follows:

Top Winslow Homer gallery crowned by clerestory lantern.
Above Sectional perspective. **Overleaf** Great Hall.

Mr. Payson's Homers have never been far from our thoughts as we designed the new building that will house them. From the outset it was our intention that these and other masterpieces of the State of Maine Collection, beyond simply being made available to the public, should be appropriately celebrated by the settings in which they are displayed. The diversity of the collection—and indeed of the Homers themselves—clearly advocates a variety of such settings: spaces ranging from intimate to grand, and lighting from natural to artificially controlled. But there is equally a need for coherence in the totality of the museum experience and a comprehensible order in the arrangement of its parts. To achieve these goals, the new galleries are composed of a multilevel aggregation of identical spatial units that are variously combined, vertically as well as horizontally, to form larger spaces of diverse configuration within the unifying order of the structural frame. Thus, from the moment of entry into the Great Hall, the visitor will encounter a rich but disciplined elaboration of interior space accompanying and supporting the exhibition of works of art.

In considering how best to capture the special quality of "Portland light" for the benefit of paintings and sculpture, we rejected the conventional method of admitting daylight through translucent ceiling panels as employed in most museums built during the past century. Instead, we returned to an earlier, simpler, and in my view superior prototype, the domed clerestory—a configuration first and most brilliantly exemplified by John Soane's Dulwich Picture Gallery. The particular merit of this configuration is that controlled daylight entering from above

suffuses, shapes, and animates the space as it illuminates the works of art within. Fixed louvers mounted in the clerestory lantern shield the gallery from direct sunlight while permitting up to forty foot-candles of daylight—considered by conservators to be the optimum—to reach paintings hung on the walls below. Here then the fundamental elements of architecture—space and light—are placed simply and directly in the service of the museum experience.

Just as the internal space of a museum mediates between the art object and the visitor's eye, so its external form mediates between the museum as an institution and the community it serves. In our design of the Charles Shipman Payson Building, which fronts on one of Portland's major public squares and is literally surrounded by landmark structures, this was a particularly crucial issue, presenting delicate iconographic and environmental problems. Already standing on the museum's property were three architecturally significant buildings: the McLellan-Sweat Mansion (1800), a handsome example of the Federal period that is open to the public as a house museum; the Charles Quincy Clapp House (1832), an elegant and unusual Greek Revival building now occupied by the museum-affiliated Portland School of Art; and the L. D. M. Sweat Memorial (1911), a characteristic gallery building of its time that still houses a significant portion of the museum's collections. All three of these important buildings have been preserved and integrated into the expanded museum complex—a complex comprising 15,000 square feet of new gallery space (five times the floor area of the Sweat Memorial), a 200-seat auditorium, a research library, museum shop,

Top Third-floor gallery with view of spaces beyond.
Above Aerial view of Payson Building and environs, showing historic structures on museum's property.

Top View across Congress Square toward Portland Harbor. **Above** View of stepped building form and garden from High Street. **Overleaf** Congress Square facade.

and administrative, storage, and work space required to serve this greatly enlarged institution. The total floor area of new construction is 57,600 square feet.

The distinguishing feature of this design problem was the need to provide these extensive new facilities in a form that would respect and render eloquent the living presence of history on and around the museum site. Our solution prescribed a stepped building form that, while fronting boldly onto Congress Square, grants primacy to its smaller neighbors within the museum precinct. To complete this strategy of accommodation, the new building is shaped in plan to create outdoor garden spaces that provide a sympathetic landscape setting for the entire ensemble.

In the Congress Square facade of the new gallery wing, we have thought it appropriate to assert strongly and even provocatively the identity of the museum as a major institution in its city. The scale and iconographic character of the elements composing this facade are graded in ascending order from ground to roof. The street-level arcade is intimate and repetitive, with a single exception made for the entry arch, which penetrates to the second floor as one of a series of large semicircular openings. These in turn announce the major theme, which is fully developed at the top of the wall, where an alternating rhythm of incised large circles and smaller squares refers to the spatial order of the building's interior. The projection of this wall above the roof allows it to engage the sky and thus to assert its special role in defining and ornamenting Congress Square. This facade, indeed the entire exterior of the

HAY
NO U
TURN

new building, is built of water-struck red brick with gray granite trim—materials indigenous to Maine and commonly found in the vernacular architecture of Portland. Our purpose in employing them here was to extend and reanimate a tradition of masonry building that has, for more than two centuries, shaped the distinctive personality of this city. This is a role appropriate, we believe, to a regional museum housing works by Hartley, Hopper, Marin, and Wyeth, not to mention Mr. Payson's Homers.

In a talk in 2013, marking the thirtieth anniversary of the opening of the Payson Building, I explained my thinking in greater detail, starting with a series of diagrams with accompanying text that explains the step-by-step evolution of the design.

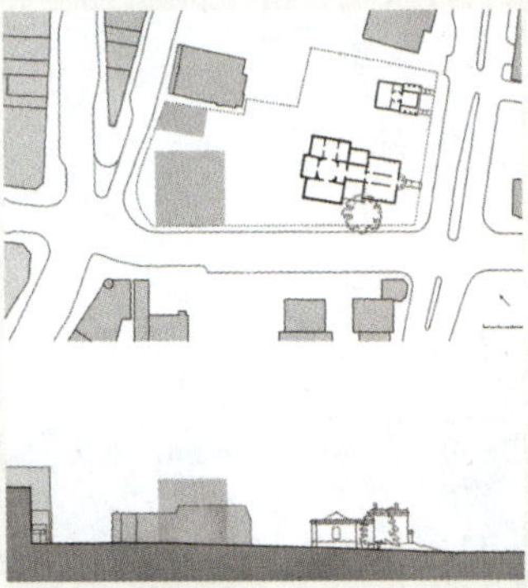

← Of the five buildings standing on the museum's property when we were awarded this commission, three were to be preserved: the McLellan House, the Charles Quincy Clapp House, and the L. D. M. Sweat Memorial. These architecturally significant buildings, together with a magnificent copper beech tree, were from the outset recognized as integral and essential assets of the museum's campus. Indeed, their presence was the single most important factor conditioning our design.

→ The museum property included important frontage on Congress Square that became available after removal of two commercial buildings. The square then needed to be contained on this side by a street wall commensurate in scale with the dimensions of the space, the heights of neighboring buildings, and the prominence of the location as seen from a considerable distance along Congress and High Streets. Analysis of these factors led us to conclude that the new museum building should present to Congress Square a building facade measuring approximately 120 feet in length by 60 feet in height.

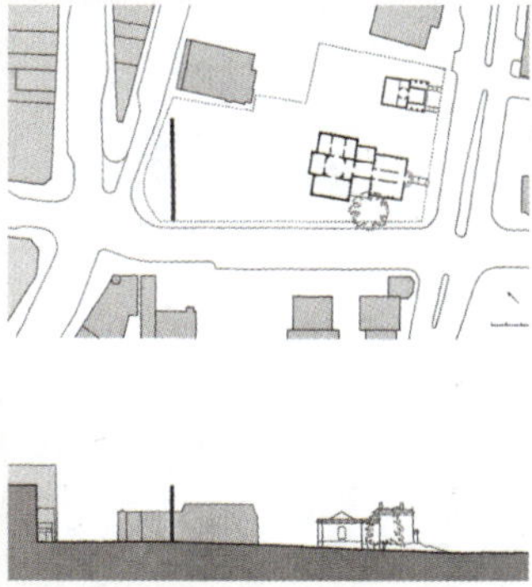

→ Behind the street wall, we needed to establish an organizing discipline within which to plan the museum's new exhibition galleries. A spatial grid was proposed, made up of two elements: a 20-by-20-by-12-foot parallelepiped defining the smallest desirable unit of gallery space, and a 20-by-6-by-10-foot parallelepiped defining an interstitial space between each gallery unit. The accretion of these elements horizontally and vertically resulted in a three-dimensional grid defining well-proportioned spaces of appropriate scale and suggesting an intrinsic distinction between circulation spaces (rectangular) and places of repose and contemplation (square).

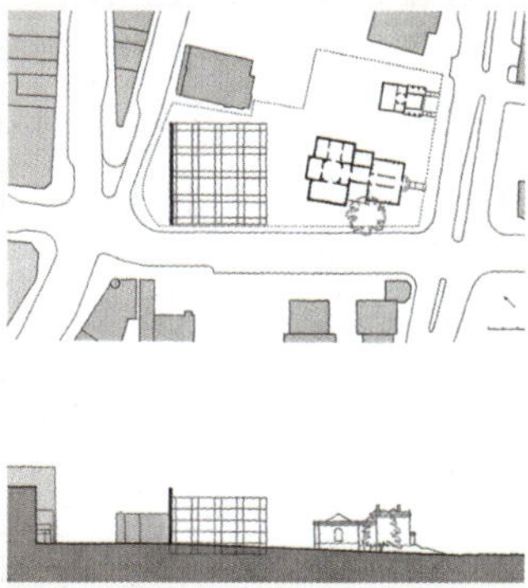

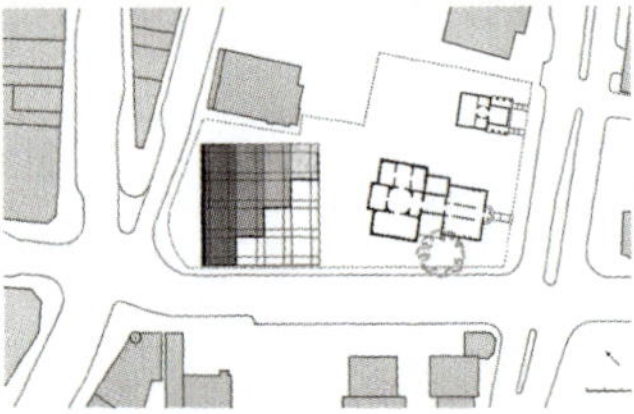

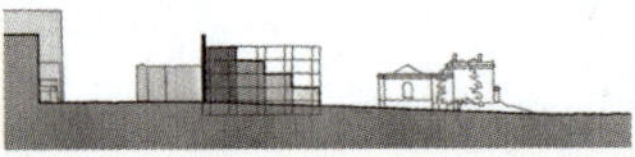

← Within the discipline established by the spatial grid, we needed to devise a building form that could accommodate the museum's functional program and also respond appropriately to the diverse conditions of its site. While on its Congress Square face the building needed to assert a unified, large-scale presence, the High and Spring Street sides required a recessive, fragmented form granting primacy to the much smaller historic buildings within the museum's campus. These objectives were achieved by starting with a four-bay-wide, four-story-high block facing Congress Square, then stepping the building down and back through each unit of the spatial grid as it approached the L. D. M. Sweat Memorial.

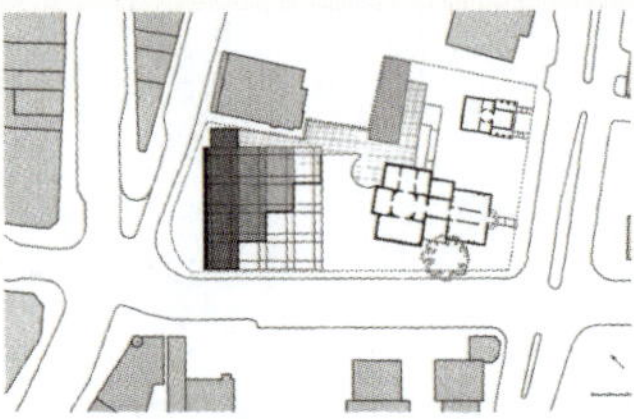

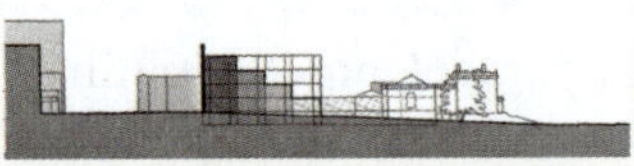

← The new building needed to be linked internally to the existing galleries in the L. D. M. Sweat Memorial. This connection was achieved by means of an infill structure that also contains an octagonal sculpture gallery and an adjoining wing with space for necessary administrative and service functions. The infill building was shaped in such a way as to complete the definition of two outdoor garden spaces within the museum's campus—one facing onto High Street and the other onto Spring Street. These provide a sympathetic landscape setting for buildings that together bear witness to nearly two centuries of architectural history in Portland.

The very first move in the process I've just outlined, positing a major facade overlooking Congress Square, caused me to rethink the obligation of this regional museum not just to acknowledge but to celebrate the traditions of its place, and prompted me to envision the Payson Building as *joining* rather than setting itself apart from those traditions. This was an entirely new beginning for me in that it was the first of my built works to pursue a contextually integrative design strategy drawing on local vernacular precedent. Portland is a city built of brick and granite, a city rich in the kind of unpretentious, serviceable architecture that achieves a certain eloquence through its modesty and directness. But vernacular buildings tend to be background buildings, and the museum leadership clearly wanted a foreground building. The Payson Building was intended to initiate a kind of cultural revival in Portland, and therefore, although inspired by vernacular precedent, it had to speak in a way that would transcend that precedent. In facing this challenge, I was obliged to think about the cultural meaning that could be carried not only by indigenous materials but by the craft involved in the making and assembling of those materials, so that a work of architecture could both embody and move beyond the traditions from which it sprang. My effort to achieve this dual goal is seen most prominently in the Congress Square facade, which one critic described as giving evidence of an architect's doodling—thus implying a relaxed casualness that was the exact opposite of my actual interminable agonizing over this inescapably rhetorical frontispiece of the Payson Building.

Top Main facade, with entry and arcade.
Above Commercial Street, with nineteenth-century brick and granite buildings, 1979.

In the end, the Congress Square facade became the two-dimensional external manifestation of the conceptual schema that defines the spatial structure of the museum, as experienced sequentially while moving through its galleries. While the admission of daylight through domed clerestories is surely the most important distinguishing feature of the building's interior, I'd like to remind you also of another feature that brings me back to my deep affection for Portland. The museum's director, John Holverson, and I wanted the interior to affirm its connection to its place not only by means of material and detail but also by providing glimpses of the city at various points along the way. Thus, after passing through the half-domed entry, entering the Great Hall, and moving up to the second floor, one cannot rise to the third without passing by the arched windows that offer views into Congress Square, after which one mounts a stairway leading to a glazed landing, with views into the garden and the harbor beyond.

Just as the Payson Building is seen from the outside as the museum in the city, so from the inside the visitor encounters the city in the museum.

The way the stairways always engage the corner—so that halfway up, you see out—is critically important. It is important because you need to persuade people that it's worth walking up four floors, and one way of doing that is by making it an interesting walk. The scale of those stairs is something I learned from Borromini. In the Palazzo Barberini in Rome, he made a staircase of a scale such that when you walk up it, you feel as if you're floating. So the stairs in Portland are exactly the same proportion of tread to riser as that Borromini stair: 16 inches by 5 ⅓ inches. And you do feel that you're floating up.

Then you have an event at midpoint that takes you back to the city before you go on to the next gallery. I like the fact that you're not just immersed in art but are brought back to the connection between art and life, art and the city. The Payson Building is very much about connecting the experience of looking at art with the experience of being in this particular place.

In retrospect, the Payson Building marked a hinge point in my professional life as significant as that marked by the Hancock Tower a decade earlier—though of a very different kind. Whereas the tower in Boston had challenged me to discover how the skyscraper could be imagined as a contingent rather than an autonomous presence in the city, the museum in Portland challenged me to discover how the well-established vernacular traditions of a place could inform a contemporary work of architecture. It caused me to think about history in what was for me a completely new way—as something not to stand aloof from but to embrace and explore as a stimulus for fresh invention. Eschewing historicist pastiche, the Payson Building exhibits both the awkwardness and the ardor of that first embrace. More than a quarter-century after its completion, despite or perhaps precisely because of its many idiosyncrasies, the building still seems to celebrate the exploratory mode of its creation, and that is a source of enormous satisfaction to its architect.

Above Half-dome entry flanked by arcade.

BRICK

Conversation with Paolo Conrad Bercah
New York City, February 1998

The Portland Museum of Art, which opened in 1983, was your first brick building. Since then you have used brick in a number of projects, including the Moakley Courthouse in Boston and the Anderson School in Los Angeles. You obviously have an affinity for this material. Why didn't you use it earlier?

My changing attitude toward brick is another symptom of the evolution in my sensibility and thinking about architecture over the years. The pedagogy of the Graduate School of Design under Gropius gave me little reason to care about brick. Furthermore, because Harvard is a largely brick campus, brick was associated in my mind with the past, with neo-Georgian and a kind of stylistic eclecticism—all the things that, in the brave new world, we were going to get away from. It wasn't until Portland that I became interested in brick as a material that carries the memory of a certain tradition in the craft of building. Prior to that I simply wasn't interested in architecture's capacity to carry memory. Even when using a material that was contextually sympathetic, I was interested only in the architecture's asserting its newness and dissociating itself from tradition. In those early years of practice, I was still in thrall to the prescriptions and proscriptions of the Gropius pedagogy.

But then Louis Kahn said to the brick, "What do you want, brick?"

Yes, Portland came after I had become very much interested in Kahn's work. The whole idea of going back to what he called Volume Zero—in effect, going back to prehistory to find the sources—I found compelling. For me it was a way of acknowledging that a future entirely disconnected from the past is futile and impoverishing, but without having to abandon the modernist rejection of historical styles. In other words: Yes, we have to look to the past, but we're going to go back to the very beginning. I think that was part of Kahn's consciousness. I know it's part of mine, that taste for the earliest phase of any stylistic development. It's a natural outcome of both my own sensibility and the time in which I live that I tend to be more responsive to vernacular precedent than to so-called high-style precedent, and I found the vernacular buildings of Portland very engaging.

In my youth brick had been just another material for keeping out the weather, to be used in accordance with modernist principles of design but without specific concern for the tradition of its use, the cultural implications of its use, and the craft implications of its use. But in Portland I became very much involved with all of those issues and with the ways in which architecture, through the use of an indigenous material, can both embody and transcend the traditions of a place.

In what way did you draw on the vernacular tradition in Portland?

Almost all the elements of the museum's building envelope can be found in the vernacular architecture of Maine, including the arcade and the half-dome at the entrance. I got into hot water when I had to go beyond what could be carried over from the vernacular tradition. Early on, I determined that the Congress Square facade should be expressed as a quasi-detached screenwall. This idea did not take long to emerge, but it was extremely difficult to find the voice for that wall. It is really the wall of the square, and its scale has to do with the need to enclose the space of the square. It is articulated so as to enrich that space by declaring the importance of the institution housed on the other side. But the problem is that the building is small, and the wall wants to be tall. I had to find a way of articulating the wall that was coherent with the vernacular precedent I was using, so I arrived at the idea of arcuation—of creating arches. Arcuation is something that brick can readily do, whereas trabeation is something that brick cannot so readily do; it cannot be a flat beam. Therefore I decided that trabeation had to be handled by granite lintels, while arcuation could be handled by brick.

All of that was pretty easy. What became much more problematic was how to give expression to the wall as it rose above the roof of the building behind. I believed that the wall should engage the sky; therefore it had to have openings so you could see its thickness and realize that it was rising above the building and asserting itself as a wall, not as just as the front surface of a solid object. That is why it is separated by an arcade from the front.

What about the upper part?

That took a long time to design. Once again I fell back on my weakness for weightlessness. I felt the need to express the tradition of arcuation yet at the same time to go beyond that tradition, to push it to an expression you would never find in a simple vernacular building. My solution was to carry the arch around to inscribe the circle in brick. It is very peculiar outcome, highly mannered but also minimal. The wall is all about weight, substance, and bearing, and suddenly these strange things happen. You have to understand that it was the first time in my life that I ever thought of a facade as a facade. Before then, we did not think about facades; the word *facade* was never used.

It seems as if during the early years of your practice, your method was to deal first with the plan, then with the section, and last with the front of the building. Did this way of working come from Gropius?

Yes, and it was a characteristic weakness of the modern movement. The curious thing is that Le Corbusier, who was the architect most studied when we were in school, was a master of facades, but we never thought of him in those terms. We occasionally looked at him in terms of composition, but we had completely overlooked what Colin Rowe, Fred Koetter, and company later made him out to be—essentially a facade architect. We did no analytical studies; at Harvard under Gropius, such activity was strongly disapproved of. Facades were thought of as a product of facadism, which was the corrupt practice of superimposing a stylistic dress on a building. Truthfulness was a big issue, and the term *facade* was assumed to mean untruthfulness.

Because it suggested a mask?

Yes, a mask that concealed the truth. When I said that the Portland Museum was the first time that I consciously designed a facade, what I meant was that it was the first time that the exterior wall had a life of its own, transcending though not rejecting its duty to tell the truth about the building behind. By separating the wall from the body of the building and extending it upward beyond the top of the building, I was saying that its main obligation as architecture is to be an appropriate enclosure for the square, one that mediates between the space of the square and that of the museum. It needs to offer something to both. It has to present the museum as an institution, and it has to enclose the square in an appropriate, lively, and engaging way. From the inside it fulfills another obligation, which is to allow people moving through the museum to glimpse the city.

The building in fact has a pronounced frontality that reminds me of the Palazzo Farnese. One would expect to find a piazza in front of it. Yet what is in front is not a real square; it is more like an intersection.

Yes, but it is trying to be a square—it wants to be a square—and the facade is aimed specifically at enhancing its quality as a civic space. It's an act of citizenship on the part of the museum to present itself in a way that dignifies the space. Like most American civic spaces, it is not a piazza in the Italian sense; it is fragmented, diffuse. But the museum aspires to anchor it.

How did you come to the building's stepped form?

That was my response to the split personality of the site. On one side it engages the square, framed by multistory commercial buildings, while on the other it engages the remnants of a residential neighborhood, with very small-scale but historically important buildings. The whole scheme of the museum is based on the need to address those two scales. But I discovered right away that the mere stacking up of blocks from one story on one side to four on the other didn't suffice, for a very simple reason. If you were to look at the stepping-up in section and imagine the facade not being there, you would see that the stepping-up actually turned the high side of the building into a back, and it had to be turned into a front again, so that the museum would front on rather than back up against the square. Hence the need for a separate screen-wall facing the square.

I'm beginning to see a similarity between the front of this museum and the back of the building that housed the *scenae frons* in Roman theaters. There, too, the back became a front, and the facade was simultaneously front and back.

Yes, you are right—I had never thought of it that way. In this case, however, there were two reasons I couldn't go with the highest block as a front to the square: one was that it was the back of a stepped volume, and the other was that it wasn't high enough. In order to solve both problems, I needed to disengage the back wall from the volume of the building. The schema of the building allowed me to do that because it involves squares separated by interstitial space, and the last interstitial space became the occasion for separating the facade.

So the back became a screen that created a front to the square.

Yes. A screen-wall has the capacity to be a facade. But while the wall needed to be disengaged from the volume,

Above Elevation of Congress Square facade, Portland Museum of Art, showing American bond with six-course headers, every mortar joint drawn by hand.

it also needed to be engaged with the building. The vaulted arcade and half-dome entry were very important to me; I wanted the wall to be more than something just planted in front of the building.

Did you ever consider a material other than brick?
The building was originally conceived in granite. At first we thought, "This is a great institution, and granite is the most noble material." There is a tradition of granite post-and-lintel in Maine, but we couldn't afford it. So this is another example of the schema being adopted very quickly and the development of the architecture taking a long time. I spent months fussing with the facade. But the decision to go from granite to brick was the crucial one and opened up new possibilities, because brick lends itself to arcuation and a gentler, non-trabeated kind of engagement.

In Portland I was very preoccupied with the relationship between tradition and invention; I was interested in showing how architecture could reanimate and reinterpret a local tradition in contemporary terms. I didn't want to build a foreign object. While this was the smallest building I had done up to that time, in the context of Portland it was too big, too important, and too local in its connotations to set itself apart as a modernist icon. At the same time, I didn't want to mimic the past. The challenge of this enterprise was to find a way to use brick and granite that would both respect and transcend the traditions of its place.

You are fond of saying that architecture is an art of indirection, meaning that the architect doesn't make a building but produces an elaborate set of instructions that are executed by people who actually do make

the building. With respect to your works in brick—the Portland Museum, the Boston federal courthouse, the Anderson School—are you satisfied with the way they were executed?

Yes, very satisfied. The craft of those buildings, embodying the care and skill of the masons, adds a great deal to their quality as works of architecture. One of the most important discoveries of my late career has been that you can still get beautiful brickwork if you ask for it, and that it's worth getting.

THE INFLUENCE OF SOANE

Excerpts from Commentary Prepared for the Documentary Film *Sir John Soane: An English Architect, An American Legacy* (2005)

Discovery of Soane is part of getting to know history. After all, as Philip Johnson said, "You can't not know history." My generation in architecture came close to not knowing history because of the proscriptive pedagogy we were subjected to. But in the end it's true: you can't not know history. You can't be an architect traveling around the world looking at things without becoming engaged by history.

So sooner or later—I think it was in the early sixties—I visited the Soane Museum in Lincoln's Inn Fields. I saw that wonderful breakfast room. I saw that enchanting paneled room where the Hogarths are hung, with its successive layers of panels and pictures until finally you open the last layer and you're looking down into a garden. The idea that an architect could have so much fun! You sense his sheer joy in finding new ways of making spaces and new ways of shaping the experience of a place.

I didn't visit the Dulwich Picture Gallery until the late seventies, when I had already started to think about the Payson Building. I was immediately struck by two things: first, the wonderful scale of the spaces, and second, the wonderful light in those spaces. I felt right away that Soane had discovered the best way of lighting a picture gallery, whereby daylight comes in through domed clerestories, then strikes the sloping planes of the ceiling surface and is reflected into the space. I was astonished to learn that this strategy, which Soane invented and utilized so skillfully in Dulwich, had seldom if ever been used subsequently in an art museum until I used it in Portland.

Since the nineteenth century, the fashion in museum and gallery design has been to introduce daylight into the space via skylight and then through a horizontal translucent plane. The resulting light is a very good light, but it does not bring the space to life the way Soane's domed clerestories do, because the light is coming through a translucent surface rather than reflecting off the surfaces of the sloping ceiling. That reflected light is not only more lively; it is also a better light for the paintings. Today many people feel that contemporary museums are big performances taking away from the art. But Soane succeeded in getting the best of both worlds: he created spaces that are wonderful to be in and full of life and light, yet are also wonderful as settings for the pictures that are hung in them.

In Portland I emulated Soane quite directly. As in the smaller galleries at Dulwich, the spaces of the Payson Building are square, the clerestories octagonal, and the planes that make the transition from the square at the base to the octagon above are brought to life by the light that falls on them. The walls below are deliberately made so that curators can deal with them as they wish and paint them different colors; above that line, where the wall surface stops and the domed surface begins, at a height of about ten feet, it's always white. All this is exactly as in Dulwich. The louvers in the clerestories, however, are something you won't find in Soane's gallery. These have a very specific purpose: namely, to prevent sunlight from falling directly onto the walls below the domes, which is essential for conservation of the pictures. At different times of day you get very interesting shadows from the light coming through the louvers onto the inside surfaces of the domes. So you get the benefit of the sunlight and the wonderful liveliness of direct light and shadow without compromising the conservation of the art.

The twenty-foot-square unit of space in Portland is almost identical with the square units in Dulwich. When a larger rectangular space was needed, Soane made it by elongating one domed unit, whereas I made my rectangular spaces by aggregating a series of square domed units. The program of the Portland Museum called for its galleries to be flexible, so it had to be made in such a way that the spaces could be aggregated in varied ways and changed over time in response to curatorial changes. The walls are sixteen inches thick—because walls should be thick!—but those walls are hollow, and within them are columns that occur rigorously at the intersections of the square grid and the rectangular interstitial spaces. You could take out all the walls in the building and reorganize them in different ways. This flexibility is deliberately not made explicit, because I did not want the columns to separate themselves from the walls. To do that would have put too much emphasis on the discipline of the grid that governs the structure of the building. I didn't want to express that discipline directly; I wanted the space to flow

Above Domed clerestory at Portland Museum of Art.
Page 200 Main gallery at Dulwich Picture Gallery, London.

freely. I wanted more of a game, if you will, between the consistency of the square domed clerestories and the variety in the placement of the walls.

One of the reasons Dulwich appealed to me so much is that the domed clerestory was affordable; it could be done with drywall. Drywall is a material without quality, but it did allow me to create a rich array of spaces at a modest cost. The one surface throughout the Payson Building that is deliberately enriched materially is the floor. Thanks to our use of sheetrock on the interior walls and brick on the exterior, we could afford this bit of material richness. We wanted to have some surface inside the building that would speak to the regional character of the museum just as the brick and granite spoke to its regional character on the outside. So for the floor we chose pine and granite. The choice of floor material was a very important part of giving the museum a distinctive character without in any way limiting curatorial flexibility. It's no accident that only in the floor can one see the underlying geometric discipline of the building explicitly expressed.

Soane's gallery at Dulwich is a one-story building. In order to achieve a building of a scale that I thought appropriate to its frontage on Congress Square, I needed to be able to step up from the scale of the houses on one side to the scale of the commercial buildings on the other. The Soanian domed clerestories define a module that could be stacked vertically as well as horizontally. And that's the whole secret to the design.

Another aspect of the Payson Building that betrays the influence of Soane is the handling of brick. Particularly on the Congress Square facade, the recesses in the brick and the way the large circles and openings are made all reflect lessons that I learned from Soane—specifically, that you don't just cut a hole in a wall; you first set the stage by creating a change of plane within which an opening then takes place. This strategy is particularly evident at his Royal Hospital Stables, from which I learned so much about brick and how to bring it to life as a way of making architecture. Soane was quirky, a mannerist, not a rulebook architect. As I struggled to find the right voice for the Congress Square facade, Soane's very lean interpretation of the classical language not only appealed to my sensibility but also seemed to resonate with the vernacular architecture of Portland, much as Soane's buildings resonate with the vernacular architecture of Georgian London.

Above Royal Hospital, Chelsea, Stables, London, 1814.

DOWNTOWN NEW BRUNSWICK, STAMFORD SOUTH END

Corporation as Catalyst: Two Headquarters Buildings

A characteristic feature of American corporate expansion in the half-century following World War II was the construction of emblematic headquarters facilities, often in the form of multi-building campuses in rural or suburban settings. Less common, but to me more interesting, were headquarters projects located in declining urban areas, with the dual aim of catalyzing urban regeneration while accommodating corporate growth. Two such projects, both motivated by their sponsors' sense of civic responsibility, engaged my attention during the decade between the mid-seventies to the mid-eighties.

The pharmaceutical giant Johnson & Johnson was founded and has always kept its headquarters in New Brunswick, New Jersey. During the 1970s, confronted by an urgent need for more office space, the company's management considered relocating its headquarters to a suburban location but ultimately decided not to abandon the small city of which it had been, for almost a century, the leading corporate citizen. To meet its needs, J&J acquired a fifteen-acre site straddling a railway viaduct and giving its corporate campus a newly prominent presence in the heart of the city. At the same time, the company sponsored an urban development initiative aimed at revitalizing New Brunswick's declining downtown. Our firm was then given a dual assignment: to design the headquarters complex and to help envision a plan for renewal of the city in which it was embedded.

Although a slender sixteen-story tower announces **Johnson & Johnson World Headquarters** (1976–83, with W. Stephen Wood; Laurie D. Olin, landscape) on the city's skyline, most of its office and accompanying support spaces are housed in an adjoining array of linked pavilions, three to four stories in height. This strategy of fragmentation serves a twofold purpose: internally, it

Top Pavilion atrium at Johnson & Johnson World Headquarters. **Above** Pavilions and executive tower, flanked by public promenade. **Page 206** Aerial view of complex.

gives identity and focus to the company's several operating divisions, each organized around a skylit atrium; externally, it gives the headquarters complex a lively but not overbearing presence in a richly landscaped park that offers its amenity both to the buildings within and to the surrounding city streets.

As with Johnson & Johnson in New Brunswick, the **Pitney Bowes World Headquarters** (1979–86, with Theodore J. Musho; Laurie D. Olin, landscape) in Stamford's South End is the product of management's decision to remain in the city—and neighborhood—where it had been founded six decades earlier. As with the New Brunswick project, our corporate client also sponsored a comprehensive planning study with the aim of strengthening both the physical and the social fabric of its hometown.

Although the Pitney Bowes building's floor area almost exactly matches that of Johnson & Johnson, both the schema and the voice of its architecture are entirely dissimilar, reflecting the distinctly different character of its site and a distinctly different attitude of senior management toward the structure of its corporate community.

On the street side, the building's six-story height is divided into two three-story sections, the lower of which is set back to form a monumental colonnade that offers a generous spatial figure celebrating an active engagement with the adjoining public road. Conversely, on its park side, the building is shaped to form a large concavity that embraces and preserves a wooded knoll, behind which the mass of the headquarters is almost completely concealed when viewed from the adjoining public park that occupies the tip of the South End's peninsula. The street-side colonnade and the park-side crescent are joined by a five-story-high colonnade along the building's west end, offering an invitation to the park.

Top Aerial view of Pitney Bowes World Headquarters.

Above Monumental colonnade and main entrance.

Opposite Left Facade embracing wooded knoll.

Opposite Right Central galleria with clerestory.

Internally, the Pitney Bowes headquarters is enlivened by a 300-foot-long, four-story-high galleria that functions as a main street along which are arrayed meeting rooms, a cafeteria, and other spaces serving the entire staff. This interior gathering place makes an engaging civic gesture to the corporate community it houses, complementing the civic gestures made by the building's exterior to the larger community in which it is embedded.

In my 1974 lecture at Harvard (page 150), I expressed concern about the tendency of corporate clients, when building in cities, to give priority to satisfying their own internal requirements as opposed to fulfilling larger urban design goals. As lead designer of the two headquarters buildings discussed herein, both commissioned in the late 1970s, I was pleasantly surprised to find that concern misplaced. Both of these corporate clients were motivated by a strong commitment to the cities in which they had been founded and had thrived. Both sought to make their new headquarters a catalyst for urban regeneration by sponsoring comprehensive planning studies and lending support to contemporaneous community-based enterprise. In so doing, both set examples of enlightened corporate citizenship.

WHERE I STAND

Excerpts from Inaugural Lecture as Chair of the Department of Architecture at Harvard Graduate School of Design, October 28, 1980

HGSDNEWS

Henry N. Cobb Appointed Chairman of the Architecture Department

Inside

Summer 1980
Volume 8, Number 4
Published Quarterly

Harvard Graduate School of Design
Gund Hall, 48 Quincy Street
Cambridge, MA 02138
Second class postage paid at Boston, MA
USPS 912-280

Editor: Yvonne V. Chabrier
Assistant: Jody Feinberg
Designer: Hiestand Design Associates
Printer: Puritan Press, Inc.

Dean-designate Gerald M. McCue has announced that Henry N. Cobb, a founding partner in the New York firm of I. M. Pei & Partners, will assume the chairmanship of the Architecture Department on July 1, 1980. Cobb's appointment was approved by the President and Fellows of Harvard on May 5 and by the University's Board of Overseers on May 19.

McCue, who currently heads the Architecture Department and will become dean of the School on July 1, stated that Cobb was selected from over 50 nominees considered in an international search over the past several months. Cobb emerged as the top choice, McCue said, "because of his outstanding creative work as an architect whose consistently adventurous exploration results in meaningful and interesting design solutions." McCue also cited Cobb's "strong interest in architectural theory and discourse and his perceptive and incisive teaching in the studio," as important factors in the selection, and noted that Cobb's "demonstrated leadership in shaping the careers of those around him makes him especially suited to serve as chairman."

Ron Higgins, head of the Student Forum and the student representative on the Search Committee—which included Professor Gerhard Kallmann, Associate Professor David Handlin, and Landscape Architecture Chairman Peter Walker—said the Committee was unanimous in favoring Cobb's appointment. "We were looking," he said "for someone who would respect the diversity of views on the faculty and among the visiting critics, someone who would appreciate the fact that the GSD's strength lies in this diversity, particularly at this time in history when it is so easy to get caught up in a particular fad or ideology. At the same time we were looking for someone who could bring to the Architecture Department the kind of coherence that a conductor brings to an orchestra. I think

continued on page 2

I am acutely aware that my appearance on this platform must provoke expectation of a different kind from that which greets the other lecturers in this series. Unlike them, I am no longer simply a visitor to this school, no longer a guest from whom one hopes to gain a glimpse, however brief, into the workings of a lively mind and the issues with which it is engaged. Though the impact of such a discourse may indeed be deep and long-lasting, the intervention of a visitor is by its nature a hit-and-run affair, begun and ended in the span of an hour. But my situation is quite the opposite. This occasion inaugurates, symbolically if not literally, an engagement that is intended to continue, if all goes well, for a period of years. It thus marks the opening of a dialogue and the launching of an enterprise. Hence the obligation I feel this evening to introduce myself in a more than superficial sense, to tell you where I stand and why—to declare, however tentatively, my intentions.

I should start with intentions—and here I will be brief. First, although it may seem to go without saying, I want to affirm my support for the goals so eloquently set forth by Dean McCue in this room just a few days ago. Among these, none seems to me more important to the future of our school than a renewed commitment to teaching and research in disciplines governing the design of towns, cities, and regions. We must acknowledge the essential interconnectedness between these disciplines and the discipline we call architecture. We must recognize that every design initiative, at whatever scale, is a fragment embedded in a larger context, and that neither the fragment nor the context can be well understood without reference to the other. Thus the room is a fragment of the building, the building a fragment of the street, the street a fragment of the town, the town a fragment of the region.

If these propositions are true, a program in architecture is indeed impoverished if its students and faculty cannot draw nourishment from—and equally give nourishment to—those who are engaged in shaping the physical world at the larger scale. After all, they too are architects—indeed should perhaps be so designated, as Dean Hudnut proposed more than a generation ago. Architect of cities, architect of regions: though their techniques, procedures, and areas of special knowledge are no doubt distinct, they nonetheless have much in common with the architect of landscapes and architect of buildings. But whatever titles one may give to these design disciplines, their shared concern for the quality of the physical world clearly advocates their close association, including joint faculty and at least in part a shared curriculum, within a single graduate school. In the difficult but exciting task of achieving this, I shall help in every way I can.

With respect to the architecture program itself, I can report that I bring to this school a mind burdened with a few biases and a great many questions, but no preconceived answers. Because our program is already strong, in both its faculty and student body, we can indulge ourselves in the important luxury of open discussion and searching inquiry—a process that is perhaps in itself more useful, more invigorating, more consequential than any array of answers that may ensue. For, as Dean McCue has suggested, the quality of our community is defined precisely by its capacity to promote and sustain a creative tension between conflicting ideas and value systems. This is not to anticipate an impasse or stalemate: on the contrary, I see a good deal of change ahead in both the substance and the format of our program. But such change will, I hope, be more for the purpose of pursuing questions than of settling into answers. I do not foresee a future characterized by certainty.

Very well, you may say, but surely one must bring to the chairmanship at least a few firm convictions, a few fixed attitudes, a few aspirations that may serve as guides to action. Indeed one must, and I will not deny that certain qualitative preconceptions have determined, for example, the range of questions that I am disposed to ask and the sequence in which I would ask them. To be as explicit as I can, I am guided by a desire to see embodied in the architecture program four qualities that seem to me essential to the fulfillment of our educational mission. The first of these is coherence, by which I mean evidence of a clearly defined set of values and intentions that informs the program, locating its moral and intellectual center. This does not imply the imposition of a dogma, either aesthetic or philosophical. The metaphor appropriate to my meaning is a structural skeleton, not an enclosing wall—a skeleton constituting an internally coherent frame of reference within or against which individual participants, both students and faculty, may discover and elaborate their own personal positions and intentions.

The second quality I would seek is rigor, by which I mean a program that is both demanding in its content and economical in its means. When we consider the high cost of education in both time and money, the importance of rigor is self-evident.

Third, our program in architecture should be characterized by openness: it must be accessible to the extraordinarily diverse initiatives, touching the realms of both theory and practice, that are abroad at this moment in history. Yes, I will acknowledge that an attitude of openness may engender a loss of focus, may invite a self-indulgent narcissism, which in turn may enervate the imagination of the architect. But these are risks we must learn to live with, as it is unthinkable that we should shut our eyes and minds to the diversity of attitudes and intentions now operative in our field.

Finally, I would seek an elusive quality perhaps best defined as audacity. By this I mean that combination of energy, courage, intuition, and will by which any human enterprise may be transformed into a creative act. In particular, audacity fuels the leap of imagination, the break from convention, the fathoming of the unfathomable that is intrinsic to every work of art. According to Pasternak's Zhivago, "The root of beauty is audacity." Can an educational program admit this attribute? I think it can and must, for therein resides our best safeguard against complacency and the sterility of dead ideas. We need the nettle of audacity to challenge us in every aspect of our program.

So much for my intentions. About them I have said clearly not enough, and yet in the circumstances perhaps more than I should. If I have risked some premature judgments, it is in order to indicate the character of the enterprise as I perceive it. Further than this I can scarcely go at so early a stage in my education about education.

Now I want to say a few words about our art. What do we mean when we refer to architecture as a social art? We mean, I believe, that the subject of architecture is the human condition, and that architecture makes its strongest appeal when, having satisfied all requirements of use and technique, it memorably portrays that condition while shaping our experience of the physical world. We may then go on to ask how this conception of architecture as a social art has been operative in our time and, more specifically, what meaning it has had for me. I suppose it is fairly well known that I have spent my life in a group practice that has been notable for its involvement in large undertakings. For better or for worse, this was my intention, formed before I had graduated from this school, and for better or for worse, it has been an intention fulfilled. As a consequence, I have experienced in a most direct, continuous, and intensely challenging way the pressure placed upon architecture by a phenomenon that has transformed the human condition in our time. I refer to the prodigious growth of institutions within the fabric of society.

Institutions of government, institutions of business, institutions of education, institutions of culture—all have proliferated and expanded during my lifetime on a scale that optimists see as enriching and pessimists as cancerous. I tend to be an optimist, but I cannot deny that there is a good deal of evidence on the other side. Much of the negative evidence—and far too little of the positive—is embodied in our architecture, reflecting as it often does our society's desperate incapacity to so conceive its institutions that they may liberate rather than oppress the communities they are meant to serve. For architects, the burden of this problem seems inescapable, since its source lies not primarily in our discipline but in the program of society. We must therefore accept it, absorb it, contend with it; and ultimately we must devise, if we can, strategies within our art that may promote a more perfect symbiosis between a community and its institutions. Much of my life as an architect has been devoted to a search for such strategies, and it is in terms of this search that I propose to discuss several examples of my work. [Herewith followed a discussion of the college at Fredonia (page 80), John Hancock Tower (page 110), and Portland Museum of Art (page 170).]

In this brief discussion I have sought to acquaint you as best I could with my concerns and intentions as an architect—not for polemical purposes but in order that you with whom I am privileged to share this community may be able to place me in relation to your own points of view. And this is part of a larger aim: to foster a critical dialogue within our school—a dialogue that may invite the participation of many voices and diverse viewpoints while perhaps finding some focus, without undue constraint, in the conception of architecture as a social art.

With this aim in mind, I want to state quite explicitly what I have certainly hinted at throughout this talk: I hold to the opinion that architecture cannot escape an active engagement with the issues and conflicts that comprise the human condition. We cannot stand above or apart from those issues—be they social, ethical, cultural, technical, ecological—because it is only by engaging them that we may find a significant subject for our art. And lacking a significant subject, any art however disciplined, however finely wrought, is soon reduced to a mere cipher.

Having acknowledged this, it is equally clear that we must not confuse, as perhaps we occasionally have during my lifetime, the subject with the art. The satisfaction of user needs, the response to societal demands, the conservation of resources, the invention and refinement of building technologies—these in and of themselves cannot make an architecture. All are necessary, but none is sufficient. Very well, but what then is sufficient? What qualities distinguish architecture from mere building, and how are those qualities to be attained? To these questions, many answers have been attempted, but few tell us as much as we can learn by consulting our own intuitions. Even Le Corbusier's famous statement in *Vers Une Architecture* is more stirring than informative and hints at no precepts or procedures for achieving the transcendent qualities it espouses.

This, then, is why we are here in this school instead of taking correspondence courses in engineering and the social sciences. We are here because we understand that there is no prescriptive mechanism, no recordable body of knowledge, that can adequately equip us for the making of architecture. Instead, we must learn architecture by doing it, so to speak, in a process that is long, arduous, inefficient, awfully expensive—and absolutely indispensable. A particular virtue of this method—as attractive to the teacher as to the student—is that it is characterized by an inquiry whose outcome is never predictable. As one sociologist has remarked, "The design studio is probably the most rich and advanced system of teaching complex problem solving that exists in the university."[1] All of us who participate in this process, whether as students or teachers, are actors in what has been aptly termed a "theater of inquiry"—in which each of us strives to acquire that habit of mind by which the architect, through a process at once conceptual and pragmatic, is enabled to form intentions and act on them. This is not indeed a matter of seven semesters in a graduate school; it is the unceasing labor, and the very great joy, of a lifetime. But here at least we may begin.

1 Quoted in Colin Rowe, "Architectural Education in the USA," *Lotus International* 27 (New York: Rizzoli International, 1980), 45.

THEORY AND PRACTICE

Skyline Conversation with Peter Eisenman
New York City, April 1982

This is the second in a series of interviews I am doing with architects who are also educators: deans, chairmen, or professionals who are seen by the public at large to have a dual role. The questions I would like to cover fall basically into four areas.

The first concerns the definition of architectural education. Does it involve both the training of students for the profession and a definition of the discipline of architecture? And how do these two interact?

The second concerns the relationships between education and the profession. What do you feel is the relationship of the discipline and theory of architecture to professional practice? What, for example, is the relationship between your teaching and your practice?

The third concerns the relationship of education and the practice of architecture to what I call "cultural power." We should consider what seems to be a different relationship between the cultural power structure and the education and profession of architects than exists in other professional disciplines.

Finally, the fourth concerns the particular position of Harvard—its traditional role in relationship to the curricula of other schools, to the Boston community, and to other more "East Coast" and international concerns.

I see those four questions as so closely interlocking that elements of all are bound to creep into the particular discussion of each one. To start with the first, it is very hard for me to talk about education in terms of general theory since, although I am a practicing educator, I am not a professional educator. Of course I have been teaching off and on as a studio critic for the past twenty years, but studio criticism is an activity that, while it may provoke a good deal of thought about education, does not force the issue in the same way as the responsibilities of creating a program and faculty do. Thus I have really come to grips with the problem of architectural education only very recently and in a particular setting.

With that cautionary preamble, let me begin by referring to the fascinating interview with Michel Foucault that appeared in the March issue of *Skyline.* Toward the end, in commenting on the distinction between those sciences that are certain and those that are uncertain, Foucault places architecture in a third category, which the Greeks call *techne* and which he defines as a "practical rationality governed by a conscious goal." I agree with this definition, and I think it explains why architecture as a discipline has never been entirely comfortable, nor perhaps even welcome, among the rigorous knowledge-based disciplines that traditionally inhabit great universities. Unlike those academic disciplines, architecture does not have as its object the advancement of knowledge independent of the application of that knowledge. By its nature, architecture fulfills itself in practice—in the enterprise of applying a practical rationality to a conscious goal. In fact, practice is so inescapably central to our discipline that training for the profession of architecture necessarily involves an attempted replication of the conditions of practice though the methodology of the design studio.

This suggests a paradox inherent in the whole idea of locating architectural education within a university-based graduate school. Such a context would seem to separate the enterprise of architecture from its vital sources of nourishment in the "real world" of practice; however, its entrepreneurial, practice-oriented character would seem to devalue architecture as an intellectual discipline and cripple its capacity to establish a fruitful discourse with other, less "contaminated" disciplines inside the university. It is because I am fascinated by this paradox and by the challenge of trying to resolve it for the benefit of architecture that I have put one foot in the academic world. For me, this predicament, this paradoxical situation in our discipline, is also precisely what makes architecture in the end the most noble of the arts and sciences—an enterprise inescapably committed to the synthesis of idea and technique in the realm of practice.

There is another paradox: in law and economics—two disciplines that also have practices that are certainly related to the general culture—the theory of law and the theory of economics probably have more influence than their practice. In architecture, the theory is undervalued because it does not matter.
Yes, why is that? In another part of the same interview Foucault pointed out that what is significant about the emergence of architectural theory in the eighteenth century is not that architects were interested in theory but that the clients, those who held power in society, were interested in architectural theory.

Why did that change? Why are clients and society today not very interested in architectural theory? If this is true, I have a problem with your idea that architecture is the most noble discipline. It could be argued that economics and law are more noble because in both cases the theory—that is, the rationality of the discipline—is almost more important than the goal. Why is it that in the eighteenth century architecture was thought of this way and is no longer?
There's a hidden assumption in that question: that architecture becomes more noble as the role of theory becomes stronger and as goals can be defined

independent of practice. I don't think I could agree with that. The point I was trying to make is that interest in theory reflects a view by those who have power about the role of architecture in the shaping and controlling of society. In the eighteenth century people who held power became interested in architectural theory because they saw in it a means of control. I would not like to convert that remark—which is not a critical observation but rather an objective one—into your heavily value-laden suggestion that architecture becomes more noble as its theory is seen as a means of control.

It may be that society is interested in economic theory, or the law, as a means of control, but I was not suggesting it in that way. That was *your* value-laden statement; I never said "control." I was merely questioning the nobility of architecture; it is thought of as having a mystique, a nobility, because it is an art—whereas economics and the law are not.
I would agree that art is indeed an aspect of its nobility; it is also an aspect that protects architecture in some sense from rigid theoretical formulation. This is both a weakness and a strength.

Are you saying that because the mechanisms of control have shifted to other disciplines, architecture has lost its capacity to control in a way that it did in the eighteenth century and therefore has lost its theory?
I don't think architecture ever had the capacity to control; it was manipulated. It was never the architect who controlled. Rather, those who exercised power saw in architecture a mechanism for control of society in a period of accelerating urbanization. Architecture is inescapably pragmatic; hence it is in the vise of society,

and of those who hold power in society, in a way that law and economics are not. It is paradoxical that on the one hand architecture, by definition, gives three-dimensional form to the society from which it springs, portraying it in a form that is so vivid and so influential that it has the status of a cultural artifact; and that on the other hand, this cultural power does not invest architects or architecture with the kind of direct manipulative power that one might say lawyers and the law of economics and economists have in the shaping of society.

You said that architecture today does not have the capacity to shape society as much as law and economics do. Using Foucault's argument in a purely utilitarian way, this may have happened precisely because architecture has lost its theoretical condition as a pure discipline; because of this, it does not shape society but rather is subject to it. Perhaps if we did not see it as an enterprise but rather studied architecture for its own sake, as a discipline, then that might be an enterprise that could be fulfilling enough in itself. Is that a possibility for you?

Yes, I certainly do not mean to say that there is not the potential to shape the culture through the investigation of architecture as a discipline. As a matter of fact, it seems to me imperative at this moment that we acknowledge the importance of investigating the discipline of architecture. But in the end the relevance of that investigation will be as it informs practice and not as it creates theory.

Do you mean that for you, theory—if it does not inform practice—has no benefit in itself?

Yes and no. Because I am a practicing architect, the excitement, the intellectual stimulation, that comes from digging beneath the surface of practice into the discipline naturally comes from its anticipated reflection back into practice. But I would acknowledge that architectural theory can have a value independent of practice to the extent that it may initiate a discourse with other disciplines. Furthermore, I think the argument for educating architects in a graduate school of a great university rests entirely on the notion that it is necessary to investigate the discipline of architecture. Otherwise, the atelier system, the apprenticeship system, the internship system, all can be shown to be more effective. What is important about a university is that it provides connections among the disciplines that enrich each of them; those connections can be made only if we somehow can investigate architecture at a level of theory that allows discourse with other disciplines.

If theory only leads to practice—that is, to goal orientation—then you might say it contributes to the present malaise that we are experiencing. It does not matter if there is any theoretical investigation. Everything is concerned with selling, with the media. We seem to have no corrective, no notion of what the discipline is against which to measure results.

My argument would be that an independent theoretical discourse, without the establishment of some framework against which you can measure deviation, leads inevitably to the corruption of practice itself. You said that theory should lead to practice, that it must be goal oriented.

I said that in architecture, theory fulfills itself in practice.

If it fulfills itself only in practice, you have the corruption of practice itself because you cannot measure theory outside of practice.

I disagree. Corruption occurs, it seems to me, when theory ceases to inform and be informed by practice. I would argue that neither theory nor practice can acquire much cultural significance unless each regularly draws nourishment from the other. Theory uninformed by practice is likely to be as corrupt as practice uninformed by theory. This does not mean that theory ought not to place itself at a certain distance from practice. The best way to show what I mean is by reference to criticism, which is surely the logical vehicle for cross-fertilization between theory and practice. As long as criticism operates, as it generally does, at a purely evaluative level—as long as it merely measures performance with respect to accepted criteria that are themselves unquestioned and uninvestigated—it must remain a very shallow undertaking. At this level, criticism may indeed corrupt practice and very quickly empty architecture of ideas. To achieve any real cross-fertilization between theory and practice, criticism must examine the questions asked as well as the answers given. The failure of our culture to produce this level of criticism is deeply disappointing, and it is this failure, I would argue, that has led to what you call the present malaise.

To take a more optimistic view of current practice, I think quite a few architects are fruitfully engaged today in a third type of criticism: that discussed by Jorge Silvetti in "The Beauty of Shadows" [*Oppositions* 9, Summer 1977] and identified by him as "criticism from within." It is exactly there that theory fulfills itself decisively in practice by way of a critique that occurs in the act of making architecture. For me this is probably the most important type of criticism: architecture criticizing itself in its own language. Certainly this is the most promising aspect of the present moment in architecture—the one aspect of postmodernism that clearly transcends fashion, although many architects of my generation would not like to admit it. I am not trying to pretend, by the way, that the element of fashion does not enter in; it is surely there, but beneath the surface of Charles Jencks's "isms," there is clearly a more interesting investigation in progress—an effort to explore, through criticism from within, the sources of meaning and value in our art.

Let us go back for a moment. You said earlier that education involved the necessity of investigating the discipline—partly to create a discourse with other disciplines. You also talked about your responsibility for creating a program and faculty, as opposed to teaching in a studio. There are two possible approaches to this responsibility. One is to make a program in the abstract that defines or corresponds to a definition of the discipline, then to go out and find a faculty to teach that program. Or conversely, one gets the best faculty one can find and allows that faculty to create the program through its teaching. What are your feelings about these two views?

Both are necessary, and neither is by itself sufficient. I see my own intervention as shaping the program but also as bringing people to Harvard who will themselves shape the program. It is the chemistry that results from these two different kinds of initiative that will determine the success or failure of the project. And I want to make it clear that I do not think of this project as resulting in a quantifiable product—some kind of perfect instrument for the teaching of architecture. I am really interested only in the quality of the activity. To paraphrase

Foucault's remark about liberty, learning is not a condition; it is a practice.

So you are saying it is a process?
Yes. There is absolutely no doubt that the intellectual-energy content of the process is far more important to me as a goal than the formulation of any pedagogical theory. I do not see Harvard as becoming the repository of a single theoretical position, a dogma, or least of all a style—although I naturally do not preclude the possibility that important and influential ideas may emerge from the activity taking place. My focus is on stimulating activity, and in particular the activity of investigating the discipline, which seems to me crucially important at this time. While I want this activity to be critical of practice, I do not want it to be alienated from practice. So my goal at Harvard is to generate both an intensive investigation of the discipline and a critical awareness of the conditions of practice. In this mix I see the promise of a school that would shape as well as serve our profession.

I would say that since the time of Walter Gropius, the influence of the Graduate School of Design has been very limited and also hermetic, in the sense that its influence has been very much localized in the Boston area. Harvard has not been an influential school for twenty years. Perhaps it is because Harvard has not been as interested in the investigation of the discipline as it has been in the training of people for the practice. This is in contrast to the fact that the education of lawyers, businessmen, and doctors at Harvard has had a national and international influence during the same period. It is precisely in the area of architecture that Harvard has not been influential—unlike the University

of Pennsylvania and the Philadelphia school at a certain time, Cornell and the Colin Rowe school of contextualism at another time, the Cooper Union formalists and John Hejduk at another time, Princeton and Michael Graves, and even the kind of influence of Yale's star system.

Would you agree, one, that this is true—that Harvard's influence has been local and seems to be parochial—and two, that one of the reasons for this is that the investigation of the discipline, which you see as a necessity, has not been the paramount concern in the training of architects at Harvard for the past twenty years?

Rather than generalize about this, I would prefer to identify some of the specific strengths and weaknesses of Harvard's program during the thirty years since Gropius's retirement. The dominant figure of this whole period was clearly Gropius's and Joseph Hudnut's immediate successor, Josep Lluís Sert, who was dean for sixteen years, from 1953 to 1969. Quite early in his tenure—it was in the late fifties, I believe—Sert made a move that I would argue was probably the single most influential pedagogical initiative of the postwar era: he established an interdisciplinary program in urban design. The significance of this invention—and "urban design" was truly Sert's invention—lay in its effectiveness as a vehicle for increasing the power of the architect by legitimizing his intervention at the urban scale.

For a few years in the early sixties, this initiative certainly renewed Harvard's position of leadership. It remains important because—again we return to Foucault's point—it is the contemporary parallel to eighteenth-century architectural theory: an ideological construct that places architecture at the threshold of power, shaping public space, controlling the way people move and congregate, determining how they live in aggregation. After all, architecture comes close to power only when it deals with problems of aggregation.

Sert may have invented urban design, but it was without ideology. I would like to define ideology similarly to the way Charles Rosen does in his book *The Classical Style*: ideology is the notion of a developed theory that precedes practice; practice follows from theory, as opposed to theory being something that results from practice.

In a general sense I would agree with you that urban design was a strategic idea, although I don't devalue it particularly on those grounds. I would also agree with you that the present predicament of this construct is the consequence of its having been born as a strategy and having remained a strategy.

In the collapse that took place at the end of the sixties within the universities, the architecture schools were the first to be thrown into disarray, precisely because they were the least able to fall back onto a "high ground" of theory that could protect them. Indeed, the unique case of survival at Cooper Union was due precisely to the fact that John Hejduk had somehow given his program a theoretical and ideological base that enabled it to survive, while other schools—Columbia, Harvard, Yale—were falling apart. It is indeed ironic, as well as sad, that Harvard, having successfully expanded the horizons of architectural practice by embracing the urban scale, was on that account especially vulnerable to distraction and confusion when the revolution came.

If you consider capitals of power in architecture—Los Angeles, Houston, Chicago, New York—Boston is not thought to be in that category.
This is not due to the architects; it is due to the situation of the clients.

It does not seem that Harvard has influenced the activity of the architects who are the recipients of that power. Consider the realm of publications, for example. The Yale journal *Perspecta* stood alone for many years as one of the few critical vehicles for discussion of architecture in the country.
Perspecta was the product of a phenomenon that must never be underrated, as it remains the single most important aspect of a graduate school: good students were at Yale. It was exclusively a product of that situation. Why did Yale attract those students? Paul Rudolph was there; he was pursuing a different strategy from that of Sert. While he was initiating the urban design program, Sert seems to have imposed at Harvard a more narrowly prescriptive program in architecture than Rudolph did at Yale. Although Rudolph's personal ideology and work were enormously influential at Yale, they were always—and quite intentionally—balanced by the work of a diverse group of visiting faculty. His was the model of an "open" school, and the resulting discourse was enormously stimulating.

One could say that accreditation requirements for schools are focused more on the training of students than on the manufacturing of knowledge, and that the reason we have a homogenization of schools tending toward education as training—rather than toward the definition of the discipline and the creation of knowledge—has to do with the practical and utilitarian views of the accreditation board.

The question of accreditation is difficult for me. The issues involved are troublesome but in the end not very interesting. I am uncertain whether the profession is justified in creating the apparatus of accreditation. I suppose it is marginally justified, just as the registration of architects may be marginally justified, on the grounds of protecting the public health and welfare. But whether accreditation is doing anything for us in terms of improving the performance of our profession I cannot say. Certainly with respect to the program at Harvard, accreditation requirements do not have one iota of influence on my thinking. But having said that, I must acknowledge that as a practicing architect my sense of what is required in the training—as opposed to the education—of architects is probably not much at odds with the standards set by the accreditation board. I am guided by the fairly elementary notion that people coming out of our school, as a minimum requirement, should be equipped to make themselves useful in the profession.

But there are a lot of different and interesting ways to be useful.

In fact, you are touching on something of great importance. In my view, our educational system has failed to convey to students the idea that there are many ways of being useful. Too often we deliver into the world graduates preoccupied with unfulfillable dreams, dreams that they will take with them—fruitlessly and bitterly—to their graves. Instead, we should be arming our students with the capacity to invent, pursue, and fulfill realizable goals, to discover their own modes of usefulness. This is in part a problem of skills and in part a problem of attitude, habit of mind. It is a problem that preoccupies me a good deal at Harvard.

This brings up an interesting point about the training of students. In Italy there are six thousand students studying architecture at the University of Venice, twenty thousand at the University of Rome. These people have no unfulfilled dreams of professional practice because 90 percent of them are not planning to join the profession at all. They consider architecture a discipline; in the same way, a student in the nineteenth century would educate himself in the law without any intention of becoming a lawyer. It seems to me that the reason there are unfulfilled dreams is that we promise training for the profession. Instead we should be saying, "We will give you only an education; what you do with it is your business." Would you comment on that?

It has to do with the tradition of American education; our tradition of professional education definitely has a service aspect to it. I do believe it is appropriate for a professional school to take the position that it is training people to respond to a perceived need in the program of society. But that is only a minimal obligation. You are suggesting that there are two educational constructs—one general and one goal-oriented—and I am suggesting that one is contained within the other, that they are not mutually exclusive. While I endorse the notion that a minimal obligation of a graduate school is to prepare the student to be useful to the profession, I also feel that one does not do that very well unless one is doing other things along with it.

Let us go back to your idea that there is a dialectical relationship between the discipline and the practice of architecture. Consider Charles Rosen's thesis that prior to neoclassicism, theory evolved from practice—that people built buildings and then tried to rationalize

them or have them define a set of ideas after the fact. For example, Palladio built his buildings, and then near the end of his life he redrew the buildings to confirm a set of ideas; his theory came from his buildings. Neoclassicists started from the other end: they began with a set of ideas, a theory of the discipline, and then tried to make practice conform to those. According to Rosen, this was the beginning of ideological practice.

We have gone back and forth since that time. You could say that the eclecticism of the nineteenth century was an attempt to return to a point where practice came before theory, and that Beaux-Arts academicism was a reaction to that eclecticism. You could say that modernism was a reaction to both, and that it set up a theoretical discourse—not a formal set of rules but an ideological discourse—in social, political, and moral as opposed to purely formal terms. The ideological practice of the Beaux-Arts was formal; the ideological practice of modernism was certainly moral, economic, and social. Today we have reverted, in one sense, to an eclectic period—even though people would like to call it a postmodern period—suggesting a new or revisionist ideology. Unfortunately, the practice of postmodernism is not defined by a theory.

First, would you say that this dialectical relationship of discipline to practice is, in fact, cyclical? Second, would you say that one does not have an ideological discipline or an ideological practice unless one can define a body of theory? Third, would you agree that history remembers only ideological practices?

I do not know whether the relationship is cyclical. I would answer yes to your second question, but I would modify it to say that theory informs practice, and practice informs theory in ways that in the end are much more casual than your construct suggests. With reference to the third question, there is absolutely no doubt in my mind that the architectural practices that remain in cultural memory have ideological content, but the ideological content may not always or necessarily be embodied in theory.

I would say that Robert Venturi has an ideological practice. That is, his practice started in a way from his book [*Complexity and Contradiction in Architecture*, 1966], which set forth—whether intentionally or not—an ideology. His practice then tended to elaborate on and confirm those ideological propositions. On the other hand, Richard Meier has what could be called an aesthetic practice. He starts from a set of forms that have for him an a priori value. The value that he gives to these forms preempts any ideas that may already be inherent in them.
I am not sure that the evidence would support the distinction you draw. Whatever the process, Meier's buildings are loaded with ideological content. It may be quite true that his process was one of becoming interested in forms that had been produced by one ideology and removing them from that ideological base, manipulating them, and putting them into his own construct, but the result is certainly architecture with ideological content.

When does architecture not have ideological content? If I were to discuss the practice of I. M. Pei, Henry Cobb, James Freed, et al., I would argue that until now it has been a practice that I would call *professional*. That is, it is concerned primarily with the production of an architecture that mediates between a client's demands and a concern for the public domain rather than with the demonstration of an ideology or an aesthetic strategy first and foremost.

Aren't you simply defining strategies in practice that in the end are mere reflections of diverse ideologies? To pursue this line of thought a step further, I certainly would not want to formulate an educational program with the goal of favoring one strategy of practice—be it "ideological," "aesthetic," or "professional"—over another: this would be inappropriately prescriptive, it seems to me. Nevertheless, I do believe it is essential that our teaching program promote an awareness of ideological content in architecture, whatever the mode of practice. Furthermore, I believe that a graduate program such as ours has a special obligation to develop a capacity for self-criticism in the profession, and this can happen only when the investigation of the discipline includes ideological as well as formal and technical issues. While it is essential to acknowledge that we are preparing students for the practice of a profession, it is equally essential to engender more than one idea about what the practice of that profession might be. That is my definition of generating a capacity for criticism. As I said before, we must aim to shape as well as serve the profession.

I would have said that, until your assumption of the chairmanship at Harvard, your architecture, while certainly at the highest level of professionalism, was not necessarily in the realm of ideology. However, your notion of education certainly has a component that is ideological. Would you say that this attitude, which you have come to realize as necessary in education, will in turn affect your practice of architecture? Should it? And if so, how do you see that happening?
At various times and in various circumstances our practice could be characterized as commercial, professional, aesthetic, and ideological—or so at least it seems to me.

Perhaps indeed it is just this that best defines our shared aspirations: the notion that we can and do engage the world at many levels within the broadest possible conception of professional practice. It is important to us that we have the capability and desire to tackle both the Portland Museum and the Mount Sinai Hospital reorganization and expansion.

What does all that have to do with my enterprise at Harvard? Simply this: if we accept the proposition that education and practice are mutually interdependent, and that each is at least potentially a vehicle for critically examining the other, then a commitment such as mine is surely a logical way to engage both aspects of the relationship. There is nothing original in this, but I do believe that the time is right for me to make some contribution to education and that this is likewise a moment when my practice could benefit from the critical distance thus obtained.

But how would you define this benefit? After all, architects have always thought they understood their discipline without resorting to what you call the "critical distance" of the academic world. Most professionals in commercial practice would say, "What is the problem?"

In the aftermath of the modern movement and its failed dreams, it seems to me, there is a very real danger that architecture may retreat once more into the sycophantic role of an uncritical "service profession." This corruption will be avoided, I believe, only if architecture can strengthen its capacity to criticize as well as cater to the received program of society. But this capacity cannot be nurtured through practice alone. It requires a more rigorous procedure than the conditions of practice permit—a procedure that could allow us to question the questions as well as questioning our answers. This then is the benefit to be derived from achieving critical distance from practice: it allows us, perhaps, to investigate and comprehend our discipline in a way that may help us to strengthen the profession and thus forestall the corruption of practice.

Rafael Moneo has suggested that architecture could be seen as the invention of convention—invention as design and convention as some sort of system or rationality. If we were to take these two aspects as the beginning of the definition of what architecture might be, could they become fundamental for the training of architects? First, one would have to define convention and invention; second, one would have to define the relationship between convention and invention and how they relate to practice, so that convention does not preempt invention but rather the reverse, that design is in fact the tool that invents the discipline. How do you feel about that?

I feel pretty good about it.

Forgive me for that one-line answer. It's not that I don't find Moneo's construct and your proposal interesting. In fact, I find them both quite persuasive. But all this talk has exhausted me, and I am happy to let your statement stand—it's a good ending, I think.

Perhaps it's time to remind ourselves that according to Valéry, Degas in his old age ascribed most of the world's ills to thinkers and architects. If he was right—and who's to say he wasn't?—I stand condemned. And you, Peter, stand twice condemned. For this I salute you.

DOWNTOWN DALLAS

Fountain Place, 1982–86
with Michael D. Flynn, P. V. Banavalkar (structure), Dan Kiley (landscape)

Three towers designed by our firm and standing within a few blocks of one another bear witness to the rapid growth of office space in downtown Dallas during the decade from the mid-seventies to the mid-eighties. The first two, One Dallas Center (1977–79) and Arco Tower (1978–83), are governed in plan by the geometry of the equilateral triangle. Fountain Place, the last to be completed and certainly the most interesting of the three, is governed in both plan and section by the geometries of the square and double square.

As its name suggests, Fountain Place is more than a building: although only partially executed, it was conceived as a five-acre, mixed-use development, with twin office towers and a hotel rising from an expansive water garden populated by a densely planted forest of bald cypress trees. The developer, an exceptionally bold and imaginative entrepreneur, asked for two things that he rightly considered essential in order to overcome the disadvantage of a marginal location at the outer edge of downtown. First, he wanted office towers that would be distinctive and memorable on the skyline; and second, he insisted that the development should be so conceived as to produce an attractive and memorable place in a city whose public realm was at that time notoriously impoverished—a city of skyscrapers surrounded by bleak streets and embedded in a sea of parking. Much to the developer's credit, the first tower together with half the water garden was completed in the face of a recessionary oversupply of office space. Sadly, owing to weakness in the office market, the second tower had to be abandoned.

Dan Kiley's delightful water garden at Fountain Place, made possible by the evacuation of one-half the volume of the tower up to a height of sixty feet above the ground, exemplifies an interesting but too-little-understood

principle of place making: in a space that lacks definition by means of enclosure, a powerful and spellbinding sense of place can be engendered by the creation of a "forest" in which people are magically swallowed up immediately upon entering.

Fountain Place is a metamorphic tower, by which I mean a tower whose form changes continuously from base to top in accordance with preestablished geometric rules. In this case, a subtractive design process starts with a cubic volume at the base and is then carved by means of cuts that conform to the diagonal of a double square in both plan and section. I explained the discipline governing these procedures in "A Note on the Architectonics of Folding."

> In Fountain Place, *folding* is a manipulative procedure that shapes the panels comprising the building envelope and thereby shapes the entirety of the building volume. The pleasure of the fold lies in the invigorating clarity that it imparts to the volume while preserving visual continuity and surface tension in the envelope. However, the main purpose of this note is not to argue *why* folding may be desirable, but rather

Top Left and Right Tower as seen from different viewpoints.
Above Skyline view. **Opposite** Terraced water garden at base.
Page 240 Photomontage of twin-tower model in downtown Dallas.

to explain *what* folding is and *how* it can become operative architectonically at the scale of a building—that is to say, within the discipline of constructed material and detail.

Bending is a manipulative procedure applied to objects; *folding* is a manipulative procedure applied to surfaces. Hence, when we refer to a sheet of paper as being folded, we are engaging in an elision. The full statement would be that the sheet of paper is being bent while each of its surfaces is being folded. It is important to understand that the fold in one surface is distinct from the fold in the other. Because paper is dimensionally thin, we feel justified in eliding this distinction by compressing the statement "the paper is being bent and its surfaces folded" into "the paper is being folded." However, when we increase the material thickness from that of paper (approximately one-hundredth of an inch) to that of curtain-wall construction (eight inches minimum), we can no longer afford to elide this distinction: we must acknowledge explicitly that the curtain wall as a constructed object is being bent, and that we will achieve an architectonic manifestation of folding only if we can compress the visible architecture of the wall into an exterior surface approximating zero thickness.

Buildings exist at a scale so large that they cannot be monolithic like a single piece of paper that is folded or a single stone that is carved. Hence the building envelope must be constructed by assembling multiple elements, between which there will inevitably be joints. The fundamental requirement for an architectonic manifestation of folding is that folds can occur *only within* and *not between* the elements

Above Diagrams of surface folds, with corresponding views of tower.

that comprise the surface to be folded. A fold always describes the manipulation of a continuous surface contained within each element of which the building envelope is composed. A joint is a void between two elements and hence cannot be folded; a change of plane located in a joint is a break, not a fold.

In the building envelope of Fountain Place, there are no breaks; all changes of plane take the form of folds located within the panels that comprise the curtain wall. The operation of folding is enabled by a net of painted aluminum muntins subdividing each 6-by-12-foot panel that constitutes the basic element of the wall. Without exception, all changes of plane in the curtain wall are produced by folds located on these internal muntins. Besides fulfilling the aforementioned requirement that folding take place only within and not between elements, this disposition of folds allowed the curtain wall manufacturer to shop-fabricate the folded panels, thus assuring a high degree of accuracy in these multifaceted elements of the building envelope. Each folded panel is composed of at least four and as many as seven panes of glass, separated by the muntins on which all folds occur. The shop-fabricated folded panels were then disassembled for shipment to the building site, where they were reassembled and installed on the exterior in the same manner as adjacent unfolded panels.

Both the logic of construction and the logic of use favor an orthogonal geometry in shaping and assembling the elements that comprise a building envelope. Fortunately, however, folding as herein described is entirely unconstrained by the orthogonal geometry of the curtain wall panels in which it occurs. Diagonally oriented folds, as exemplified by those occurring in Fountain Place, are not only feasible but desirable: they impart unexpected drama to the building envelope—and thence to the building volume—by uniting orthogonal elements through an operation that is oblique to their own order.

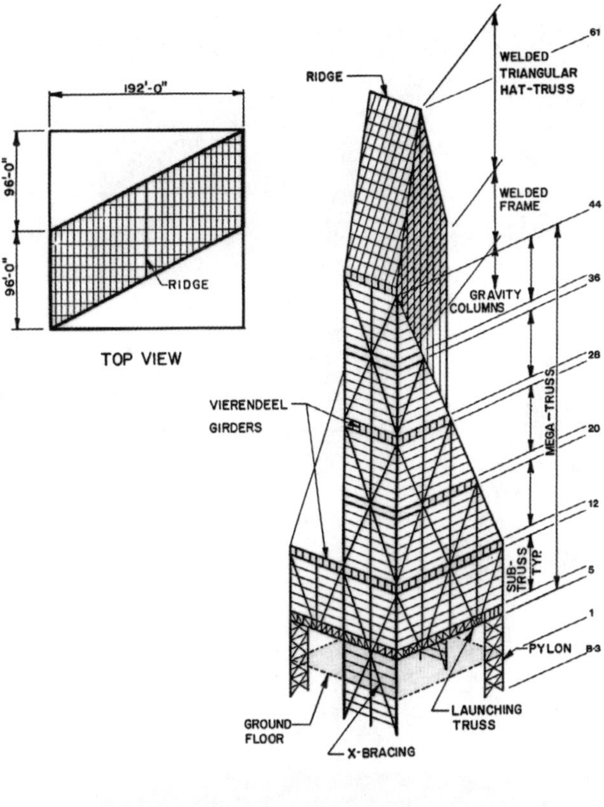

Above Schematic diagram of exterior structural frame.

CRITIQUE OF FOUNTAIN PLACE

Excerpt from *The Charlottesville Tapes*, 1982

On November 12 and 13, 1982, twenty-five architects from eight countries gathered in Jefferson's Rotunda at the University of Virginia for a two-day conference at which participants were asked to present one previously unpublished project for criticism by their peers. The proceedings were taped, and a full transcript was subsequently published in book form as The Charlottesville Tapes, *from which the following is drawn.*

Henry N. Cobb The project that I am going to show today is still in a very early stage of design. It is located in Dallas, a city that is not easily loved. Actually, I love all cities, including Dallas, but I love some a little more than others.

This is my fourth building project in Dallas, and it reflects two concerns: a concern about imagery and a concern about place. To my mind they are equally important. Let me first speak about the issue of imagery. Downtown Dallas is a city of box office towers that, owing to the flight path of a nearby airport, cannot exceed about sixty stories in height. Our clients are understandably concerned that their project, which is to contain three million square feet of rental office space, should not become lost in this crowd of nearly indistinguishable commercial buildings. They asked for a strong and memorable image on the skyline, an image that would be intrinsic to the building's form without resorting to fancy hats or applied ornament. The design strategy we adopted to achieve this goal is governed by its own internal logic: a subtractive procedure applied to a prismatic tower 190 square feet in plan and 720 feet high. This pure prism is carved from the top down with incisions that adhere rigorously to the geometry of a double square in both plan and section. The resultant twin skyscrapers are actually identical but appear to be different, as one is rotated ninety degrees in plan with respect to the other. Major incisions in the base of each tower reintroduce the diagonal geometry and create a spatial rather than volumetric presence at street level.

Now, about the issue of place. I have to point out that this project is a collaborative effort of two others with my firm, Harry Weese and Dan Kiley. Harry and Dan are both involved in the design of this six-acre site, but the generating idea is really Dan's. For forty years he has dreamed of building a water garden planted with a dense grid of trees, and he has finally found his opportunity here. We decided to make one surface out of which these two skyscrapers would grow. It's only a few inches deep, but it's all water except for a few granite walkways that are almost flush with the water's surface. On fifteen-foot centers over all six acres, we will plant what you might call God's little skyscrapers—five hundred bald cypress trees—which will create, we believe, an unforgettable place. We feel that it will match the unforgettable image of the twin towers on the skyline.

Although I have been designing tall buildings for thirty years, these are, I suppose, my first real "skyscrapers." I will acknowledge that I set out quite deliberately in this project to find my own way of making a skyscraper image: these are skyscrapers made by carving away rather than by building up. In this sense, they remind me of Roland Barthes's comment that skyscrapers of New York have made it a deep city, not a high one—a city excavated rather than built. I designed these towers by saying, "Damn it, I'm going to start with a point at the top and work down from there."

Michael Graves I don't know why I wasn't upset by John and Philip's building, but I am upset by yours, Harry—I guess because you present it in a way that implies there's an internal logic to the geometry, to the form, yet I see no logic at all.[1] If it is possible for minimalism to be picturesque, you've done it. I don't understand the slashes through the building on the diagonal. What I see are two towers that make a kind of pastiche or stylistic motif of a house—but there's no sense of place here. I'm thinking of towers by people like C. F. Hansen, where there are a series of pavilions all the way up. I don't understand how you are so populist on the ground floor and then so abstract and into your own internal language in the towers themselves. If you bend over backwards to make a place on the ground for everybody, then those bloody-awful towers also ought at least to provide a place to have a drink or to have lunch or to do something beyond looking out through the green-awful glass.

Robert Stern A few things occur to me. One is that despite the fact that your building has the image of a skyscraper, it really doesn't have the anthropomorphic or representational qualities that most of the skyscrapers of the twenties and thirties that define the type seem to have. The second thing that troubles me has to do with your, or Dan Kiley's, ground floor. I'm not convinced it's actually a place for people at all. I think that unless you have a gondola, you're not going to be able to circulate between the trees; it's really a nonplace.

The third observation concerns your criticism of Dallas. I agree that many parts of Dallas are alienating to the pedestrian, but it is the obligation of any architect who recognizes that problem to make a gesture that would

1 Johnson and Burgee had presented their as-yet-unbuilt project for International Place, Boston.

eventually return the city's streets to the people. In cities like New York and Boston, the street is the place where people come together. In the sense of the refusal to create architectural space at the periphery of the city block, I didn't understand Philip's scheme, and I understand yours even less.

Peter Eisenman I want to answer Michael. You seem to suggest that picturesque is all right if you do it the way Johnson does it, but if you pretend to an internal logic—that is, abstraction—it is a no-no. I hope we're not saying that internal logic is out and picturesque is in, or that abstraction is out and anthropomorphism is in, because no matter how much anthropomorphism you try to build into a skyscraper, it can never be a little house. To a human being at the ground floor, it is an abstraction.

Michael Graves There was something that Rob [Krier] said about an overall abstraction of the architectural frame, which then could be embellished with images of a figural quality—I think that's a little closer to the mark for me. In other words, that there are elements within any building's vertical dimension that we can identify with.

Henry N. Cobb I did not really mean to put so much weight on the idea of internal logic. The aim of this experiment is really to achieve a memorable image using the language of abstraction.

Jaquelin Robertson There seems to be not only a split between the Europeans and the Americans—between the Kriers and the skyscraper builders—but also a major generational gap among the Americans here. I find Harry's dilemma very touching—and I mean that in the best sense. This project confirms that he has become one of the master builders, one of the most refined builders in the country, of this kind of curtain wall technology—equivalent as a technician in glass to a master stonemason in the Middle Ages.

Yet these very minimalist but enormous sculptural buildings that he is doing are missing certain crucial things with respect to urbanism. Here, almost as if to expiate for the great, shiny cliff above, there is an attempt to produce a Persian garden below, which is, I assume, intended as a kind of earthly paradise in the desert of Dallas—water and shade. But Persian gardens don't have that too dense, too consciously geometrical and relentless relationship of water to trees. Like Bob Stern, I think you will need rubber boots to get about in there. There is a one-liner aspect to that placemat-like, synthetic garden with trees planted on fifteen-foot centers; it has the same problem of minimalist rigidity as the building itself. Together they become less humane, not more. Dallas still prevails.

This is a profound problem facing younger American architects: the inability of the abstraction and minimalism inherited from the recent past to address urbanism. To my knowledge, this kind of super-scale, abstract sculpture has not added anything to the American city. Which takes us back to Leo's question: do architects have some larger sense of the governing order to which they are committed and toward which they shape each building? Or are they always "ad-hoc-ing," hoping that the beauty of the individual object will have a major impact on the city? I think that the city will not, cannot, be made successfully in this way. We must find another strategy.

THE TALL BUILDING IN THE CITY

Conversation with Paolo Conrad Bercah
New York City, February 1998

While the Fountain Place and Hancock towers both play with the same geometry and are materially similar, they are very different in character. How would you define that difference?
I would go back to a statement Yeats made: "We make out of the quarrel with others, rhetoric, but of the quarrel with ourselves, poetry." The posture of Fountain Place is autonomous and its gesture is rhetorical, that is to say boldly assertive in its quarrel with the world. The posture of the Hancock Tower is contingent and its gesture is poetic, that is to say profoundly ambivalent in its quarrel with itself.

How does the Hancock Tower, despite its prominence on the skyline, escape being rhetorical?
By its understatement. Among tall buildings that is a very rare trait. Most are designed to be rhetorical, the more dramatically so the better. By contrast, the Hancock

Tower is as relentlessly unrhetorical as a tall building can be. It is not an advertisement for itself.

You have called Fountain Place your first skyscraper. I gather you wouldn't apply the term to the Hancock Tower or the cruciform building in Montreal. What is the distinction?
Fountain Place is the first of my buildings to scrape the sky in the figural sense. I have never been particularly interested in that aspect of tall buildings, but in Dallas I wanted to create a gesture on the skyline that would distinguish the tower from the flattops around it. It is nothing if not an advertisement for itself. What sets it apart from most self-advertising skyscrapers is that the formal strategy by which its skyscraper image is obtained is subtractive rather than additive. This is curious, since we have spoken about my interest in aggregation, and aggregation by definition is an additive process. But my preference for subtractive design strategies is perhaps an expression of my anxiety about the fact that I am so deeply implicated in aggregation. Fountain Place conceals the aggregation of sixty floors behind a formal strategy that doesn't refer to those sixty floors at all.

It becomes an enormous sculpture.
It does, and that's arguably a weakness. Only sculptors are envious of it. A sculptor friend of mine once upbraided me, saying, "How come you got to do this sculpture that's a thousand times bigger than what I can do?" But I think it's an impoverishment of architecture to reduce it to sculpture; it's a disservice to both arts. While it's arguable that the sculptural approach to the tall building at least helps make it more interesting and less alienating, in the end it's a deception, a trick of the trade. It limits

a building's capacity to mean something as architecture, and I'm acutely conscious of that limitation.

So you're dissatisfied with Fountain Place?
No, I'm perfectly satisfied with it. In the circumstances, I think it's definitely the best I could do. If you spend much of your life designing office buildings, you're living on a very thin diet, architecturally speaking, and you extract from it whatever you can. Fountain Place is a lively presence in the city because it changes as you move around it, almost as if it were doing a dance. And as you get closer, you discover something else that I consider even more important: the building doesn't just occupy space; it shapes space.

What do you mean by that?
A tall building of necessity *occupies* space, and in a gridded city of blocks and streets, most buildings, even those with spectacular skyline profiles, do only that. For example, as much as we may admire its image on the skyline, the Chrysler Building only occupies space at street level; it doesn't shape it. Similarly, the Empire State Building merely occupies space. However, as the main tower at Rockefeller Center demonstrates, a tall building can be more than merely an inert object in the city. The Rockefeller Center tower adjoins a civic space, and its relationship to that space is much more actively engaged than the passive relationship of blocks surrounded by streets. The latter is a neutral relationship in which the civility of the building consists simply in its taking its place within a city block. There's nothing in principle wrong with that. But a modern city that contains only huge office buildings filling blocks is ultimately an impoverished city because the public realm that exists in the

streets separating those enormous blocks is insufficient; it doesn't provide a rich enough life. In the historic city that richness of space and life was provided by squares with churches, palaces, town halls, and so on. But those things are absent in the downtown areas of most American cities. The proliferation of office space to the exclusion of other uses has had a devastatingly deadening effect.

So what can this monstrosity, the tall office building, do to make amends for that and enhance public life? It's not enough to put a fancy hat on top. It's wonderful to make a fancy hat, but it means nothing to people who, for example, are on the street next to the Chrysler Building. You have to go all the way across town, to Fifth Avenue and Forty-Second Street, to really enjoy that hat, and even then it's fleeting. So a tall building has to offer something more. If you assume that the profit derived from a tall building is sufficient to allow it to invest in shaping rather than merely occupying space, and if you assume that the morality of development demands that people who build tall buildings dedicate some of their resources to making civic space, then the question for architecture becomes: what kind of space should that be, and what role does the building play in shaping it?

These are the very same issues you addressed at Place Ville Marie.

Yes, and in every subsequent tall building project. I don't think that I have done a single tall building that was merely surrounded by streets and did not have a an active relationship to the public realm in which it is embedded. The shaping of public space in these projects has taken many different forms, and those forms are often more interesting than the buildings. The water garden at Fountain Place, for example, is more interesting than the building. And at Commerce Square, in Philadelphia, the way in which the buildings contribute to the shaping of a public space is much more interesting than the buildings themselves. The figure is the *space*, not the buildings. As in Place Ville Marie, but in a completely different way, Commerce Square is an exploration of a kind of transfiguration: the two towers, which are figures on the skyline, are transfigured as they move toward the ground in such a way that they frame both the public space of the street and the new public space within. This public space is the figural component of the project at street level. The towers become residual solids as they meet the ground; they are in the service of the public space. That is very, very important.

So there is a parallel in this respect between Fountain Place and Commerce Square?

Yes, despite the enormous difference between them as works of architecture. They are both twin buildings—or were intended to be, although in Dallas the second tower remains unbuilt—and both aspire to shape active public space at street level. Yet they do so in exactly opposite ways, and the reason has to do with the context in which each is placed. Philadelphia is a city of well-defined streets and squares. Our desire was to respect that tradition by making buildings that would contribute to the strengthening of the grid of streets and to an extension of the tradition of squares. In Dallas, however, in the vicinity of Fountain Place there is no clearly defined array of streets, blocks, and squares; there is just a vast, disordered expanse of highways and parking lots. In that situation the creation of a public square would have been more or less meaningless. Dan Kiley's solution—and it is by far the most interesting thing about the project—was to create a field of trees that would permeate the entire site, giving it a strong identity and appeal without enclosing walls or streets. The effect is amazing: as soon as you step ten feet off the street, you are swallowed up in a different world. It is like walking into a forest; it has that kind of magic. The strategy really works in that particular city, and it was the economic leverage of the building that allowed that water garden to be created. Through the mechanism of transfiguration—again, comparable to if very different from that in Montreal and Philadelphia—the building becomes a void in the lower sixty feet. This huge cubic volume, 192 feet on a side, having been carved away to create a memorable image on the skyline, is then carved away even more dramatically at street level to create the sixty-foot-high openings through which the garden extends. The building becomes residual as it meets the ground; it is placed in the service of Kiley's landscape.

So I like to think that in both Dallas and Philadelphia, as in Montreal, I was able to show how tall buildings can do something important for the life of a city by shaping civic space.

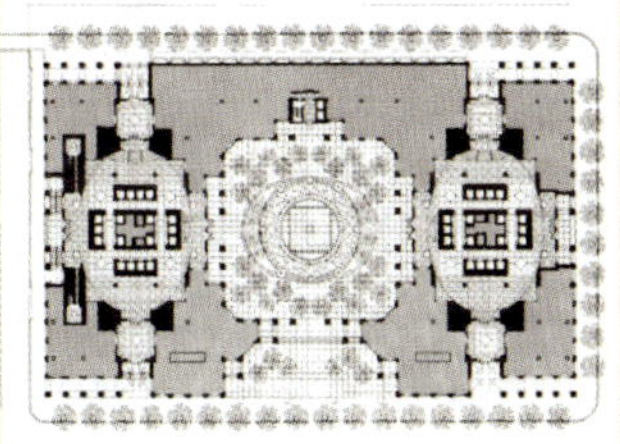

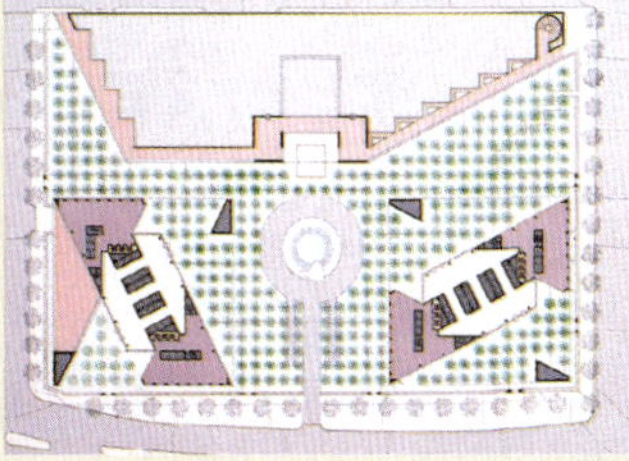

Above Commerce Square, Philadelphia (1992), and Fountain Place, Dallas (1986), at same scale.

AMERICAN ARCHITECTURE 1958–83

Lecture Marking the Twenty-Fifth Anniversary of the Jewett Arts Center at Wellesley College September 20, 1983

My purpose here is not to offer a critical assessment of recent work but to attempt an overview of the major issues and events that have shaped American architecture in the past quarter-century, as seen by one who has been active in practice throughout this very unsettled period. In doing so, I am going to turn a blind eye for a moment to architecture's seductive imagery and consider instead its uncomfortable predicament in the culture of our time.

Architecture serves human needs and shapes human experience. This inescapable duality informs the entire practice of our art. All architecture is produced by a synthesis of these related but separate intentions—a synthesis through which architects aspire to, and occasionally reach, the highest realm of art: that realm wherein, having satisfied all requirements of use and technique, architecture may illuminate and give meaning to the human condition while shaping our experience of the physical world. Why should I bother to propound these simple truths, which may seem obvious enough to be left unsaid? I do so because if we want to understand the complex currents and extraordinarily diverse products of contemporary architectural practice, I believe we must place them in the context of two disturbances that have profoundly unsettled architecture during the past quarter-century. The first is a revisional movement in the program of society, raising questions about how architecture serves human needs. The second is a revisional movement in the formal language, the substance of our art, raising questions about how architecture shapes human experience. From what I said a moment ago, it is not difficult to imagine that the simultaneous occurrence of these two disturbances has provoked widely divergent interpretations of that crucial synthesis through which architecture must make its ultimate and strongest appeal.

The ongoing revision in the program of society has affected all of us, whatever our professions. But its impact on architecture is not, I think, well understood. A significant episode in this process—one that must be vivid in the memory of everyone who experienced it—was the campus revolution that swept through American universities in the decade from 1963 to '73, reaching its apogee in '69 and '70. This was one of the more dramatic symptoms of a growing dissatisfaction with the way in which existing institutions in society were meeting human needs. As a consequence of this dissatisfaction, the value systems and ethical conduct of many institutions—governments, universities, and corporations among them—came under attack. Substantial rearrangements in the institutional structure of society were proposed and sometimes enacted—changes that redefined the relationships between individuals or communities and the institutions by which they had often felt themselves oppressed or neglected rather than well served. But many questions were raised regarding both goals and process that remain unanswered, and nowhere is this condition of unresolved crisis more evident than in the field of urban planning and design—the whole complex of interlocking issues that bear upon the form and quality of buildings, neighborhoods, cities, and regions. This crisis has affected the practice of architecture in many ways that can perhaps best be summarized by saying that it has left architects without a clearly defined subject for their art. For architecture is, after all, a representational art—an art of portraiture, if you will—and what is portrayed in it is precisely the multiform structure of desired relationships between human beings, their institutions, and the natural world. When that programmatic structure is disarranged, as it surely has been, when there exists no clear consensus as to a normative standard of conduct governing those relationships, then the architect is indeed an artist without a subject, responding to pragmatic requirements of use but deprived of that larger sense of purpose upon which all great traditions in human culture have heretofore been built. This has been and remains a central predicament of architecture in our time.

The disturbance that I have been discussing—the contemporary uncertainty in the program of society—clearly lies outside the discipline of architecture. As I have said, it concerns the subject of our art. Now I want to turn to the second revisional movement that has unsettled my profession in the past quarter-century—a crisis located within the discipline itself and touching its very substance, the formal language of architecture. To understand the character of this disturbance, it is first necessary to recall that the modern movement from its inception proposed a new language of architectural form constituted not from the classical tradition, which was deemed to have lost its value, but from the use of newly available technical means to achieve newly defined programmatic ends. Now, however much, with the wisdom of hindsight, we may deplore the chiliastic delusions and exclusivist proscriptions that characterized the modernist revolution, we must acknowledge that the invention and deployment of this new language was indeed a formidable achievement. The trouble was that the new language by means of which architecture had been rescued from a former condition of decadence was itself, because of its separation from tradition, all too easily subject to decay. What had not been anticipated in the positivist program of modern architecture was that its very usefulness, its adaptability to any definition of need, would make it fatally vulnerable to devaluation by the overwhelming economic imperatives of modern capitalism. Thus the functionalism that had been intended to place architecture at the service of society was all too soon and too often converted into a functionalism of market efficiency in which both the users of buildings and the larger public were ill served.

From this, I think it is clear how the two revisional movements that have shaped American architecture in the past quarter-century—the revision of program and the revision of language—though separate are nonetheless intimately related and have tended to reinforce one another. For the devaluation of the modern language of forms through economic exploitation naturally came to symbolize, indeed came to be seen as, the physical embodiment of that perceived tyranny of institutions that engendered such intense revulsion during the decade of the sixties. And this explains, for example, the almost mythic status that has been accorded to a single event—the dynamiting of Pruitt-Igoe, a low-rent housing project in St. Louis that was demolished at the insistence of its own occupants only a few years after receiving a national award for excellence of design. These revisions—of program and language—also account, at least in part, for the astonishing growth of preservation movements and the virtual eclipse of large-scale urban renewal in the past decade. We Americans have suddenly awakened to the value of collective memory as recorded in architecture and in cities. This new awareness has caused us to ask that growth and change should henceforth be incremental and conservative rather than comprehensive and radical.

The mention of collective memory brings into focus another problem that beset the modern movement in architecture as a consequence of its rejection of virtually the entire repertoire of forms inherited from the past. All art is necessarily the product of a particular dialogue, in the mind of the artist, between memory and invention. By severely limiting the role of memory in this equation, the modern movement, while in one sense reanimating architecture, in another sense impoverished it. This impoverishment began to worry some American architects at the very outset of the postwar building boom in the early fifties. For example, Paul Rudolph observed in 1952 that he had returned from a European trip "with the reinforced conviction of the necessity of regaining the 'form sense' which helped to shape Western man's building until the nineteenth century. Other periods," he continued, "have always developed means of tying their architecture to previous works without compromising their own designs. This," he concluded, "is also our task."[1] Although these con-

1 "Three New Directions: Paul Rudolph, Philip Johnson, Buckminster Fuller," *Perspecta* 1 (Summer 1952), 21.

cerns clearly informed much of Rudolph's own work—most notably the Jewett Arts Center at Wellesley—they remained largely unacknowledged in the mainstream of architectural practice for another decade.[2] But in 1966, with the publication of Robert Venturi's seminal manifesto *Complexity and Contradiction in Architecture*, a younger generation of architects began to give voice to their growing dissatisfaction with the modernist vocabulary, which they felt had drastically limited the communicative power of their art. Against the famous aphorism of Mies van der Rohe that "less is more"—an aphorism that had become emblematic of modernism—Venturi proposed that "less is a bore," and this led in turn to Robert Stern's postmodernist war-whoop, "More is more!"

The battle of slogans is trivial but nonetheless suggestive evidence of a crisis of language that has engulfed architecture with ever-increasing intensity for the past fifteen to twenty years. Unlike the crisis of program, this debate is largely internalized within the architectural profession though often communicated to a wider public through critical commentary in the press. The recovery of history, and particularly of the classical tradition, is a central theme in this crisis. Yet it would be a mistake to think of it as merely a historicist-versus-modernist debate. It is rather a widening exploration, from which no possibilities are in principle excluded, of the means by which architecture shapes human experience. Although much of this exploration may be seen as against modernism, it would be more accurate to characterize it as beyond modernism, in the sense that it builds upon the

2 Rudolph later turned his back on the Jewett Arts Center and declined to attend the twenty-fifth anniversary event at which this talk was delivered.

experience of modern architecture, without which it would in fact be inconceivable.

Through this brief review I have tried to indicate, in a necessarily generalized way, how architecture has been engulfed in the past quarter-century by two simultaneous and interrelated revisional disturbances—one in the program of society, which is the subject of our art, and the other in the language of architecture, which is its substance. Although the issues giving rise to these disturbances embrace very different territories of human sensibility and concern, we may observe that many of them find common ground in one underlying problem that has acquired, therefore, an especially profound significance for architecture in our time. This problem concerns the dynamic interaction—the ongoing dialogue, as I referred to it earlier—between memory and invention, between the values associated with treasuring the known and those associated with probing the unknown in our evolving human culture. Just what is the nature of that dialogue, that eternal and inexorably cumulative discourse, and how should it be nourished, enriched, employed for the benefit of humanity? This question is as old as civilization itself, but it has perhaps never been so central to the shared concerns of diverse spheres of interest in society as it is today. And it should come as no surprise that architecture, the preeminently social art, with its inescapable commitment to the synthesis of functional, technical, and symbolic realms, finds itself now the principal arena for addressing this question. It is a question to which many answers are possible, while none is certain; and this surely accounts in large part for the astonishing heterogeneity of our recent and current architecture.

Architecture cannot, after all, escape its time. As Daniel Bell has remarked, “Today there is no center; there are only peripheries." Perhaps this is why, in the exuberant pluralism of what is called "postmodern" architecture, we can find little evidence of that perfect synthesis of intentions, that distillation of essences that alone can render our art sublime. The last American architect to enter this highest realm of art was Louis Kahn in several of his late works. I think immediately of the library at Phillips Exeter Academy. There, with a serene authority born out of the most profound understanding, Kahn has given expression in architecture to the essential spirit of scholarship—an intensely individual pursuit that nonetheless both draws from and adds to the collective consciousness of mankind. One cannot use or even visit the library without being moved by its assertion of a probity transcending all instrumental concerns. Marvelously, this one building takes exception to virtually everything I have had to say about the contemporary condition of architecture. It is the perfect concrete example with which to bring this all-too-abstract discussion to a close. For Kahn's building shows us once again what every great work of art shows us: that there exists still and always a realm of knowledge, inaccessible to all our sciences, that is illuminated for us only by the engaging particularity, the material presence, the sublime reality of art. To discover this realm of knowledge—to give meaning to the human condition while giving shape to the physical world—this remains the ultimate task of architecture, the building art, at this or any time.

ARCHITECTURE AND THE UNIVERSITY

Gropius Lecture
Sanders Theater, Harvard University
April 25, 1985

Walter Gropius, architect and teacher whom we honor in memory on this occasion, was chairman of the Department of Architecture during my own student years at the Graduate School of Design. That was in the late forties, just following World War II. A decade earlier, Dean Joseph Hudnut had brought Professor Gropius to Harvard from England, and together they had instituted a new program of professional education that was destined to powerfully influence the practice of architecture in our time.

I do not intend to dwell at length here on the history of the Hudnut-Gropius era at Harvard. Like all too many partnerships between men of great ability, what had begun in a mood of optimism and harmony ended sadly in disappointment and discord. But in view of my stated topic this evening, I cannot fail to observe that Harvard's sponsorship of that joint enterprise constituted an intervention by this university of a kind quite without precedent and still without parallel in the annals of architectural education. We can get some glimpse of the dramatic character of this intervention by reflecting for a moment on the events surrounding Walter Gropius's arrival in March 1937 to take up his new post in Cambridge. This was, we may note, an occasion of more than merely local interest. As a world-renowned architect and leading advocate of what was then called the "New Architecture," as the founder and first director of the Bauhaus, and as a German citizen who had distanced himself from Nazism, Walter Gropius personified ideals and aspirations that engaged the sympathy of many Americans in that era. Hence his arrival was a quasi-public event, reported by the press and accompanied by a number of receptions at which the distinguished immigrant was invited to declare his beliefs and intentions.

On one such occasion, at the Boston Architectural Club on April 14, 1937, Professor Gropius issued a summary statement to the press that began as follows:

> Today we are in a position to prove conclusively that the outward form(s) of modern architecture and design are not the whim of a few architects or artists hungry for innovation, but the inevitable consequential product of the intellectual, social, and technical conditions of our age. The transformation from manual to machine production so preoccupied humanity for a century that instead of pressing forward to tackle the real problems of design, men were long content with borrowed styles and formulistic decorations. [But now] a new conception of building, based on realities, has developed and with it has come a new and changed perception of space. It [has] dawned that an architect cannot hope to realize his ideas unless he is able to influence the general production of his country, its trade and industry, in such a way that a new manner, a new school results, which succeeds in acquiring authoritative significance.[1]

Now, if you could distill zeitgeist theory in a test-tube, you couldn't get it any purer than that! The same document concludes several pages later with these words: "Though some will continue to find sympathy and others antipathy for the movement we call 'the New Architecture,' no one can any longer ignore its intellectual basis—an essentially vital basis, whose scope so far transcends considerations—one might almost say 'details'—like

1 Walter Gropius, Summary for the Press, "The Development of the New Architecture," 1937, Series I (19), Walter Gropius Papers, 1925–1969 (MS Ger 208), Houghton Library, Harvard University.

fitness for purpose or functional truth. Its spiritual necessity, its power of persuasion can no longer be disputed, and the youth of today is inspired by it."[2]

And so we were. For fifteen years, from 1937 to 1952, a generation of young men and women flocked to Robinson Hall in response to this new vision—the vision of an architecture liberated from the tyranny of dead styles, an entirely new architecture in which art, technology, and social purpose would be powerfully joined for the benefit of humanity. Whatever judgment history may ultimately pass on the Hudnut-Gropius era at the Graduate School of Design—and it will surely be a mixed one—this much is certain: in thus opening its doors to the New Architecture, Harvard cast itself in an unequivocally critical and activist role. And in doing so it vividly demonstrated the power of a great university—at least of this great university—to shape as well as serve our profession. As a witness to this episode, and indeed as a product of it, I could not help but be preoccupied during my own term as chairman with the sense of that latent power that resides in the university and that I would wish to see employed for the benefit of architecture. But beyond this I have been increasingly concerned to understand those reciprocal energies that flow, or could be caused to flow, between the university and our discipline—energies that if effectively mobilized might contribute to the strengthening of both. Hence my topic this evening, architecture and the university: a topic that I hope may be appropriate to this occasion when we remember Walter Gropius and to this place that more than any other symbolizes the collegial fellowship of this, our university.

To bring my theme into focus, I am going to cast it in the form of two very simple but I think not oversimplified

2 Gropius, 4.

questions: Of what use is the university to architecture? And of what use is architecture to the university? If these questions seem blunt or even hostile, I would argue that they are nonetheless questions that we would do well to ask here among friends—friends of architecture and friends of the university—as they will surely be asked of us one day by those who do not share our loyalty to either. For as President Bok observed in his incisive critique of law schools just a few years ago, we live in an era characterized by "wide discontent with all our major professions" and at a time when "the public seems critical of all institutions."[3] Who can doubt that both the discontent and the criticism are justified? And who will deny that we inhabit an over-professionalized and over-institutionalized world—a world in which the elaborate and self-perpetuating forms of our social mechanisms too often threaten to suffocate the substance of their tasks? In such a world we are obliged to be skeptical of all professions and all institutions and especially of those—among which I count architecture and the university—that aspire to the highest goals. For we can hope to approach these goals only if we are willing to subject our pursuit of them to the most searching and ceaseless self-criticism.

After this introductory harangue, you must be wondering whether my discourse this evening can conceivably have a positive outcome. I think it can, but first I must ask you to bear with me while I push a little further through the thickets of negativism. We need to face squarely and unflinchingly the fact that architecture is a misfit in the university. Now, it is true that our profession is not entirely alone in this. Indeed, it can be argued that all professional schools are more or less misfits in the

3 Derek Curtis Bok, *The President's Report*, 1981–82 (Cambridge: Harvard University, 1983), 24.

university as classically defined—as defined, for example, by John Henry Newman in his famous discourses on *The Idea of a University*. Newman, writing in the middle of the nineteenth century, maintained that the one great purpose of a university was to provide a "Liberal Education," which he defined with characteristic eloquence as that "process of training, by which the intellect, instead of being formed or sacrificed to some particular or accidental purpose, some specific trade or profession, or study or science, is disciplined for its own sake, for the perception of its own proper object, and for its own highest culture."[4]

In a university so conceived and so dedicated, there could be no place for the specialized, quasi-autonomous professional school. Yet surely one of the achievements of the modern university—and nowhere more brilliantly demonstrated than right here at Harvard—is that it has been able to enlarge its conception of its task to include those areas of knowledge, or perhaps we could better say those ways of knowing, that are both instrumental to and nourished by certain modes of acting that human society has come to see as central to its well-being. Each of these linked modes of knowing and acting, which we call professions, is characterized at least to some degree by the ancient wisdom that "practice is the basis of theory."[5] Hence in welcoming professional schools into their scholarly precincts, universities have inevitably had to face the problem of how to connect themselves intimately and productively to ongoing professional work while still preserving an appropriate critical distance from current

4 John Henry Cardinal Newman, *The Idea of a University* (London: Longmans, Green and Co., 1929), 152.

5 Jaroslav Pelikan, *Scholarship and Its Survival: Questions on the Idea of Graduate Education* (Princeton: Carnegie Foundation for the Advancement of Teaching, 1983), 49, 90n19.

practice. The mechanisms developed for making these connections while maintaining that distance have been various and by no means uniformly effective. Probably the outstanding success story is the teaching hospital, in its role as a link between medical schools and the medical profession. Yet even this seemingly superb institutional invention has come under attack in recent years as being obstructive to progress in the sociology if not the science of health care. But to return to the subject of our concern here, it is notable that in the case of architecture, although some serious efforts have been made to invent comparable mechanisms linking the schools to the profession, none has been more than marginally successful. This failure is not a cause but a symptom of the condition of misfit that I am trying to define. When we look for causes, we can identify two distinct circumstances that lie at the root of the problem.

The first of these is that architecture, though it encompasses in practice many modes of thought and action, is at its center a visual art. And while scholarly study and appreciation of the arts may flourish in a university, the practice of an art, insomuch as it engages suprarational processes that are essentially alien to the intellectual mode of scholarship, is condemned to remain a stranger there. This condition is not specific to architecture; it defines the predicament of any art that aspires to practice in an academic setting. But in the case of architecture the problem is compounded by a further circumstance that contributes to the peculiar misfit I am speaking of. For whereas in other arts or professions important contributions can often be made through individual work or at least through institutional mechanisms that are more or less compatible—as is the teaching hospital—with the norms and style of the academic world, in architecture the opposite is true: important contributions almost always require an operative apparatus that cannot be accommodated within the structure of the university and almost always involve engagement with a broad array of activities and interests that seem entirely alien to its norms and style. Deprived of that apparatus and that engagement, architecture is reduced to a kind of shadow of itself. And although history records a few examples of such shadows that have moved the world—the contributions of Piranesi, Boullée, and today perhaps Léon Krier come to mind—these remain extraordinary exceptions that in the end serve only to prove the rule.

Thus architecture in its engagement with the university seems caught in an unresolvable paradox: on the one hand separated from its vital sources of nourishment in the "real world" of practice, while on the other hand devalued as a discipline by its entrepreneurial, practice-oriented character and thus gravely disadvantaged in its struggle to establish a fruitful discourse with other less "contaminated" disciplines within the university. In fact, the record shows that American schools of architecture—and we should not forget that the university-based architecture school is an American invention—have always existed precariously on a kind of ideological seesaw between the two terms of this paradox, tipping now toward the norms of the practicing profession, now toward those of the academic world, but rarely and only fleetingly able to create the kind of engagement between the two that would enable one to assert that the university has been in any real sense useful to architecture or architecture useful to the university.

At this point it may be objected that I have created a meaningless straw man in this vague concept of reciprocal usefulness—that it is in fact a trivial notion and should not be allowed to divert us from the only important question: Do we or don't we provide a sound program of training for entry into the profession? To answer this question affirmatively, as I hope we can, is only to invite another: Inasmuch as there are no fewer than ninety-one accredited schools of architecture in North America, with a total enrollment of close to 21,000 students, and inasmuch as three-quarters of these students are enrolled in five-year undergraduate programs, thus clearly establishing such programs as the norm for training in our field, is there any compelling reason why Harvard should persist in offering a graduate degree program that delivers another seventy or eighty aspiring architects each year into an already overpopulated and undervalued profession? Or to phrase the question another way, even if we acknowledge that training for the profession is a necessary activity of our school, in the sense that without it we would lack an absolutely indispensable link to the practice of architecture, does it therefore follow that such activity is sufficient in and of itself to justify our school's existence?

Now, lest I be misunderstood, I want to assure you that in asking this question I mean no disparagement of our professional degree programs. On the contrary, I believe we are entitled to take a good deal of pride in their present condition. Architecture is a highly competitive profession, and the competitive record of our faculty, students, and young alumni during the past few years has been impressive. For example, projects designed by members of our faculty, competing in a field of almost eight hundred entries, this year won three out of four Architectural Design Awards, including the coveted First Award, in the annual competition sponsored by *Progressive Architecture*. And our students, competing against the cream of the crop from graduate schools across the country, last year won two out of three traveling fellowships awarded by the Skidmore, Owings & Merrill Foundation. (This year we were not allowed to enter, so as to give other schools a better chance!) And both of the two Rome Prize Fellowships in architecture—the most significant recognition a young architect can receive—were won this year by very recent graduates of our master of architecture program. It seems to me that even at the risk of displaying a certain chauvinism, we should permit ourselves the luxury of savoring these facts. What they tell us is that measured by undeniably objective standards, ours is not just a good school of architecture—it is perhaps second to none. And judging by the spirit and substance of Professor Moneo's lecture last month, our department is destined to become even stronger under his forthcoming chairmanship.

But this condition of strength does not erase, indeed it all the more obliges us to confront, the question of sufficiency that I raised a moment ago. It is, we will find, a question that answers itself as soon as we admit, as we surely must, that what has made our training good is precisely our knowledge that training is not enough. We know that education that is merely instrumental is by definition insufficient. We know that while preparation for practice is a central mission of our school, we cannot adequately fulfill that mission unless we are doing other things as well. Yes, but what things? Well, naturally, useful things—things that are useful to architecture and useful to the university, And so you see we are driven inexorably back to the two questions that I began with—questions of reciprocal usefulness that, after all this verbal squirming, still remain unanswered. Let us finally address them now, one at a time.

Of what use is or could be the university to architecture? We can come close to answering this question by considering another: Why do architects teach? We teach, of course, because we enjoy participating in the enterprise of higher education—an enterprise concisely summed up in Whitehead's maxim that "the task of the university is to weld together imagination and experience."[6] But we teach for another reason as well: because involvement in a professional school helps us to gain a critical distance from our practice. And if we notice that the activity of teaching is today more appealing than ever to practicing architects, we may ascribe this appeal to an enhanced awareness of the necessity of obtaining that critical distance, as an aid to practice, in an era of acute cultural ambivalence—our strange contemporary era that has found no better name than "postmodern." A notable aspect of the postmodern period has been the erosion, amounting sometimes to eclipse, of those normative standards upon which architecture, more than any other art, has traditionally been dependent. This erosion has afflicted standards governing both the program of society, which is the subject of our art, and the language of built form, which is the substance. Hence, surrounded as they are by conditions of uncertainty in every aspect of the culture, yet caught up in an ever-more-frenzied cycle of production and consumption, architects who would resist the trivialization of their art are now obliged to seek through hard critical inquiry those guiding principles that in other times were often readily available to them through received tradition, prescriptive theory, or some form of contemporary cultural consensus.

And this at last brings into view the answer that I want to propose to the first of my pair of questions. For it suggests that the usefulness of the university to architecture

6 Alfred North Whitehead, "Universities and Their Function," *The Aims of Education and Other Essays* (New York: Macmillan, 1967), 93.

no longer resides, as it once did, in the promotion and elaboration of particular belief systems, theoretical constructs, or modes of practice. Rather, usefulness now resides, or could reside, in the capacity of the university to sponsor a critical discourse about architecture—a discourse powerful enough in its thrust and broad enough in its scope to act as a bridge between the very diverse modes of thought and action that enter into the making of architecture. Such a discourse would join the instrumental and pragmatic to the speculative and ideal. It would be founded upon scholarship that is both reflective and speculative, conducted with a rigor and audacity that would engage the interest of other disciplines in the university and command their respect. It would be a discourse distanced from practice but never alienated from practice. Above all, it would be a discourse that does not shrink from addressing those fundamental questions that define the contemporary predicament of our profession and our art.

Among these questions, none surely is more poignant or more pervasive than that concerning the perpetual transaction in architecture—the ongoing dialogue, if you will—between memory and invention, between those values associated with treasuring the known and those associated with probing the unknown in our evolving human culture. Just what is the nature of that dialogue, that eternal and inexorably cumulative discourse, and how should it be elaborated, enriched, and employed for the benefit of humanity? This question is as old as civilization itself, but it has never been so central to the shared concerns of diverse spheres of interest in society as it is today. And it should come as no surprise that architecture, the preeminently social art, with its inescapable commitment to the synthesis of functional, technical, and symbolic realms, finds itself now the principal arena for addressing this question. It is a question to which many answers are possible, while none is conclusive, and this surely accounts in large part for the astonishing heterogeneity of our recent and current architecture.

Returning now to my theme, I want to be very precise about the claims I make for the kind of discourse about architecture that I am suggesting might take place within the university. As I indicated earlier, I do not regard the university as well fitted for direct intervention in the making of architecture. Its institutional structure and procedures, not to say the modes of thought that prevail there, do not lend themselves to such activity. Nor would I wish to see universities engaged in the formulation of prescriptive theory to be promulgated as a guide to practice. History has amply demonstrated that such prescriptions, with their corollary proscriptions, invariably lead to the corruption rather than the advancement of our art. What I want to see taking place in the university is an activity of a much more subtle and complex kind—an activity that acknowledges and forcefully promotes a mutually nourishing interaction among scholarship, speculative inquiry, and practice. It is in my mind an activity dedicated more to the pursuit of interesting questions than to the formulations of definitive answers. Thus it is an activity that informs and is informed by practice but does not aim to direct practice. I do believe that the cultivation of this activity—this critical discourse, as I have called it—is of no little importance to the future of architecture. I further believe that it is a useful activity that ought to find its natural home in our university, where, apart from its intrinsic worth, such a discourse could surely help us to overcome the most dangerous shortcoming inherent in all professional education: namely, that "necessary technical excellence can only be acquired by a training which is apt to damage those energies of mind which should direct the technical skill."[7] Again, I have borrowed the words of Alfred North Whitehead, who in the same essay goes on to declare: "The way in which a university should function in the preparation for an intellectual career, such as modern business or one of the older professions, is by promoting the imaginative consideration of the various general principles underlying that career.... A university is imaginative or it is nothing—at least nothing useful."[8]

I turn now to the second of my pair of questions: Of what use is or could be architecture to the university? Consideration of this question brings us hard up against the misfit status of our discipline that I touched on earlier. The truth is that owing to this condition of misfit, schools of architecture, while located at the university, can seldom be said to be in and of the university. At Harvard, the most balkanized of institutions, this problem is exacerbated by isolationist tendencies inherent in an "every-tub-on-its-own-bottom" administrative policy. Hence the Graduate School of Design, with its curious studio-based teaching methods, its paucity of scholarly research, and its dedication to serving the highly "contaminated" professions of architecture, landscape architecture, and urban planning, must appear, to borrow the language of *Peanuts*, as a kind of Pig-Pen character in the university family—that is to say, disreputable and more or less useless but to be tolerated with appropriate condescension and frequent expressions of dismay. Probably we should accept this situation and be grateful for it. But I trust you will not think me hopelessly quixotic if I declare that something else is possible. For in my view those aspects of architecture that

7 Whitehead, 96.

8 Whitehead, 96.

makes it a misfit in the university are precisely those that ought to make it truly useful.

Before attempting to give substance to this hypothesis—and I am all too aware that I may fail in the attempt—I think it is worthwhile to review briefly how the present situation of architecture in the university evolved, how it became what it is today. First, it is important to reiterate that although the pedagogical methods employed in the training of architects have evolved principally from European models, the idea that such training should be located in a university, rather than within the profession or in specialized academies, originated not in the Old World but in the New. And it should come as no surprise to learn that one of the earliest proponents of this idea was Thomas Jefferson, for whom both architecture and higher education were passions of a lifetime. Jefferson argued that universities in the new American democracy should include not only the liberal arts but the scientific and technical disciplines as well. And when these thoughts matured into his project for the University of Virginia, architecture was included in its curriculum. Indeed, one of Jefferson's principal arguments for his "academical village," as he called the Virginia campus, was that the several pavilions framing the Great Lawn would serve as useful models for students of architecture. His other argument for this classical "village," interestingly enough, was that "if we don't have beautiful buildings, we will lose all our best characters to Harvard and Yale."[9] Thus spoke the Gentleman from Virginia! Unfortunately, Jefferson's enthusiasm for architecture as—again in his words—"the one art we can excel in," and hence worthy of a place in the

9 Frederick D. Nichols, professor of architecture, University of Virginia, telephone conversation with author, March 28, 1985.

university, did not find sufficient support to survive him at Charlottesville.[10] Nonetheless, his idea had clearly taken root, for it was to bear fruit half a century later in the curricula of the land-grant colleges, those altogether splendid American inventions brought into being by the Morrill Act—a funding bill enacted by Congress in 1862 with the stated purpose "to promote the liberal and practical education of the industrial classes in the several pursuits and professions in life."[11] Stimulated by this munificent legislation, the first American schools of architecture were inaugurated within several early land-grant colleges and universities. Our next-door neighbor, the School of Architecture at MIT, founded in 1868, was the very first of these, with the schools at Cornell and Illinois following a few years later.

Thus was established what has since become the prevailing mode of preparation for the profession of architecture in North America—the undergraduate professional degree program located within a usually public university. By and large, the older privately endowed universities, with their commitment to liberal education at the undergraduate level and to scholarly research on the graduate level, did not follow this pattern. During the latter half of the nineteenth century—the period when land-grant colleges were being established across the country—these older institutions were focusing not so much on training for the useful arts as on the advancement of scholarship through graduate study. Although law, medicine, and divinity—those intellectual centerpieces of the European university since medieval times—were generally

10 Nichols.

11 Turpin C. Bannister, ed., *The Architect at Mid-Century: Evolution and Achievement* (New York: Reinhold Publishing Corp., 1954), 96.

welcomed to such institutions as graduate professional schools, architecture was greeted with ambivalence, as a discipline whose base of knowledge and mode of practice did not unequivocally entitle it to a place in the university.

At Harvard architecture was first introduced in 1874 by Charles Eliot Norton as part of the subject matter of his lectures on the history of art. Instruction in architecture with the specific aim of preparing students for professional practice began with the offering of courses by Herbert Langford Warren at the Lawrence Scientific School in 1893. By 1897 architecture had become a full-fledged undergraduate department in the Faculty of Arts and Sciences, and in 1906 it acquired graduate status as a department of the Graduate School of Applied Science. In 1919, still under Warren's dedicated stewardship, architecture became a separate graduate school, a status it retained until 1936, when under Dean Hudnut it was combined with the School of Landscape Architecture and the School of Planning to form the present Graduate School of Design.

This capsule history is of interest to us here only insofar as it provides a factual skeleton enabling us to reflect on the relevant implications of its several episodes. In its origin, the study of architecture at Harvard seems to have emerged, as is so often the case in the life of great institutions, more from the personal enthusiasms and commitment of a few key individuals than from any general consensus in the university. The charismatic appeal and wide influence of Charles Eliot Norton must surely be counted the moving force in bringing architecture into the university and in stimulating its appreciation as one of the arts in which was to be found, in Norton's words, "the expression of a nation's highest moral aspiration."[12] But the evolution from dedicating the eye and mind for the enjoyment of architecture to professional training for the practice of architecture could have been accomplished only through the active interest and support of President Eliot, whose conception of the university as a consortium of graduate schools built around Harvard College was broad enough to embrace both the liberal and the useful arts. As is well known, it is to Eliot that we owe Harvard's initial commitment to professional education, an enterprise that by now, through its schools of law, medicine, divinity, education, business, and government—and dare we say design?—virtually defines its stature as a great university. Under President Eliot, Harvard gave enormous and purposeful impetus to the burgeoning culture of professionalism that was rapidly coming to characterize the American university system. And it is safe to assume, I believe, that architecture was seen by him as a desirable if perhaps peripheral item in the array of services offered by the university to society. In this he gave support to the utilitarian ideal of professional education as primarily a service, an instrumental training that has as its primary if not its sole aim the preparation of young people for entry into practice. This is indeed a noble conception, but it is also a narrow one, entirely neglecting as it does the possibility that architecture as a mode of knowing and acting might have some meaning for or be of some reciprocal service to the larger purpose of the university. And curiously, the modernist revision of the pedagogical program in architecture as conceived by Hudnut and Gropius served only to reinforce this narrowness of purpose. For it explicitly limited the institutional role of the Graduate School of Design to "the preparation of students for

12 Eduard F. Sekler and William Curtis, *Le Corbusier at Work: The Genesis of the Carpenter Center for the Visual Arts* (Cambridge: Harvard University Press, 1978), 4, 309n6.

professional competence."[13] The removal of all advanced study in the history of architecture to the Department of Fine Arts was emblematic of this heightened emphasis on instrumental training, with its concomitant disengagement from any scholarly work or discourse that could connect the GSD to other disciplines or branches of learning within the university. To a significant degree, however, and in a variety of ways, this isolationist posture was reversed in the succeeding era under Dean Josep Lluís Sert. By his persistent and effective advocacy of an expanded role for the visual arts in the curriculum of the college, by his invention and energetic promotion of an interdisciplinary program in urban design within the GSD, and not least by his own considerable production as an architect, Sert brought design powerfully into focus as a central concern in the life of the university. What nonetheless joined the Sert era to its predecessor—and separates it decisively from our own—was its participation in the essential ethos of modernism: an ethos predominantly positivist, determinist, and confident of its capacity to offer for every problem a definitive solution.

But for the past fifteen years at least, our culture has been evolving toward a very different ethos: an ethos in which the only thing that is certain, whether we speak of physics or philosophy or architecture, is that the time of certainty is behind us. In this new era, when we have become acutely conscious of the relativism of truth, there has been, in the words of Christopher Norris, a "turn toward a more 'conversational' ethos for philosophy"—and we could say equally for architecture—suggesting,

13 Joseph Hudnut, Memorandum on the Proposed Graduate School of Design, 14 January 1936, Records of the President of Harvard University, James Bryant Conant, 1933–1955 (UAI 5.168.XX), Harvard University Archives.

again, in Norris's words, "a turning-away from positivist rigor and truth claims."[14] And this brings me back now to my admittedly shaky hypothesis. It seems to me that the misfit status of architecture—both as an art and as a complex, practice-oriented profession—might now in fact commend it as a most useful participant in this more conversational discourse that may be emerging in the university. For have we not arrived at a moment when the world of scholarship may at last be ready to listen to Nelson Goodman's contention that "the arts must be taken no less seriously than the sciences as modes of discovery, creation, and enlargement of knowledge"?[15] And may we not have finally arrived at a time when the several sciences could profit from understanding the peculiar capacity of architecture to invent, define, elaborate, criticize, and question the relationships between human beings, their institutions, and the natural world? And is this not a time when we who bring architecture to the university are most acutely aware that our art can and must do more than simply fulfill the expectations of the culture it finds itself in? Architecture can indeed be both thought about and practiced as a radical critique of the culture—a critique carried out in the language of forms rather than the language of words. Surely architecture so conceived and so practiced has something useful to bring to the ongoing discourse within the university: something useful drawn from that realm of knowledge—inaccessible to all our sciences—that is illuminated only by the engaging particularity, the material presence, the marvelous concreteness of our art.

14 Christopher Norris, "Philosophy as a Kind of Narrative: Rorty on Postmodern Liberal Culture," *Enclitic* 7, no. 2 (Fall 1983): 145.
15 Nelson Goodman, *Ways of Worldmaking* (Indianapolis and Cambridge: Hackett Publishing Company, 1978), 102.

As an architect who can make no claim to scholarship, I find it difficult to articulate, let alone defend, this hypothesis. Nonetheless, it commands my intuition with such force that I am emboldened to put it forward here, however tentatively. And should my intuition prove correct, then architecture might indeed find a use, hitherto unimagined, that would place it not merely *at*, but unequivocally *in* and *of* the university.

In addressing the two questions that I began with concerning the reciprocal usefulness of architecture and the university, I have all too clearly been manufacturing dreams—dreams that are barely hinted at in our present reality. Could these dreams become realities? Well, against all odds I remain an optimist. Surely we can find some reason for optimism in recent developments at the GSD: under Dean McCue's leadership, our school has redefined its mission and greatly strengthened its commitment both to scholarship and to the professions it serves. The president and governing boards have responded to these initiatives with enthusiasm and have given our school their support, both moral and material. New faculty appointments have been authorized and new programs approved.

In short, our school is moving on an upward trajectory, which could, if all goes well, place it in a new and hitherto unattainable orbit. Whether we reach that orbit depends on further initiatives that must now come from within the design professions and from within the university. We in the professions must open ourselves to critical and speculative inquiry at a level of intensity that we have heretofore seldom welcomed. We must acknowledge that such inquiry is essential to the vitality of our art in an era of pervasive uncertainty, and that it must be conducted in a spirit of ongoing dialogue rather than as a quest for one-sided, ultimate answers. And we in the university, for our part, must be more willing than we have so far been to acknowledge that the world of scholarship may have something to learn from modes of thought and action that cannot but appear alien to it. As my use of the first-person plural suggests, we, the faculty and students of the GSD, are the design professions, and we are the university. Hence all of the obligations I have cited are ours, and in meeting them we are challenged, above all, to take care that the privileged cultural position and special intellectual resources of our university are so utilized as to make our school preeminently the home of high adventure, a place—again the words are Whitehead's—where "the adventure of action [meets] the adventure of thought."[16]

I am reminded of a motto that we all learn in childhood: "Nothing ventured, nothing gained." It is a motto I would like to see emblazoned on every architrave in Gund Hall—but of course there are no architraves in Gund Hall!—and indeed on every architrave in the university. Perhaps, if we pay attention to these words—nothing ventured, nothing gained—they may yet save us from falling prey to those negative and defensive habits of mind that seem to lurk so persistently in the shaded groves of academe. For there is no doubt in my mind that architecture and the university can be truly useful to each other only to the extent that both can become enterprises characterized not by complacency but by self-criticism, not by silence but by active discourse, not by comfort but by discomfort, not by refuge but by risk. These, so I believe, are the essential preconditions for the moment when we may at last be able to declare that architecture is worthy to inhabit the university and that the university is worthy to embrace architecture.

16 Whitehead, "Universities and Their Function," 95.

TRAFALGAR SQUARE, LONDON

Sainsbury Wing, National Gallery
Competition Proposal, 1985–86
with Paul Marantz (lighting)

In May 1984, at a Hampton Court dinner celebrating the 150th anniversary of the Royal Institute of British Architects, the Prince of Wales delivered a talk that concluded:

> What, then, are we doing to our capital city now? What have we done to it since the bombing during the war? What are we shortly to do to one of its most famous areas—Trafalgar Square? Instead of designing an extension to the elegant facade of the National Gallery which complements it and continues the concept of columns and domes, it looks as if we may be presented with a kind of municipal fire station, complete with the sort of tower that contains the siren. I would understand better this type of high-tech approach if you demolished the whole of Trafalgar Square and started again with a single architect responsible for the entire layout, but what is proposed is like a monstrous carbuncle on the face of a much-loved and elegant friend.

The "monstrous carbuncle" to which Prince Charles referred was the winning entry submitted by Ahrends, Burton and Koralek in the 1982 competition for an extension to the National Gallery.

Subsequent to the "carbuncle" speech, the Environment Ministry withdrew permission to build the premiated scheme, and a major gift from the Sainsbury brothers prompted reconsideration of the building program. In 1985 the trustees decided to start afresh with the two-stage international competition in which I became a finalist.

In their design submissions, the six competitors had to deal with two distinctly separate issues: the external posture of the new wing in its urban setting, and the internal spatial articulation of the picture galleries, in which the museum's superb collection of early Netherlandish and Italian tre-quattrocento paintings were to be displayed. Here I will neglect the interior and limit myself to the external aspects of my proposal, as set forth in my report to the architect selection committee, excerpted below.

In shaping a building volume for the Sainsbury Wing, I have remained faithful to the tentative conclusions drawn from my initial site analysis as presented to the committee last September. Principal among these was the observation that a curved building face derived from a rotational geometry constitutes the most appropriate response to the site's complex urban setting at the intersection of Pall Mall and Trafalgar Square. This proposition has now been given specific form as a semicircular screen-wall articulating the most prominent corner of a building volume that otherwise simply fills the available land area (as indeed it must if it is to provide the required accommodation). This curved screen-wall, by virtue of its position, its shape, and its ornament, is the indisputable architectural cynosure of the new building. Standing as it does at an extraordinary pressure point of London's public realm, the screen-wall is the natural vehicle for deployment of an architectural apparatus composed of classical elements and intended to communicate in a quite precise way the institutional role of the new building as not merely an extension but a significant augmentation of the National Gallery.

The fulfillment of this intent requires a design strategy that shows appropriate deference to the main building by acknowledging its best features while at the same time compensating for some of its salient weaknesses. Among the latter, the most disturbing to me is the misleading impression conveyed by the Trafalgar Square facade with respect to the hierarchy of space that lies behind it. The internal primacy of the exhibition galleries is nowhere evidenced; indeed it is contradicted by a fenestration scheme that gives

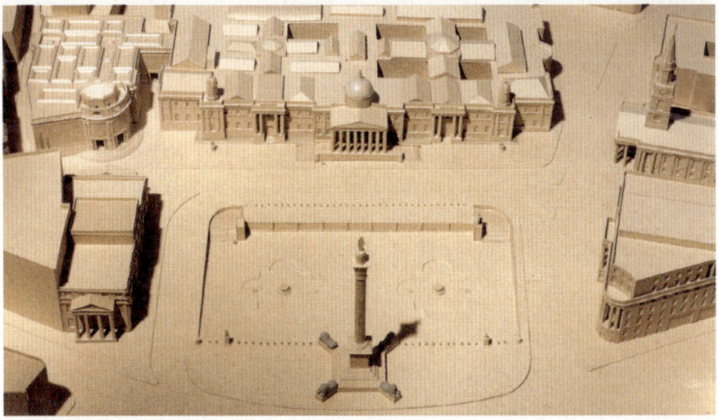

Top Perspective view of National Gallery competition proposal, 1986. **Middle** Model of proposal in Trafalgar Square. **Bottom** William Wilkins, National Gallery, 1838.

the ground-floor offices the status of a "noble floor," while the main gallery level above has the appearance of a secondary upper floor of a vastly overextended country house. Only the blindness of this upper range of windows hints, rather ineffectively, that something else might be afoot.

Fortunately, however, this confusing and unsatisfactory two-story array is overlaid with a colossal Corinthian order, giving the facade both a distinctive character and an appropriately public scale. Clearly this order, with its well-defined entablature and base, is the strongest unifying feature of Wilkins's facade and constitutes the one element (other than Portland stone) that the new building unquestionably needs to have in common with the old if both are to be perceived as belonging to a single institution. In considering how best to introduce this colossal order into my design, I experimented first with columns, both engaged and freestanding, but found through models that they inevitably challenged the primacy of the existing central portico—a primacy that I firmly believe should be maintained. The less assertive and actually more characteristic pilaster therefore recommended itself, and the decision to employ this motif then laid the foundation for all subsequent steps in the design.

Adoption of the colossal order of the main building as the governing element in the facade of the extension brought me immediately face-to-face with the problem of entry: as it happens, the base of the colossal order is too high to be easily accessible from street level and too low to allow for a gracious entry beneath it. While wrestling with this difficulty, and being preoccupied also with the importance of

Top Main entry elevation, plan, and sections.
Above Michelangelo Buonarroti, Palazzo dei Conservatori, Rome, 1564.

establishing the gallery level as unequivocally the "noble floor" of the new building, it dawned on me that both problems could be solved by introducing a smaller order of columns below but overlapping the colossal one—a strategy invented by Michelangelo for the facade of the Conservators' Palace on the Capitoline in Rome. The particular merit of this strategy as I have interpreted it here is that it dramatizes the poignant duality of intention inherent in this building: on the one hand, as a major public institution located in the heart of a capital city, the building ought to invite entry and play an active, engaging role on the urban stage; on the other hand, as the repository of paintings whose significance surely transcends that of even the greatest symbols of national identity, the building ought to maintain a certain "distance" between the place of contemplation within and the distracting busyness that flows constantly around it. My aim has been to find a way of communicating this duality while striking a delicate balance between deference and self-assertion in the relationship of the new building to the old.

In pursuit of this goal, I found that the curved screen-wall by itself, though successful in its engagement with the street, was insufficient: the second half of the duality of intention that I sought to convey could be expressed only by creating an explicit awareness of a space within—a chamber having an autonomous value quite independent of the external circumstances of its urban setting. This discovery led me to explore the possibility of allowing a dome to rise from a circular drum behind the screen-wall. But once again I found through modeling that this feature would pose an unacceptable threat to the primacy of the central dome of the main building. The solution that finally emerged from this search—an octagonal cupola of low profile rising behind the pierced attic of the screen-wall—has two advantages: first, it takes its place comfortably and with dignity, but also with appropriate understatement, among the several landmarks ornamenting the periphery of Trafalgar Square; and second, it presents a profile and roof form specifically evocative of the early Renaissance in Italy.

In shaping its new presence in London's public realm, the gallery's main building and the Sainsbury Wing to the west play complementary and interdependent roles. Indeed, as I remarked in my initial site analysis, one of the perceived weaknesses of the main building—its compositional looseness and ambivalence—becomes a positive asset in the context of the Sainsbury Wing. To understand why, it is only necessary to consider how much more difficult it would have been to design a satisfactory extension on this site had Wilkins been allowed to execute his preferred design, with its imposing colonnaded porticos, in place of the cupola-capped pavilions that now punctuate the flanking wings. My discovery of the role of these pavilions in engendering a lateral movement outward from this otherwise overwhelmingly frontal facade was the beginning of my understanding of the architectural possibilities of the Sainsbury Wing. When I first discussed this discovery with the committee, I had only the most general idea where it might lead. The work accomplished in the intervening months, aside from giving me a great deal of pleasure, has given me a confidence born of conviction that the committee's wish for an exten-

Top Model of semicircular screen-wall. **Above** Venturi, Scott Brown and Associates, National Gallery Sainsbury Wing, London, 1991.

sion to the National Gallery that would be "distinct from the existing building but belong to it" can be a wish fulfilled.

Both my competition proposal and the building actually constructed, designed by Robert Venturi and Denise Scott Brown, deploy the same monumental order of Corinthian pilasters carried over from the Wilkins building. Yet it is difficult to imagine two projects more widely diverging in their postures toward the city. Whereas mine is boldly assertive, theirs is purposefully recessive. Whereas mine deploys elements of the classical language with the almost painful self-consciousness of an enthusiastic neophyte (though not without some deliberate flouting of the "rules"), theirs deploys that language with the almost offhand panache of skilled and practiced mannerists, for whom a deep knowledge of history joined with a refined sense of the contemporary predicament has bred an unmatched capacity for irony. In retrospect, I still believe that my proposal to give the Sainsbury Wing a boldly articulated multidirectional posture, as embodied in the semicircular screen-wall, was a compellingly appropriate response to its urban setting. What was missing from my project was any evidence of how it might become an intervention appropriate not only to its place but also to its time. If awarded the commission, could I have crossed that threshold and somehow joined memory to invention for the benefit of both? I would like to think so, and had I, like my fellow competitor Jim Stirling, devoted the months following my loss to further development of my project, I might have been able to answer that question with confidence. But I did not, and I cannot.

THE FIRST (AND LAST) MEETING OF THE MODERNIST READING GROUP

Conversation at the Century Association
New York City, April 28, 1986

What follows is the lightly edited transcript of a conversation provoked by my entry in the competition for the Sainsbury Wing of the National Gallery in London. As Peter Eisenman explains in his opening remarks, this was intended to be the first of a series of monthly meetings dedicated to discussion not only of architectural projects, built and unbuilt, but also of contemporary critical and theoretical writings about architecture. As is so often the fate of such initiatives, the beginning proved also to be the end. Nonetheless, owing partly to the moment at which it occurred, partly to the individuals assembled for the occasion, and partly to the project chosen for discussion, this conversation is of some historical interest. The diverse views expressed therein quite vividly—even movingly—expose not only the beliefs but also the uncertainties and anxieties that preoccupied practitioners, educators, and theorists in the mid-1980s, when both modernism and postmodernism seemed exhausted and architecture was felt by some to be adrift in a Sargasso Sea of uncritical and culturally bankrupt "hybrid" design strategies.

Although recorded, the conversation was private and not intended to be published. I have therefore sought and received permission from each of the participants—and in the case of John Hejduk and Charles Gwathmey, from their heirs—to include it here. In addition to myself, the interlocutors were Peter Eisenman, Hal Foster, Charles Gwathmey, John Hejduk, Jeffrey Kipnis, Gianfranco Monacelli, Laurie Olin, and John Whiteman.

Peter Eisenman Some people call this a modernist reading group. It's the first evening where we've tried to bring together people who think in similar ways and who might be able to disagree about things. There are several people missing—Frank Gehry, Rafael Moneo, Kurt Forster, Giorgio Ciucci—who all want to be part of this but unfortunately couldn't be here tonight. We're hoping to do this once a month, not only to criticize our own work but perhaps to have some more public effect on things that happen. The precise nature of how that will take place will be up to the group.

Harry Cobb, who is one of the initiators of this evening, volunteered to show his modernist project for the National Gallery tonight, knowing that it would elicit a good deal of commentary and good criticism. I think it was very nice of Harry to do that because it will be a model for some sort of discourse in the future. We not only want to criticize buildings; we want to criticize papers, projects, fantasies, ideas of all sorts. We're hoping that Gianfranco will bring a book, that Jeff Kipnis might bring a paper, etcetera. It's something that will ebb and flow. We have to be completely open tonight; there is no agreement to publish anything that's said, so we can be much freer than we were at P3 to speak.[1] And I hope, Harry, you'll understand that a lot of us have been waiting a long time to get a chance to talk to you about this building, and you'll understand that it's all said in good spirit.

So with that as a background, I hope that Harry's going to show us his National Gallery competition entry for London.

Henry N. Cobb I'm full of enthusiasm for the principle of this enterprise—that is to say, not the one on the screen but the one that Peter has been talking about. And my enthusiasm for it is sufficient to overcome a certain reluctance that I feel about going first, not because I don't want to go first but because Peter explicitly asked that I go first with *this project*.

This is a project that I have preferred not to think about for the past three months, having thought about it very intensely for three months prior to that. I can no longer bring to it the zeal with which I would once have talked about it. At this moment I'm not even sure that it's an *interesting* mistake, but I also feel probably it's not a good idea for me to talk about it in terms of my present feelings because they're too ambivalent. So what I propose to do for a few minutes is to give it to you more or less the way I gave it to the trustees, and then we can talk about it.

I suppose everybody knows about the site and the program. It's a site of about 20,000 square feet with a program of about 80,000 square feet. This is the way the site looked to me in July, when I first was asked to

1 "P3" refers to a conference held at the University of Virginia School of Architecture in November 1982, transcripts of which were published as *The Charlottesville Tapes*; see page 248.

meet the committee, and this is the way that I presented it in January.

The project began with a site analysis that I presented to the committee when they came to see me in New York in September. This was before the short list. At the time, I simply wanted to express some response to the site, because I knew little about the program. I limited my remarks to what I called the public realm of the National Gallery—explicitly the public realm touching on Trafalgar Square, which I showed in this diagram as a kind of purple patch. And I went through my analysis

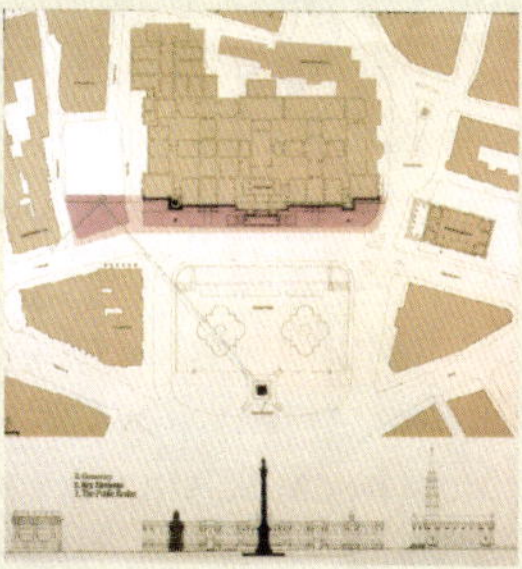

in a series of overlays in which I identified what seemed to me to be the key elements of the square and of the gallery that needed to be noticed in connection with the new building.

The key element of the square doesn't need explanation. The key element of the gallery, however, that little cupola, I did talk to the trustees at some length about. I remarked on the way in which the cupola comes into view as one approaches down Pall Mall from the west, and the way in which it presents a certain lateral energy in the facade that is invisible when you view the facade frontally but very evident in an oblique view of this kind. I talked about the importance the cupola seemed to have in any effort to make an addition to the gallery to the west.

The Wilkins building is far more interesting and far more eventful and strong seen in this view than when seen frontally because all the action of the facade, which is overly extended in the frontal view, becomes concentrated and piled up in this view.[2]

I did some research into the design of this building and discovered (and I believe that I was the first to remark on this to the trustees, because they seemed surprised by it) that if my analysis was correct—that is to say, if the possibility of making an addition to the west was invited by only one element of the existing building, namely, this cupola, which in an otherwise wholly frontal facade engenders a kind of lateral movement—then it's very interesting to see that had Wilkins built the building that

2 William Wilkins (1778–1839), architect of the existing National Gallery building, 1838.

he had wanted to build, this opportunity wouldn't have existed. He was correctly, I think, dissatisfied with this array and wanted to make, instead of these pavilions and little cupolas, another pedimented colonnade, entirely reaffirming the frontality of the facade. Had he done that—had he been *allowed* to do it, because in fact they wouldn't give him the money—this facade would have been much more self-sufficient, much stronger, and much less open to initiatives beyond it. So I got excited about that and talked to the trustees about it, and I suppose that one of the reasons that I was invited to go on had

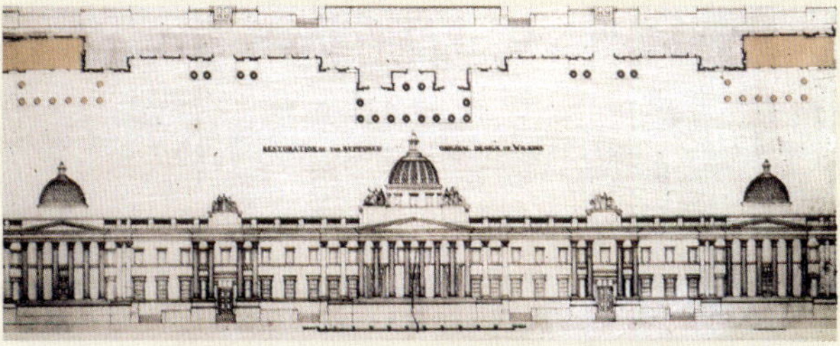

to do with this, because several of them said they understood the building in a new way.

I drew a certain conclusion from this analysis, which was that the most appropriate formal resolution for the site was one that involved a rotational geometry that could address the gallery by way of this pavilion laterally and the square by way of the Nelson Column diagonally and that would present an appropriate response to Smirke's Royal College of Physicians, which does not invite a frontal facade opposite.[3]

Eisenman Harry, why do you say Smirke's facade doesn't invite a frontal facade opposite?

Cobb Well, it doesn't seem to me that it does.

Eisenman It could be a gate.

Cobb It could be, but you see, Smirke's facade—which doesn't face the square; it faces away from it—is very

strong, and to allow oneself to confront this facade is to allow oneself to become disengaged from the other parts of the scene. So I felt it was desirable to avoid a confrontation. And for a number of reasons having to do also with giving the play to this facade, I thought that a rotational geometry would be a good way to approach it.

John Whiteman When I look at that diagram, the first

3 Sir Robert Smirke (1780–1867).

thought that enters my head is why one wouldn't think of playing off of Gibbs, because Gibbs seems at least to have learned from Hawksmoor.4 I actually think that's perhaps the best building around the square.

Cobb It is. But it depends what you mean by playing off Gibbs. I was indeed very conscious of playing off Gibbs, but it seemed to me that that was another reason why a rectilinear frontal facade was not to be desired. In other words, one needed something that did not have a front—or rather, not a single front.

Eisenman There's a strategy that could have framed and mirrored Gibbs on that side.

Cobb Yes, there is. But the gallery is a very weak building, and it won't tolerate a neighbor of that kind. The colonnade, that central pediment, is very easily challenged, and I felt that the primacy of the pediment needed to be respected. I didn't feel that a columned portico of any kind was appropriate.

Laurie Olin Harry, are you saying that in deference to the facade of Wilkins's building, you didn't dare do something as assertive as Gibbs's porch?

Cobb I wanted to be strong without presenting a direct challenge. But we'll come back to that. This is a terribly simple story; in fact, it's so simple it's embarrassing. Here's the model that we made of the square. In this view, you can see that the drum of our building has a tripartite organization that addresses successively the left-hand cupola of the gallery; then the Nelson Column; then Smirke's porch; and finally it continues around to address Pall Mall.

4 James Gibbs (1682–1754), architect of St. Martin-in-the-Fields; Nicholas Hawksmoor (1661–1736).

Eisenman How does it address the cupola?

Cobb It's rotational. It has three parts—they're forty-five degrees apart—and one of them directly addresses the cupola. You'll see it in the plan.

Charles Gwathmey You may think that's a mistake.

Eisenman I didn't say it was a mistake; I was just asking.

Cobb It may *be* a mistake.

Here's a larger-scale cardboard model. Of course, this is what has elicited from the English press a wonderful epithet that I have enjoyed: *revanchiste*.

In my report I first remind the jury of my earlier observation that a curved building face derived from a rotational geometry constitutes the most appropriate response to the site's complex urban setting. I then point out that this proposition has now been given specific form as a semicircular screen-wall, which is the natural vehicle for deployment of an architectural apparatus composed of classical elements and intended to communicate in a quite precise way the institutional role of the new building.

I go on to talk about the existing building and my decision to pick up on the colossal order, which I felt was the one element that needed to be extended into the new building, and then I comment on the fact that the

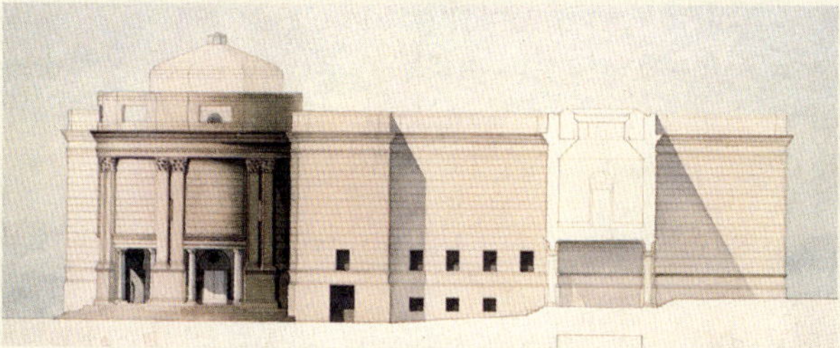

problem with the colossal order of the existing building is that the base is too high to be able to enter above it and too low to be able to enter under it. Hence my struggle with that issue and also my concern—which is partly a critique of the existing building—that the new building should assert the gallery level unequivocally as a noble floor, whereas in the Wilkins building the presence of the gallery floor and its role is completely masked; it looks like the second floor of a country house. So those concerns led me finally to this solution, the source of which is obvious.

Eisenman Can I ask a question about the piano nobile, Harry? You're suggesting that somehow there is a piano nobile, I suppose to the left, that is not picked up in the drum. Or else the drum suggests a piano nobile above it that is not picked up in the elements.

Cobb That's correct. The drum is the only articulate element of the facade with respect to the interior. I chose to treat this building as a treasure house: that is, inarticulately. I chose to extend the base—the colossal order—even though it's meaningless in terms of the interior except at the drum, where I corrected it to represent entry below and noble floor above.

Gianfranco Monacelli Could you say something about the program? Did you have any restrictions?

Cobb Well, yes, there were many restrictions, but principally there is a requirement to house about 230 of the greatest pictures in the world, all dating from the thirteenth to the end of the fourteenth century, both Italian and Northern European—actually, duecento-trecento through quattrocento. In other words, it ends with Raphael. That is the reason for the building, so everything else is secondary. There are a lot of other things they ask for: a temporary exhibition gallery, a restaurant, shops, an auditorium, and so forth.

Monacelli I was thinking in terms of height and materials.

Cobb They said explicitly that they wanted the building to be materially similar to the existing building. I think everyone proposed a building of Portland stone. And they also said that they wanted it not to be higher than the existing building.

Gwathmey The passageway through was in the brief, is that right?

Cobb Yes, and you have to preserve what's called Jubilee Walk, which is the connection between Pall Mall and St. Martin's Street. Otherwise, there were various zoning requirements from which we were excused, because they said they didn't want to confuse us with them; they're very complicated. So we were allowed to use the site as we saw fit. The program is congested, as you'll see. It's really the picture galleries; they're trying to hang too many pictures here.

Monacelli Respect for the context was implied.

Cobb Yes, that goes without saying; it was up to one to interpret. They said they wanted a building—to quote them—"that would be distinct from the existing building but belonging to it." They didn't want to overwhelm it or dominate it.

Jeffrey Kipnis What I see here are two load-bearing columns that are offset in counterpoint to relief columns with live-bearing filigree. So we have a decorative motif that turns into a load supported on dwarf columns, as opposed to relief decorative columns supporting a live load. I am interested in how you made these relief decisions, particularly the width proportions and the filigree.

Cobb Allow me to defer that for one moment, because I'm coming to that.

As you can see, this reverses the traditional mode of putting the rustication on the bottom and puts the rustication on the top. I did that for a reason, which was that I wanted the weight of the building to be on top. As I explained in my report, this strategy, which obviously has its origin in the Campidoglio, "dramatizes the poignant duality of intention inherent in this building. On the one hand, as a major public institution located in the heart of a capital city, the building ought to invite entry and play an active, engaging role on the urban stage; on the other hand, as the repository of paintings whose significance surely transcends that of even the greatest symbols of national identity, the building ought to maintain a certain distance between the place of contemplation within and the distracting busyness that flows constantly around it. My aim has been to find a way of communicating this duality while striking a delicate balance between deference and self-assertion in the relationship of the new building to the old."

All of what I did there is tied up with the intention of presenting a double message. On the one hand, the portico is very public and couldn't be otherwise interpreted. On the other hand, what is above it is very closed and has been made to express a kind of balance between the contingency it expresses with respect to its site and the autonomy it expresses with respect to what goes on inside it. I said: "In pursuit of this goal, I found that the curved screen-wall by itself, though successful in its engagement with the street, was insufficient: the second half of the duality of intention that I sought to convey could be expressed only by creating an explicit awareness of a space within, a chamber having an autonomous value quite independent of the external circumstances of its urban setting. This discovery led me to explore the possibility of allowing a dome to rise from a circular drum behind the screen-wall. But once again I found through modeling that this feature would pose an unacceptable threat to the primacy of the central dome of the main building." The solution that emerged was this octagonal cupola of low profile.

Eisenman What was the threat to the main building?

Cobb The problem for me—and this is where there is a very big difference between my scheme and all of the others—is that I'm not capable of making internally inconsistent statements. I wanted my building to be consistent with itself, yet the Wilkins building is so extraordinarily inconsistent. In various models, I tried freestanding columns and things of that kind on the drum, which I rather wanted to do because I wanted to have a porch, but what I found was that it totally demolished the existing building. You might ask, "Why not?" I suppose I was simply acceding to the expressed wish of the trustees that this building would not be seen as upstaging.

Eisenman The strength of your work has always been the fact that you never acceded to context. In fact, the strongest building for me that you ever made, Hancock, had nothing to do with the context as given, and the context had much more history and much more quality than the National Gallery. You denied and made a statement to change context, and the building has now become part of the context.

Cobb Your statement is only half-true. It's true that the Hancock changes the context, because it couldn't possibly not do so, but it is not true that it wasn't motivated by a concern for context. It was motivated *only* by a concern for context. So in that sense there's a similarity.

Eisenman The thing is, Harry, the average person would look at Hancock and say that it doesn't look like it was motivated by context.

Gwathmey There's a difference here. If it weren't for the stylistic business going on, one would question the form of the circle as a motivation for entry apart from its being a motivation for rotation. The circle would deny entry and deny frontality, and it would be a knuckle from which somewhere in the orthogonal facade there would be a connection with the original building. You took that form, and then you made it porous, and then you made it solid. But all the things that were contextually responsive from your point of view could be the wrong model. You were so responsive to the cupola, to the diagonal, and to the facade across the street that the rotation from that point of view made that connection, but from the bigger point of view it made a proposition that said this isn't the correct form for the end result, which was a secondary notation to the whole. Down the line on either side there was a frontal proposition that would have allowed you to come back to this piece and reevaluate where it was in place.

Cobb In fact, in my original site analysis, I explicitly did not put the entrance in the drum; I put the entrance to the side. It was only later, when I decided that there was nothing in this building but this drum, that it seemed unacceptable not to make whatever invitation the building was going to offer through the medium of the drum—especially because I also wanted to put the expression of the building's autonomy in the drum, and I wanted to induce an awareness of that duality.

Kipnis But there's an uneasy tension between autonomy and conciliation; there are many conciliatory gestures in an autonomous form. It seems to me that the original analysis wasn't simple—if it was laconic, it wasn't simple—and that it called for a very strong, single-focus gesture, a very strong curve without depleting detailing. What happens is, you get a very strong formal solution, and then you average away the strength in conciliatory gestures to the square, the column, and the rest of the facade, so it's just the opposite of what Charles is saying: you get the right form with the wrong articulation.

Gwathmey But the primary form could have been the back side of the curve, which would have been the erosion of the curve, and the object of the octagon could have been the object of the entry within the frame.

Eisenman That makes it more of a screen.

Gwathmey That's right. You could have taken this piece and turned it around the back, and the object would have been porous. The corners would have prevailed, and the object would have been the thing in the corner.

Eisenman Then you penetrate.

Gwathmey It's so easy, Harry! How come you didn't think of it? I'm teasing.

Olin I'll argue with Harry that once you had the thing that seemed to be a solid, if you treated it as a void, then that was the way into the project, and that the building behind obviously wanted to be a treasure box; he's right. The building behind is like a warehouse. But if that was a space instead of a solid...

John Hejduk I know it's too complicated to become personal.

Cobb Please do.

Gwathmey We all are.

Hejduk I think I've known Harry longer than anyone in this room, thirty years at least—since '56—and I think that this project here is essentially pivotal to Harry's future survival as an architect. Now I'm going to say why. Harry was, as many of us here were, caught up in the modern tradition—not modernism but modern architecture. You know, teachers do have an effect; they affected you, and they affected me, right? I want to get to a very important point. I've watched Harry now over the years, however one can watch his colleagues, and he was a man who was always interested in the urban condition, in city planning. Then there was modern architecture. And the third element was his passion for Rome and the history of architecture. It's terrible to give such a quick synopsis, but that's what I need to start with.

This in a way is a delicious trap for Harry. Because the context is again brilliantly—*brilliantly*—set up. I'm just talking about the city planning. That's number one. Number two: We used to play games in Texas many years ago, where Colin Rowe would come over in the evening—this was in the early fifties—on those hot nights, and he'd say, "Let's make little plans." So we sat up until two or three in the morning making little plans of Villa Madama, and Villa This, and Villa That, and the Robie House This, and the Robie House That, and by the end of the evening one had a huge sheet of paper three or four people had worked on with all these things, and God would never have known at the time that that was going to be the prototype for the disaster that became American architecture some thirty or forty years later. And at the end of the evening Colin would always inevitably ask, simply, "What would be wrong today"—in 1953—"in doing a Palladio villa, if you did it very well?" And you had no real argument, no good answer; all you could really say was, "It doesn't feel right for our time." That's all you could possibly say: that there was something inherently wrong about that proposition at that time, in 1953.

What this means to me—and it does mean something, Harry—is that this is your psychic test. Outside of the brilliant urban plan, outside of the brilliant understanding historically of the thing, and outside of his other work—past work, modern and otherwise—this is the first project that interests me, that I can relate to a biography. It's not so detached, in a certain way; it's not so anonymous.

He has three choices, which for me is very interesting. Say that one accepts the initial thrust of the site disposition. He can do biography—a modern building, so-called, not modern today, but a modern building within that context. Or he can do what he's done, an intelligent play on historical conditions. Those would be, I would say—and this is where the personal thing comes in—the old Harry, in both cases of the past, the modern and this. The third choice is to go—with all one's history and all one's biography and all one's knowledge and all one's intelligence—and do an exploratory piece of architecture based on the formal premises. That would interest me about Harry Cobb now. As far as I'm concerned, this project is not finished. In other words, what would be your next solution, in retrospect or introspect, to the thing that you have obviously gone into? And gone into, I think, in great depth; this is not simple in any way.

So there are the three paths. But really, I don't think there are three paths. I think now you have one. I'll tell you why I say that, Harry, because this is *the* problem of our time in a certain way. Like him or not, and like his architecture or not, one of the few people in our generation who has been able to achieve that is Rossi. Not late Rossi but early Rossi, because early Rossi was able to go back. He's a modern architect, an intelligent man, historically oriented, and he was able at one moment in his life—and I think this is why he is in fact revolutionary, relative to our time—to go back and to do structures that capture the sense of a Sassetta painting without using any of the forms of a Sassetta. And it makes him also an indigenous architect, as Mondrian is an indigenous painter: he could only be Italian, as Mondrian can only be Dutch. He's not an international painter, nor is Rossi an international architect. It has something to do with certain roots, like your roots are in New England—I suspect! This is why I'm excited about this; it has to do with the nature of your prime footing as an architect. We all go through cathartic times in our lives. This is the problem I would spend five years on. In other words, we each have our program. That's what I wanted to say.

Eisenman I'd like to add something to that, John. I'm reminded of the King's College model. On one side of King's College Chapel is a Gibbs building, pressed right up tight next to it. Gibbs, who was not a revolutionary architect of any sort, dramatized that chapel by producing a neoclassical facade of intense austerity. He was not against an architecture of his time, and he was not against the chapel, but he produced a building that contrapuntally played with it in an incredible way. He built it of the same stone that the chapel was built in. Then a century later, Cockerell produced the Cambridge library on the other side of the chapel in a basically Victorian mode, again a very strong piece but again without any paean or sympathy to either the Gibbs building or to the chapel. Now we look at those things, and we say, "It's a wonderful ensemble. There's not a more energized ensemble in Cambridge."

I think that because of our sense of the failure of modern architecture, we have lost a kind of exploratory vision, which John is talking about. But I don't sense that this building contains that vision. I'm not saying that you can't build in Portland stone, and I'm not saying you have to do a modern style. But it seems to me that the building does not have the exploratory energy of a project that would either be Gibbs on the one hand or Smirke on the other, or Wilkins, and add to that diffuse—and diffused—condition.

Laurie, thanks for coming.

Olin See you soon. [*exit*]

Eisenman I believe they chose you, Harry, because of the kind of exploratory energy that a lot of your projects have had, and that's why we respect you. And I think that somehow your critics—your worst critics, let's say; not the friends in this room—would say, "Hey, why does Harry do *that*? We can all do that better than Harry does. Why didn't Harry go with his strength and do what he does well—that is, an exploratory project?" The loss of nerve, for me, with the desire to win, is something that I think befuddled even the jury, because from what I hear, you were the favorite going in, and they were disappointed with this result—for some reason, I don't know why. I think all of us share the problem that you were faced with. In other words, if we were all in this

competition, we all would have built in Portland stone, we'd have all tried to answer the contextual problems in some way. It's a very difficult problem, especially for Harry Cobb. But my real feeling is, you didn't do what you can do well. That's what worries me about it. That's why I think John is right when he says that it's a project in the middle, because it doesn't represent the full energy of your spirit or feeling about context.

Hejduk I want to make this very clear: this is very much a Harry Cobb building. Oh, yes! Very much. No, no,

Peter, I want to get to this point, because I don't want to lose it. I'm trying to get at my *Rashomon* understanding of the biography. It is extremely close to Harry; that I believe deeply. Why I consider it a very pivotal project in his life is that this is the project that he has to work on, has to work through.

Cobb Both of you have touched on a very key point; that's why I had so much trouble coming to grips with it. It's obviously true that I wanted to win, but after all, I'm not young anymore, and I've been living with that all my life. I'm as capable as anyone else of transcending *that* problem. Therefore this is a deeper problem: John is right. I couldn't at this stage get through a certain dangerous… it's like getting into a hot tub. You want to stay there for a little while—at least I do; I'm not one of these people who gets in and gets out. I got into this hot tub, and I knew that I would want to get out of it. In fact, I told the committee when I presented it that I would want to get out of it. But at the same time, I knew that I couldn't get out of it in the framework of this competition, and therefore I chose to stay in the hot tub and do it straight, if you know what I mean.

Whiteman I don't think you're doing it straight. I might be amongst the people here who have known you for the least amount of time and am therefore perhaps less qualified to talk in personal terms. But I did used to have lunch in the building next door to the gallery five days a week for five years—until they cleaned the Poussin paintings, and then I stopped going because I couldn't take the shock of seeing them without the dirt.

The way I would like to talk about this is through the perspective of English culture, which is one of very polite but intense disrespect. England in many ways has been a place of first-rate second-rate architects, of which Gibbs is one. Your building doesn't look to me like an English building, and in many ways it looks like a challenge to an English building. You might have felt you were in a hot tub, but maybe you *were* the hot tub. See what I mean?

Let me try another way of going at it. You conceive of the project as an extension of the museum, when in fact England is often a place in which one builds buildings that are in very polite antagonism to the things they're supposed to extend.

Cobb I don't see this building as not presenting a challenge. What I was trying to do was to present a challenge in a very delicately balanced way. Obviously, I didn't succeed, because the trouble is that it's still at a point—John is absolutely right—where the game is just beginning.

Hejduk Knowing Harry's work for all these years, this is one of his most powerful…this is not a neutral project. This has power. I can only express it this way: hidden in there is a *volumetric austerity.* You know what I mean by "volumetric austerity"?

Cobb It's not a classical building at all. But what is it, is the question.

Hejduk That's the whole point.

Whiteman It's got lingerie on it that ought to be taken off. What would happen if you took the lingerie off?

Cobb Of course, I'm still close enough to it that the revanchiste/pastichiste charge is something that really stings.

Hejduk I think they're wrong.

Eisenman I don't think they're wrong; I think you have to listen to that. John, I can't be cowed by your very poetic and personal statement about this. I think that if you were to get people from the classicizing side of our friends in this world, they would say that this building doesn't do that side well. So in one sense he's right: it's not a classical building—in one sense, all right? But in another sense it is, I believe, timid about its exploratory mode. It moves out, and then it says, "Uh-oh, I can't go too far."

Cobb I'm barely able now to begin to look at this project, and therefore it's very interesting to me to hear what's said about it. But I'm not sure that it's even worthy of the commentary here tonight.

Eisenman No, no, it's a very important building. Look, Harry, John is right. One of the great qualities you have is as a person who maintains the center, in the best sense of the word. This building provokes a discourse outside the center and then realizing its energy…for example, what if you took the Corinthian paired colonettes off for a minute, and just allowed that thing to roll like an Adolf Loos building? Or had the Corinthian columns as Adolf Loos did, up to a certain point, and then allowed something else to take over. In other words, devalued them in some way.

Cobb But you see, I wasn't ready to do that.

Kipnis Wait a second: you *had* been ready to do it.

Cobb But I wasn't ready to do it here.

Hejduk You can't say that to somebody!

Eisenman You can talk about it. We're here talking about it.

Hejduk But when you start to talk about peeling this, and doing that—that's not the issue.

Eisenman That is *one* of the issues.

Cobb John is right in the sense that I'd have to do a lot more work before I would be ready for that move, you see. That's my basic problem: I'm not ready for that move.

Kipnis Could I urge you to return to that site drawing?

Eisenman I'd like to get to the plan.

Cobb Yes, we really should go on. These are the drawings which—

Eisenman But of course, Harry, with those drawings, you can't help but suggest that it's revanchiste.

Cobb Yes, well, another mistake.

Whiteman Is that really a Fibonacci curve?

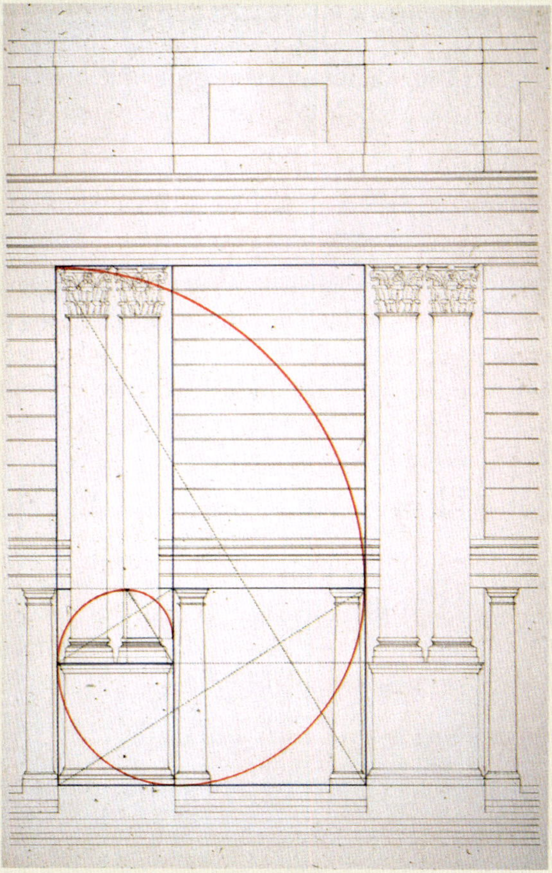

Cobb Yes. There's no mystery to it. The proportions are all there. It is very deliberate, very calculated, but not necessarily in the end very interesting. It's just there. It's a composition.

Gwathmey These are classical roots, and they're references we could all recognize: none of us would refute that, right? We would agree with it. Then—and I disagree with John a little bit—it goes into a stylistic mode, into what you erode and what you elaborate, or how you abstract, and still maintain the integrity of the piece. And you're saying you couldn't get to that, and so you did *this*.

Cobb I'm saying I wasn't there yet, and I felt that I ought to go through this. Probably, as you say, I ought to go past it.

Eisenman Can I ask a question, Harry? Take this facade piece, which is very bold. The dimension of this makes *this* problematic, because it frames it so strongly that it loses its energy. In other words, if this had been thinner in some way, and then this had been allowed to expand... my objection is in here.

Hejduk Peter, what are you saying? You're hitting details.

Eisenman I'm not hitting details—it's something primal.

Gwathmey I don't think you can recreate the craft of classicism. You can recreate the physical classicism, but that's where the interpretation comes.

Eisenman That's it—you can't recreate the craft.

Cobb This is what bothers me. I believed in the notion that that curved piece in the corner of Trafalgar Square ought to carry the meaning of the building. Where I feel bad about it is that my intentions are not realized, because in fact, the last thing that I wanted was to tip over into bombast.

Hejduk I'll take it from another line. You could be a contemporary, so-called, writer using English of our day. Let me go on! Then you can have a little bit of perversity and say, "Oh, I'm now going to write in fourteenth-century English"—or sixteenth century, whatever. Of course, you can never write in fourteenth- or sixteenth-century ink; you just can't do that. So you have one thing of being a contemporary writer using modern English, whatever that might mean. Then you move back and say, "Oh, I'm going to have a shot at this fourteenth-century stuff," knowing full well there's no replica of fourteenth-century English possible today. By doing that, you might damn well pull out of both conditions another sound.

Eisenman Let me just say one thing, John. What I liked about the Venturi project—and I only saw a bit of it—was that Venturi was doing Venturi, and I have to respect him for that. I respect him enormously because he took the challenge head-on. If I look at this facade here, and you said to me, "Who did that?" I could never say it was Harry Cobb. I could never recognize that energy, which I respect, and which is why we're here.

Hejduk That's exactly why we're here.

Eisenman I can't see Harry in that facade. I can't see the distinction. I could have found this in a book done by Letarouilly, or any number of people. I can't believe that it doesn't have the transformation. And if it doesn't do what Serlio would have done, or any number of people—

Hejduk Not yet!

Cobb I accept that criticism.

Whiteman I'm not sure that's fair. If you read it vertically, in its proportional terms, I would say that you're not there. But if you read it in its horizontal terms, in the way it turns the corner, I would say you *are* there.

Kipnis You *were* there, until you put the dress on.

Cobb That, of course, is what stings, because the notion of dress is something that I wanted to avoid.

Eisenman Harry, take Palladio, who was the master of playing with his double scale, and the Loggia del Capitano in Vicenza. Palladio's loggia is obviously one of the models for this particular piece, the giant paired order.

Cobb I certainly thought about it.

Eisenman What I would argue is this: Where is the transformation of that model?

Cobb That's a good question.

Eisenman That's the question I have to ask you. Where is the transformation? Where is something—the signature—that contaminates it? That's what all of your colleagues, your associates, and your friends have been wanting to ask about. To me, that's the real issue.

Cobb It's not a new problem for me. What this project does is expose weaknesses that might have been hitherto concealed behind modernist strategies. Contamination is something that I love. But with a certain amount of self-knowledge, I can say that one of the reasons I love it is that it's hard for me.

Anyway, let's have a glimpse at a section. This section was very important to me. The one thing that I wanted to achieve was to have that corner piece join the idea of the building as a presence in the city and the idea of the building as an internal organism. That's why I ultimately decided to enter through the drum, because I wanted every level of exposure to that element to be significant, both external and internal. Therefore I entered through it, passed out of it, went all the way through the building, and returned to it. You enter through it, and when you go through the gallery sequence, the return to it is the culminating moment. It is also the only moment in which you have a glimpse from the inside of the building to the outside.

Gwathmey Doesn't the balcony to the right of the drum, under the same ceiling notation as the stair, appear to be an addition or some unique condition that's not corresponding to the primary section that you're creating? That little extra piece is vestigial.

Cobb You're right. When you see the plan it will be even more vestigial.

Hejduk Oh, man, this section!

Gwathmey This little piece right here: look at the way it cuts the dome.

Hejduk It's a *section*. It's incredible, Charlie! No, that's a piece of modern planning.

Gwathmey It is; that's fine, I love that part. That's right, so what's wrong with it?

Hejduk Who said what's wrong with it?

Gwathmey I'm saying there's nothing wrong with it. But *this* isn't a piece of modern planning, this here.

Eisenman This is not a piece of modern planning, Harry, this juncture.

Hejduk It's a mix.

Cobb It has been remarked several times that the plan lacks generosity.

Eisenman It lacks the classical roots of the outside.

Cobb It's a modern building. I'll say briefly what my notion was. First of all, I claimed that I was going to make a virtue out of the distance of eight meters that you had to rise from the street to the gallery. I said that I was going to create a sequence. These steps were very important to me, to rise to just a certain level above the street, onto this porch, then into a space that is a transition space from exterior to interior, and finally into a very generous lobby, which is flawed in various ways.

Eisenman Harry, stop. The drum can never be transitional.

Whiteman Your description makes it sound so pleasurable, Italianate. It's so delicious in the sense of moving up and through. English architecture has never been like that.

Cobb In that sense I was presenting a deliberate challenge.

Whiteman It's a deliberate Trojan Horse, isn't it?

Cobb It is, in the sense that I wanted the experience of entry to be extended, to be elaborate, to be of a kind that would involve darkness and a gradual return to light, so that when you arrived in the gallery, the level of light, which is actually rather low, would appear to be lighter than the experience of what one had gone through.

Eisenman You mean to say that you come in and take this L-curve, and then a U-shape, and then you come back down?

Cobb No, then you go up. You go up these stairs, and you arrive here.

Eisenman But Harry, you've got to admit that's a wild sequence!

Hejduk Peter, you should appreciate that. Why? Because he talks about *de*construction this and *de*-this and *de*-that. This is *de*formation. Deformation is going on.

Eisenman You don't see deformation on the outside.

Hejduk You saw it in the section, when he talked about light and shadow and darkness.

Eisenman But you don't see the consequences on the outside. I agree with you, John: it's a plan that throws classical planning into a cocked hat.

Cobb It obviously has nothing to do with classical planning. It's a modern plan.

Eisenman It's a modern plan. It's a promenade. No, no—it is!

Cobb The problem is that they're putting too many pictures in this place and too many groups of pictures. My response was to reduce the number of different kinds of spaces to two, which I felt was adequate to the hanging requirements of the gallery. The plan lacks generosity.

Eisenman No, no. Harry, let me say this: in classical terms, you have an axis here, which then picks up an axis here, and then this axis comes through and is ended here, but this one is cut—it is absolutely cut.

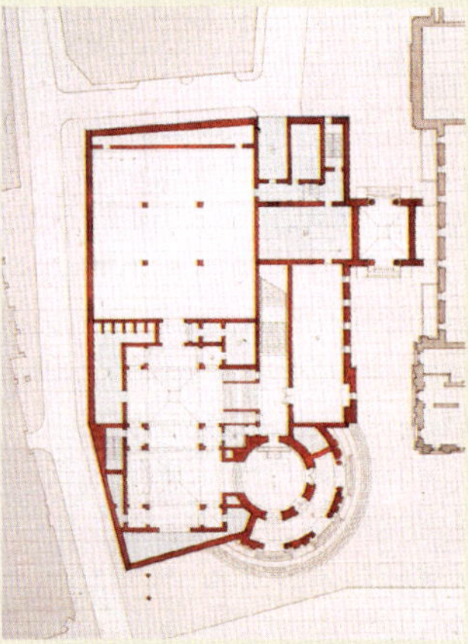

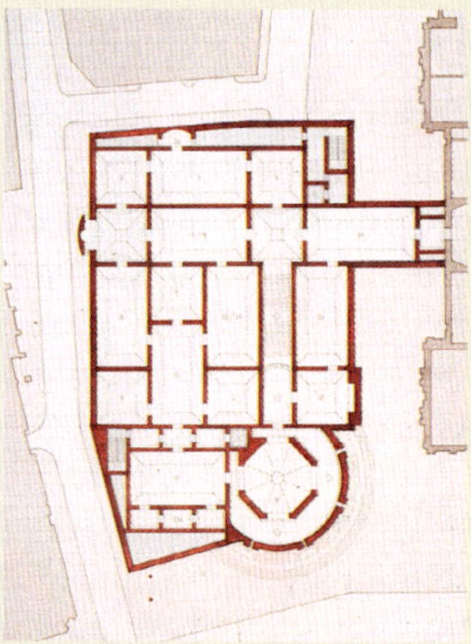

Cobb That is very intentional.

Eisenman But then you're playing certain classical games of denying axes.

Cobb All that has to do with the way in which the route through the galleries was being organized. This axis extends for about 600 feet.

Eisenman Look at this one. Look at this that you call out.

Cobb Well, all right. That's a poché. That's a little place.

Eisenman Look at this poché, where it is.

Cobb That's the Wilton Diptych. That's a special place.

Gwathmey Why'd you put it there? Why'd you put it off-center?

Hejduk Is it off-center?

Gwathmey No, it's on-center, but it's blocked.

Cobb It *is* off-center!

Eisenman It's not. It's on-center with this, but it's blocked. It's very hard to read that intention.

Cobb The intent was that only this axis would be uncontaminated. It has to do with a certain clarity. I would defend this plan in the sense that it has to do with curatorial intentions. They want—not without reason—people to be able to come from the existing building and go directly out, if they wish, or to arrive at this space and go directly into the existing building.

Gwathmey But then shouldn't this be a deformation here?

Eisenman There you go!

Gwathmey We have this as the container-closure, this is the rotation, this piece is the deformation of this, you come here, and somehow…

Eisenman Why does it take this kind of poché?

Cobb Well, I'll tell you why.

Kipnis To hang fourteenth-century paintings on?

Cobb Jeff is getting at something. I wanted this thing to be very quiet. That's why I limited the galleries: all are either five meters by five meters or five by eight. I wanted as clear a sequence as one could get, given the fact that they insist—this is a detail, but it's important—that one should be able to make connections between the northern pictures and the southern pictures. The duecento-trecento pictures are here; the Segna di Buonaventura crucifix is on the wall here, the first thing you come to; then you go through this; then you have a space with no pictures, a transition. Now you have a choice: you either go to Ucello and the Italian Gothicizing, or you go to the northern pictures.

Eisenman Why aren't the spaces of transition pochéd, then?

Cobb They are very different.

Eisenman They don't look different in terms of poché.

Cobb No, they don't. The reason they don't look different in terms of poché is the economy of the plan.

Eisenman But wait a minute, Harry. Down here there's a difference in poché. Here there are two gaskets. Why isn't there a gasket in here or in here?

Cobb I'll tell you why: because I caved in. The requirement for hanging surface was so great. In fact, I think

that this whole stairwell should have been more generous. It's very tight.

Eisenman The classical boys who play this game, like a Michael Graves, would say this is a bad plan because it's a modern plan.

Cobb It *is* a modern plan.

Eisenman So we say, "Yay, it's a modern plan!" But we've got to go one way or the other, right? Let's say we love the plan because it's a modern transformation of a classical plan, but the facade isn't both.

Hejduk Yeah, but the plan is both. It's a classical so-called modern plan.

Eisenman But the plan doesn't relate to the facade.

Cobb It does. I still have a certain confidence in this aspect of it. I wanted to deliver people by way of the room that we saw in the center. I wanted them to start the sequence. There is a distinct difference in character between the gallery spaces and the two transition spaces; they're treated completely differently, even though you don't see it in the plan. But with the exception of those two spaces, this sequence is formally treated. Then when you arrive here, I wanted to deliver a very distinct awareness that you are returning to that point.

Eisenman Not so! This is the problem, Harry. In the delivery of sequence to sequence, you get into trouble here because you're forced to do *this*, and when you're forced to do *this*, then you're forced to do it over here. To me, that is a problem. If you take this off, it's a very modern plan. Everything you say is true: there are two different spaces, and the sequence goes *bop*, *boop*, *bop*, *bop*, *bop*,

bop. But then there's a *boop* again over here. And that's not the same space.

Cobb You're right. It accommodates the arrival and the stairs and elevators and so on. To me that's not terribly significant, though. I think it's obvious what I was trying to do here: I was trying to deliver, if you will, a big bang. And I was also trying to deliver, at the moment that you had the big bang of the interior, the only place in which you also have a glimpse back into the square.

Eisenman You don't think this is a problem here? The fact that it's blocked?

Cobb Not really.

Hejduk He's locked it in!

Gwathmey But it's an accommodation lock-in; it's not a formal lock-in.

Hejduk It's a formal lock-in.

Gwathmey No, John. You can't place a diagonal square in a circle and lock in that back wall.

Hejduk It's a pincer in here. It's strange; you wind up nowhere. You never complete the form.

Eisenman We *like* that!

Hejduk You didn't say so before.

Gwathmey That's because John is so intimidating.

Hejduk I'm not intimidating. I looked at the plan, Charlie; it's a wonderful thing. You may disagree. I think it's a dilemma. The next shot at it makes a new plan.

Cobb You're being too kind, because the move hasn't

been made. The thing that bothers me about this plan is that in view of the quite clearly stated intention of a noble floor, it's too programmatically driven and doesn't have, in my anxiety to serve the curatorial interests, the kind of spatial mood that ought to be there. In fact, if you compare, for example, Jim Stirling's scheme, I think that he did succeed in giving the gallery that mood.

Eisenman Harry, let me ask you a question. I think you're being much too polite to all of us for our own good. Léon Krier thinks your scheme is the best scheme of all the schemes. He said that. Now, why does Léon Krier say that? Because he has a certain polemical bias. So he must be misreading your intention, right?

Cobb Not necessarily. He's a very intelligent man.

Eisenman He thinks it's a very classical scheme.

Cobb But then he's crazy; it's not a very classical scheme.

Eisenman That's what Michael Graves said to Léon Krier. He said, "Hey, Léon, you're crazy. It's not a classical scheme; it's a modern scheme." And he's a very intelligent man as well.

Cobb He's right. It is a very modern scheme.

Hejduk You just made Léon dumb!

Eisenman That's right, and made Michael Graves smart.

Cobb That doesn't necessarily make Léon dumb. I'd like to come to grips with something that has been talked around here a lot, and that's my explicit and unmodified use of the classical language. It's only modified to the extent that certain things have been done that are not classical, like putting the rustication on top, but otherwise it follows certain rules of the game. I did not consider this—probably wrongly, because obviously I'm playing with fire—a terribly important aspect of the project. In adopting that colossal order of Corinthian pilasters, which is the order of the existing building, I thought—and I still in a certain way cling to this idea—that it was a way of getting into a conversation with the existing building, and that it doesn't have to have any more importance attached to it than that.

Whiteman You did make the claim to me the other day that one can use the classical language to express equivocations. It seems to me that one of the things we need to get clear about are the equivocations that you might be wishing to express here, and then to talk about whether you have used or could have used the classical language to say those things. We've talked a little about the Trojan Horse. There's also a certain inertness in England about collectors and collecting, and I wonder whether the plan is indeed supposed to carry some notions about that inertness.

Cobb Not really. John is quite precise in thinking that this plan, this building, is rather characteristic of my work. It's simply an effort to work through in a fairly workmanlike, straightforward, modernist-planning way; to make a workable plan. The one place where I was trying to produce a kind of bringing-together of things that is not characteristic of modern planning is in that drum.

Hejduk What I consider the danger and the dilemma in America today—architectural America—is that we're in for a very bad time for the next fifteen years if we don't engage this argument head-on right now. All the public-relations forces, all the political forces, all the power forces are now moving head-on, saying: "We're going to make a hybrid. We lived off of modern architecture for many years, and we made a real profit out of that. And we then had another run of fifteen years of so-called postmodernism, and we got our profit out of that. What do we do now? We're damn well not going to take any risks, and we're not going to explore. So we're going to make a hybrid. And all the firms, I. M. Pei and everybody right down the line, the little ones and the big ones, can live for the next fifteen years on that hybrid."

I'm an enemy of that hybrid.

Eisenman Hear, hear!

Hejduk And that is the reason I'm here tonight, because the idea of architecture as exploration is being systematically crushed in this country. And Harry happens to be one of those gentlemen—I mean "gentleman" in the good sense of the word—who's intelligent enough to know what the scores are about, and why he's here.

Eisenman John, nobody disagrees with what you said, but I would argue that if you say that, Harry therefore can be accused of falling victim to that.

Hejduk Oh, I'm saying just that! That's exactly what I'm saying, and for this reason. This is the first time I felt close to Harry. Now, I don't mean that as a friend, I mean on another level. If he walks out of here tonight pursuing the hybrid, then we've failed.

Eisenman Hear, hear!

Cobb That's why I said at the outset that I haven't been able to discuss this project, haven't wanted to even think about it, because it's taken a little while for me to accept what is obviously true, that this in fact is a hybrid.

Eisenman John, just a second. Gianfranco has something he'd like to say.

Monacelli If I think of the way you tackled Richardson with Hancock, here you seem to approach architecture by osmosis. It's the opposite of what you did in Boston.

Cobb This is where you're on the one hand misjudging me; on the other hand you're giving me too much credit. The mode of operation in both projects is not so far apart. A hybrid solution in the Hancock would have been impossible. The weakness of the building as architecture is the obverse side of its strength; it's totally single-minded, and by being totally single-minded, it is limited—extraordinary but very limited. I was trying to do something much more complicated here. First of all, with the Hancock I made a very deliberate decision to make the building mute; that is its greatest strength and also its greatest limitation. But here I tried not to make a mute building.

Eisenman But Hancock wasn't a hybrid, Harry; that's what John is saying. John's anxiety is that the times were more ideologically charged when you did Hancock. I think the times are very ideologically charged *now*. What John is objecting to is that if we were to present you as the leader of the new...whatever...

Cobb The new hybrid!

Eisenman ...this would not be a building highly charged with the ideology of an attack against hybridism. That is the real problem: the building is highly charged *with* hybridism.

Kipnis But wait a second, we can't leave with John's poignant declaration of hatred for hybridism, which we all agree with, without any proposal whatsoever for an alternative.

Eisenman That's what this group is about. We have time, Jeff—months and months.

Kipnis I know, but I want to ask John. He articulated the motive without offering the alternative. In what direction do you see movement, rigor, motive, without appeals to hybridization? Where do you see it?

Hejduk There are some Rossi buildings…I don't know the name of the school with the library…

Eisenman Fagnono Olona.

Hejduk …the one with the metal stair. I mean, my God! Every time I look at that, I have to say, "Hey, here we use a metal stair, which is set in a symmetrical building but is an asymmetrical, beautifully exploratory detailed steel stair." And then I look at the simplicity of the basic geometry, which we all love about architecture, just a pure cement wall, and on the cement wall is a magnificent exploratory detail—a twentieth-century detail—placed in a dome. All that is again talking construction, detail, architecture. But you know the other thing it has? I said this the other night at that second talk by Doug Davis.[5] The only thing I look for now when I look at plans, sections, drawings, buildings, is: *Does that have an otherness*?

Kipnis Good. Let me move from there.

5 Douglas Davis (1933–2014), an artist and critic, was curator of *Modern Redux: Critical Alternatives for Architecture in the Next Decade*, an exhibition at New York University's Grey Art Gallery in March and April 1986 that included works by Henry N. Cobb (represented by his National Gallery proposal), Peter Eisenman, Charles Gwathmey, and John Hejduk, among others.

Hejduk Wait a minute. Then I can say, "Yes." In fact, I made a whole list of buildings that I thought had otherness. The one at the Rossi school had otherness; parts and parcels of other architects' work had it. So as I was walking out of the talk, the Franks came up to me—you know, Building 1410, House Ten [*sic*].[6] I thought they were going to ask me about the roof, because they're always asking me which roof I saw on it: did I see a pitched roof or a flat roof? I thought, Oh, God, they're going to ask me about the roof again. But you know what they said? She comes up and she says, "Does our house have otherness?" I thought about it, and I said, "There are *moments* in that house that have otherness."

No, no, I'm not being mystical. I'm being very direct. Those are the things that interest me, and they are probably explicable to a certain extent; you can get at them. I'm for the exploration into that other sense of architecture.

Kipnis Could I *please* finish saying this tonight? I would like to relate this to the criticism of this project. Investigation of otherness habitually, even systematically, occurs by interrogating self-evidencies, or what were formerly held to be self-evidencies. In other of your projects—Hancock, even Commerce Square—there were interrogations of self-evidencies (such as the relationship between, in the latter case, the exterior street and the interior courtyard) in which you have systematically questioned and brought an otherness to the orthodox way of handling the problem. But in this problem, there is not a single self-evidency interrogated, nothing that's not an articulation or a reiteration of a stipulated orthodoxy.

6 Suzanne and Richard Frank were clients for Peter Eisenman's House VI in Cornwall, Connecticut, 1975.

Hejduk Let me interrupt. There was a moment tonight when Harry spoke, just one moment, when he talked about the darkening of the light fading out, and I got a whiff, whether it was a fact or nothingness...I don't want to detach any more of this stuff, making architecture abstract, from the person—the sound of the person, how they talk, the vocabulary they use, where they come from. That's bullshit! All that is part of the biography of the buildings.

Kipnis What about his childhood, his unconscious, his sensuality? You want to take part of the person, and you leave off another part.

Hejduk I want to be inclusive, not exclusive.

Eisenman Hal, you come from another area. Maybe you'd like to say something, because you haven't said much so far in this discussion.

Hal Foster Well, I don't really know the rules of the game yet, so I feel as if I should wait. Perhaps one function might be for me later on to do a criticism of the criticism. There's a certain...I get a whiff of *Fountainhead* here. This problem of the hybrid sometimes seems as if it's merely a stylistic problem; then there's this idea of exploratory architecture, as if you as architects can somehow *do* this, in this void, in this room.

Eisenman Don't painters think they can do that?

Foster Painters, God knows—not the artists that I'm interested in. The analyses tonight of this project, its program, its history, its tradition, its unconscious, its biography, are very brilliant, and I've learned a great deal, but it's still within a very strict discipline. Perhaps, again, this is my ignorance of the rules of the game, but there's a certain institutional critique that's not operative yet in your discussion, and maybe that is an impossibility, given this project and the discipline.

Eisenman But that's something Harry is interested in.

Cobb I'm very interested in it.

Foster When you began with the site analysis of the Nelson Column—I'm not very familiar with the site, but obviously it is an extremely charged national site—you used the term *public realm*, and perhaps in London and perhaps in the site it exists; it certainly does not exist in my experience of New York, or in late capitalism. The question is, is it a given of the project, a given of the program, that you as the architect confirm this need for a national statement, or for a reconfirmation of a public realm? It's very fissured, very conflicted, in England today. Who is served here? In your discussion earlier of this institute in Chicago—let me go on for just one second! I'm sorry if this disturbs you, or if I'm way out of line—and your concern only about this figure Léon Krier, there was no consideration of what this institute really is. What is it for, and for whom?

Gwathmey We all make a lot of assumptions.

Foster I'm just an outsider, so this is my function, perhaps.

Cobb My overwhelming preoccupation as an architect—and it applies just as much to this as it does to Hancock and the Portland Museum—is the way in which institutions are represented in architecture, and that was my overwhelming preoccupation here. I suffer from a weakness of many modern architects in that my architecture is schematic. It's obvious that I didn't get beyond that in this project, beyond the schematizing, and architecture that remains at a schematic level doesn't make that otherness. By definition, to remain schematic is not to achieve that otherness. My aim here was to represent in a very precise way, through the way I deployed these elements, a certain posture of the institution in the city, and that's why the blankness above and the openness below were important to me.

Eisenman Harry, one thing you always mention is not only the posture of the institution in the city but the critique of that posture.

Cobb This is where I would criticize the intentions of the trustees. They want to be popular. I think that was one of the things Bob gave them that appealed to them. That is to say, they want to be open, they want restaurants, they want shops, they want all that stuff exposed to public view. They want to be a lively part of the city. One of the things that I quite deliberately said in this project is that the contents of this building are not something that can or should be directly or easily accessible. I said the institution, the building, has to be available and engaged with the city, but it ought to be engaged with it in such a way that it also asserts its distance. I was trying to make that distance, and I was trying to express that distance through the medium of this drum.

Whiteman I think you achieved that. When I look at the drawings, I see the connection.

Gwathmey I've listened very carefully now, and I've finally come to terms with this conversation. I've been looking at that plan, and I've listened to everybody, and I would say that from every point of view—not to make the building contradict itself—this is the intersection that's critical to the existing condition, and this is the intersection that would allow you to orient the cross-axis and the processional.

Cobb You're quite right.

Gwathmey This wall is the referential wall of Trafalgar Square—the extension of it and the resolution of it. And this is ultimately the modern object, and that modern object then would allow for erosion, resolution, and poché that is negative as opposed to filling. And this would be, in your own conversation and John's conversation, the classical cross-axial resolution internal to the plan, and then the modern resolution of context to plane and place. This distortion is not in the classical mode but in the intersection mode; it is not in the infill of this corner, which bothers Peter, nor in the plan that is the almost-rotunda but not the rotunda. The distortion of this as opposed to the internal resolution, not the external resolution, is not a modern condition. This is the closure piece, and this is the distortion piece.

Eisenman Are you saying this should be a datum, and these things…?

Gwathmey They become primary.

Eisenman And if you take this wall away, then you have figurative stuff in front of the building.

Gwathmey Exactly. And the upshot of the conversation is, we're happy.

Eisenman Then you've got another scheme. And you have not a hybrid, by the way, but something else.

Hejduk I think the remark Harry made is so important. We can't go into a museum in America today without being sold a bill of goods before we see anything. I don't

go to museums anymore because of that. I don't go to the Met, I don't go to MoMA, I don't go anywhere. You know where I go? I go down to the Philadelphia Museum, because it still feels like a museum where I can look at a painting without being hyped up the ass for this or that.

I only want to say one other thing. Somebody asked me to give a definition of "otherness" the other evening. I said, "I can't give you a definition, but I can give you an example." I've been looking for about twenty-five years at the Bacchus of Michelangelo. I've always thought it had an otherness, but I couldn't explain what that was. It had an aura, but that's still not good enough. Then six months ago, when I was in Austria, I made a discovery that knocked me over. I was showing slides, and Bacchus came up again. It's a piece of marble, it's inanimate, it's all the things architects work with. But you know what it had? I looked at it, and I realized that it had a breath—[*exhales*]—and that, to me, was an example of otherness. How the heck could an inanimate piece of marble blow a breath? That's what I think is the very technical and very analytical aspect of what the architect also is able to achieve. So it's not a mystery!

Kipnis I get a sense that we're making summary statements here. I want to add something to Hal's comment. I want to add it in such a way as to invite the architects in the room, if we can continue this, to listen to a specific den of silence that Hal points out and that I feel like I've been pointing out for some time. Harry raises the question of how architecture manifests institutions, and Hal and myself and other non-architects in this room are very interested in the fact that—[*end of tape*]

LOS ANGELES, CINCINNATI, PRINCETON, CAMBRIDGE

Campus as Community: Five Built Works

Throughout the three centuries between the founding of Harvard College in 1636 and the end of World War II, American institutions of higher education—rural, suburban, and urban—were customarily housed on more or less well-ordered campuses wherein buildings devoted to various uses were arranged around interconnected open spaces that together constituted comprehensible institutional entities. The explosive and still ongoing growth initiated by the flood of returning veterans at mid-century challenged this well-established tradition in three ways. First, it necessitated construction of more and larger buildings that often compromised the spatial structure and institutional legibility of the campus. Second, it brought new programmatic requirements that often invited major changes in the language of architecture, breaking with formal and material traditions that had theretofore given visual coherence to the campus. Finally, it caused the campus to expand its territory in ways that often provoked conflict with the adjoining communities.

My initial encounter with institutional growth occurred in 1963, with the commission to design a new academic center for the SUNY college at Fredonia (page 80), where the first two challenges were major concerns, but the third was not much in evidence. However, by the time the Fredonia project was completed six years later, a planning study commissioned by Columbia University had drawn me, along with I. M. Pei, into one of the earliest and most notorious episodes in the epidemic of university/community conflicts that spread across the United States from the mid-sixties onward. Our study, carried out over a sixteen-month period from fall 1968 to spring 1970, offers compelling evidence that in institutional and urban planning, process is often more consequential than product. Few if any of our specific proposals were subsequently implemented, and the report in which they were set forth was neither accepted nor even acknowledged by the university's board of trustees. Yet the consultative planning process documented therein did have a significantly ameliorative effect on the relationship between Columbia and its surrounding communities.

That relationship had reached a dangerously inflammatory nadir in the spring of 1968, when the university began construction of a large gymnasium in Morningside Park. The ensuing public outcry set off a student strike that shut the university down for seven weeks and forced it to abandon the gymnasium project. In an effort to extract a positive outcome from the furor, the trustees commissioned our firm to prepare a "master plan under which the campus at Morningside Heights will be arranged and developed in a manner which will not only be in its own best interests but will also take into consideration the interests of its students, its neighbors, and the City of New York."

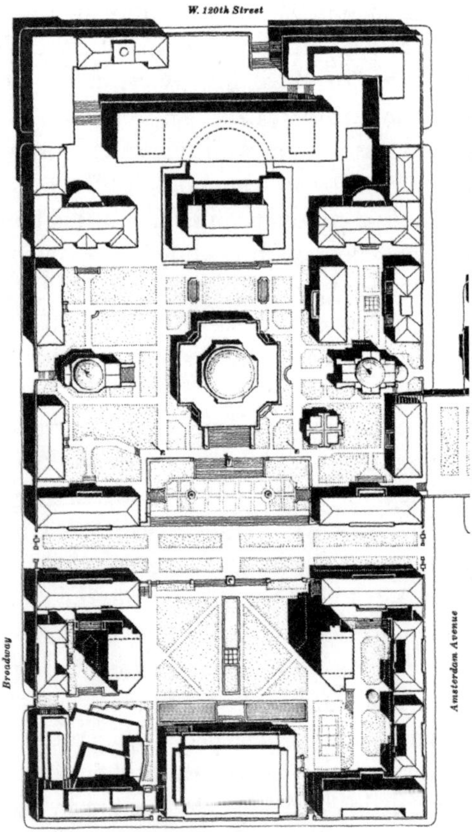

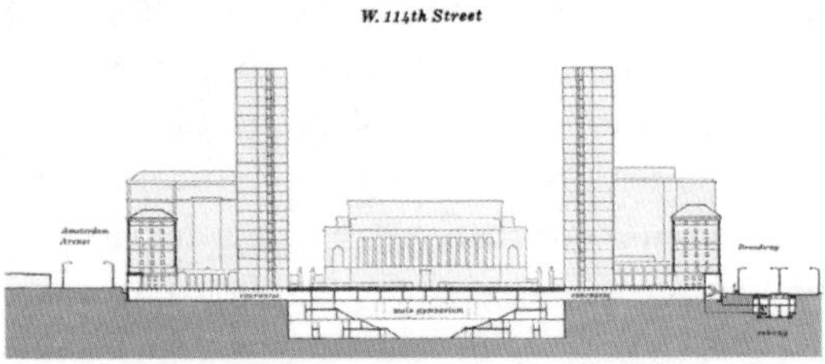

Top Columbia University campus development plan, 1970. **Above** Section, with proposed academic towers and underground gymnasium.

We recognized at the outset that before putting pencil to paper—indeed before even beginning to think about possible solutions—we needed first to listen to the many voices, both inside and outside the university, that were crying to be heard. In the event, this listening activity continued throughout the period of our work and retrospectively may be judged its most important achievement. An appendix to our report lists no fewer than 314 meetings with groups or individuals representing the university's internal constituencies and its neighbors.

The central propositions of our master plan were, first, the consolidation of existing university functions, then scattered throughout the Morningside Heights neighborhood, within the boundaries of its main campus; and second, the accommodation of all future expansion within those same boundaries. These goals were to be achieved through renovation of existing facilities and the construction of several new buildings, the most prominent of which were a pair of towers rising above a large underground sports complex (the gym!) in the South Field just north of Butler Library. Although several of the peripheral buildings indicated in the plan have since been built, this centerpiece proposal was not adopted and indeed was probably never seriously considered.

Despite its unproductive outcome, our immersion in the battle of Morningside Heights nonetheless fueled my ongoing interest in the problem of institutional growth and my conviction that its manifestation on university campuses is an important challenge for architecture. During the subsequent four decades, commissions for a number of university building projects have occasioned invigorating encounters with this challenge in all of its forms.

The five built works to be discussed herein exhibit a formal and material diversity flowing naturally from the diverse programs they serve and the diverse contexts, both physical and cultural, in which they are embedded. Nonetheless, a few themes embodying my own sensibility and aspirations consistently recur in these projects, transcending any specific program or context. Perhaps the most important of these is the primacy granted to space over object, reflecting my view that a principal obligation of every university building is to help shape a coherent spatial structure to support the life and enrich the experience of the campus. A second consistent theme is a design strategy of both fitting in and standing out, reflecting my view that both respect for tradition and openness to innovation are essential to the life of a university. And a third is my concern for the craft of building as embodying ethical values that are likewise indispensable to the enterprise of education. These consistently pursued intentions have informed each built work; in so doing, they have also obliged me to think long and hard about the purposive coalescence of form, material, and detail that constitutes the language of architecture.

The **UCLA Anderson School of Management** (1987–95, with Ian Bader) occupies a site adjoining a lushly forested creek-bed and close to Royce Hall and Powell Library, the two North Italian Romanesque Revival buildings that together define the emblematic heart of the UCLA campus. During the decades following World War II, UCLA, like most state universities, grew exponentially, and in the process its campus was radically transformed, not just in size but also in character. The need for ever-larger buildings led to a reversal in the relationship between solid and void: whereas earlier campus buildings had helped to shape figural space, newer

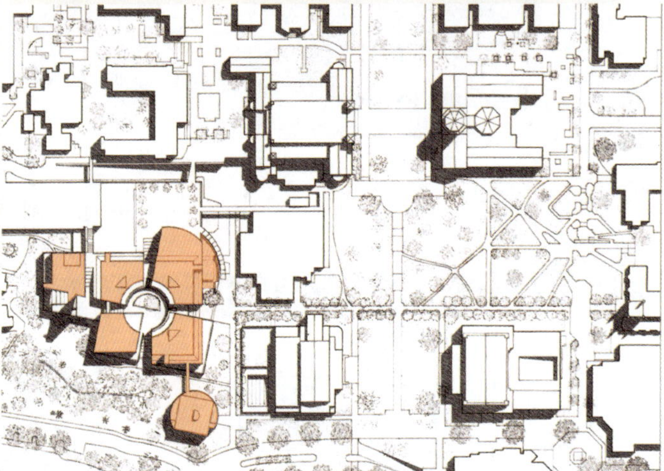

Top Aerial view of UCLA campus, 1935.
Middle and Bottom Site plan and section of UCLA Anderson School of Management and adjoining campus, 1995.

Top End wall above Anderson School exterior stairway.
Above Left Central courtyard. **Above Right** Aerial view.
Overleaf Courtyard viewed from above.

buildings simply preempted space and by their immense size and overbearing character tended to render the spaces between them residual and characterless. Our aim in the Anderson School was explicitly to reverse this trend: we wanted to show that even a very large building—and this was to be the second largest at UCLA—could be so configured as to restore the primacy of figural space over figural object and thus enrich rather than further impoverish the spatial fabric of the campus. To accomplish this, the building was conceived as a set of seven separate but interconnected fragments that together shape pathways and gathering places, not only enabling but inviting passage from the lower to an upper campus level separated by a vertical distance of sixty feet. Thus the most important characteristics of the Anderson School—intimacy and permeability—are placed in the service not just of its own constituency but of the entire university community.

Because the Anderson School is a close neighbor to Royce Hall, we thought it appropriate to employ the same Norman brick, with cast-stone trim matching the limestone trim of the earlier building. By thus respecting the material palette as well as the modest scale of Royce, we were able to shape our building into entirely new forms, forgoing historicizing stylistic tropes yet still affirming continuity with the university's origin. Further evidence that respect for precedent need not preclude formal invention is to be found in an eye-catching vertical incision that brings the sky down into the surface of an emblematic end wall of the Anderson School's exterior stairway, celebrating its axial relationship with the tower of the student union at the opposite end of a campus pathway.

If the challenge at UCLA was to make the most of a splendid opportunity, the challenge at the University of

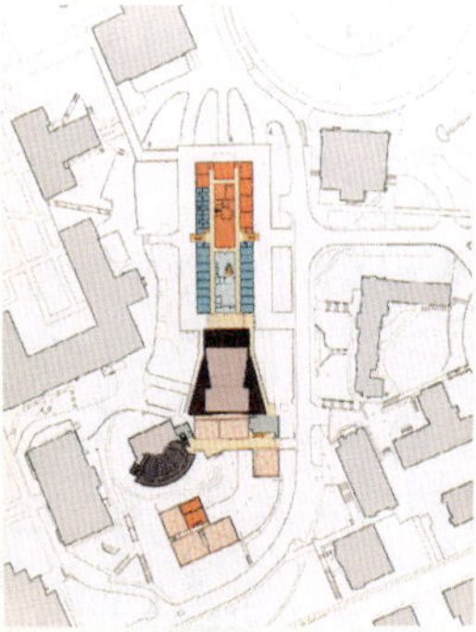

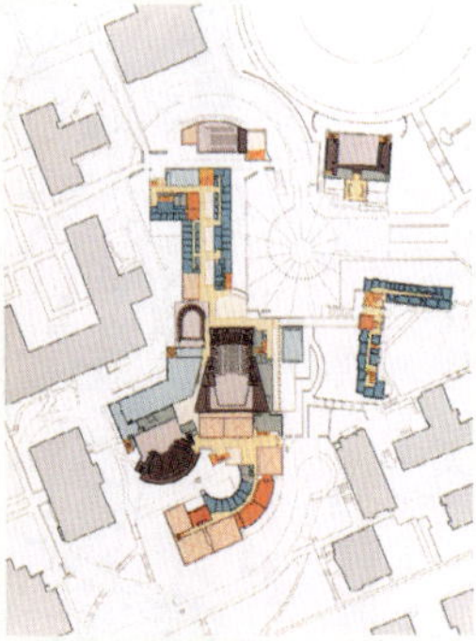

1992 **1999**

Top and Middle Plans and aerial views of existing and reconfigured CCM campus, University of Cincinnati. **Bottom** CCM Village at dusk. **Overleaf** Central courtyard of CCM Village.

Cincinnati was the opposite: to make the best of a bad situation. When I first visited the **College-Conservatory of Music** (1992–99, with Charles T. Young; Laurie D. Olin, landscape) in the fall of 1992, I found an academic community full of gifted young people and bursting with energy but housed in the most depressing environment for teaching and learning that I had ever seen. CCM's existing premises, built during the 1960s and clad largely in precast concrete, were crammed like a bone in the throat into an awkwardly shaped, steeply sloped site between a heterogeneous and disordered group of academic, administrative, and residential buildings. To make matters worse, a ring of service roads preempted the surrounding residual space, so that the school was effectively cut off from participation in the life of the campus. In this unattractive and tightly constrained setting, the school required new facilities that would more than double its existing floor space.

Thorough analysis of the costs of renovation as compared with new construction led us to conclude that existing performance and related support spaces should be retained and renovated, while the existing academic wing should be replaced. We also discovered that the need for new construction could be minimized by repurposing two neighboring buildings—an abandoned gymnasium and an obsolete dormitory—for use by CCM. These strategic decisions opened up the possibility of shaping the new academic wing, including important new performance spaces, in such a way as to frame one side of a courtyard that then became the spatial focus for a group of buildings, both new and old, that now constitute the "CCM Village" within the larger university campus. The brick cladding of the new wing, animated by recessed courses at sixteen-inch intervals, invited the

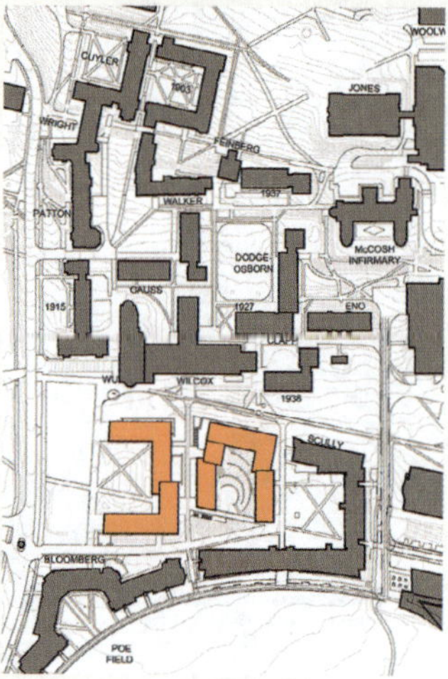

Top Sunken entry courtyard, Butler College Dormitories, Princeton University. **Above Left** View of garden courtyard. **Above Right** Site plan. **Overleaf** Exterior detail.

episodic articulation of building volume that introduces a fresh voice while also acknowledging a familial bond with its repurposed neighbors. The conversation thus initiated between new and preexisting buildings declares that a university's campus becomes stronger by embracing its history rather than erasing it.

Continuing our exploration of the mutually nourishing interaction between memory and invention, our primary goals in the design of **Princeton's Butler College Dormitories** (2004–09, with Michael W. Bischoff; Michael Van Valkenburgh, landscape) were two: first, to extend and reinvigorate the rich tradition of space-shaping campus buildings initiated a century ago by the superb residential quadrangles of Charles Klauder and Ralph Adams Cram; and second, to discover a contemporary analogue to the variety and eventfulness of massing and detail that characterize the best Collegiate Gothic buildings designed by those architects.

In pursuit of our first goal, two new courtyards, each distinct from the other in size, shape, and landscape treatment, are formed by two U-shaped buildings of varying height, one opening to the west and the other to the south. These buildings also frame an important new pathway that crosses another whose diagonal orientation provides occasions for relaxing and gently displacing the geometric order of the new residence halls.

In pursuing the second goal, we invented and deployed two unprecedented features: irregularly spaced wave-like undulations that animate the building volumes while accommodating the programmatic requirement for larger bedrooms in upper-class suites; and narrow bands of limestone—sometimes continuous and highly ordered, sometimes randomly episodic—that add richness of pattern and texture to the brick-clad surfaces of the buildings.

These features, together with the varied spaces shaped by the new residence halls, create a distinctive identity resonant with the episodic delights of earlier Collegiate Gothic buildings, yet free of mimicry. This identity is also sympathetic to the neighboring Wu Hall, which houses the Butler College dining hall and other social spaces. Wu Hall, designed by Robert Venturi and Denise Scott Brown, is an inimitable architectural star turn that I hold in very high regard—hence my decision to keep our new residence halls low in profile, both literally and figuratively.

While my profound respect for Wu Hall was a key factor in the design of Butler College, the design of the **Friend Center for Engineering Education** (1998–2001, with Michael W. Bischoff), located in a remote corner of Princeton's campus, reflects my deeply felt, if regretful, antipathy for the Computer Science Center to which it is attached. When that building was completed in 1989, its architects (both friends of mine) had expressed the hope that it would establish "a language for the development of subsequent buildings that will form a new quadrangle."[1] But the language they proposed—an intricate and to my eye fussy blend of cast stone and patterned brick wrapping a pretentiously clunky volume—was enough to drive me straight back to my modernist roots. Given my consequent decision to become a good neighbor by contrast rather than by similarity, the volumetric disposition and material character of the Friend Center—comprising a one-story classroom wing clad in precast concrete surmounted by a two-story library clad entirely in glass—seem largely self-explanatory. But one feature does require explication, and I spoke of this in my remarks at the dedication on September 29, 2001.

1 Raymond P. Rhinehart, *Princeton University: An Architectural Tour* (New York: Princeton Architectural Press, 2000), 68.

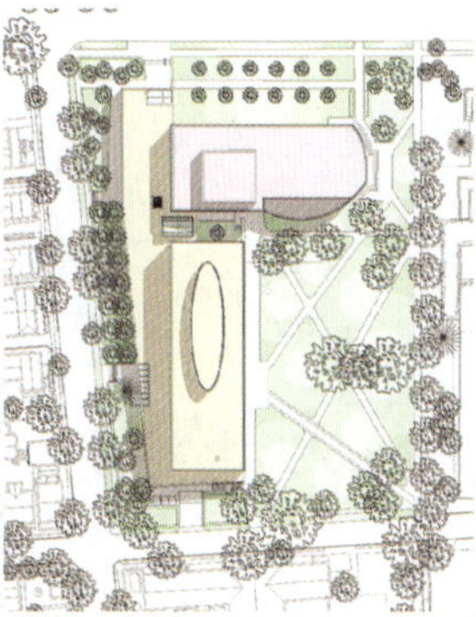

Top Friend Center for Engineering Education, Princeton University, with Computer Science Building beyond. **Above Left** Site plan. **Above Right** Library.

Top Friend Center exterior detail.
Above View from lawn. **Overleaf** Library.

As you enter and move through the Friend Center, you will observe that some quite prominent features—the glazed entry wall, for example, and the leading edge of the library mezzanine—are skewed at an angle that departs from the orthogonal geometry to which the building otherwise conforms. This deviation is not the product of an idle whim: it has its origin in our desire that the Friend Center, located as it is along the northern edge of the campus, should present itself as a good neighbor to the adjoining residential community. With this goal in mind, we wanted the building to respect, on its northern side, the alignment of William Street, which deviates slightly from the alignment of Shapiro Walk, the east-west pathway just to the south of us that appropriately establishes the orientation of this and other university buildings flanking it. Engineers in this assembly will surely wish me to be more precise: the angular rotation is exactly 5.71059 degrees. If you approach the Friend Center from the north, along William Street, you will see how important that small adjustment is in giving this building the posture of a good citizen. It then occurred to us that the same deviation might appropriately be carried into the interior so as to declare, throughout the fabric of the building, the principle that all human endeavors, and especially those of teaching and learning, may be enriched by interventions that challenge the hegemony of a prevailing systemic order. The discourse thus engendered is, so I like to believe, a small contribution made by architecture to the spirit of inquiry that animates the diverse activities destined to inhabit the Friend Center for Engineering Education.

Top Aerial view of Harvard Center for Government and International Studies (CGIS), showing mid-block garden. **Above** View looking east on Cambridge Street. **Overleaf** CGIS and neighboring buildings.

Shortly after that encounter with a contested edge on the Princeton campus, I became embroiled in a much more quarrelsome episode of university/community conflict. The **Harvard Center for Government and International Studies** (1998–2005, with Laurie D. Olin, landscape), located at the boundary between the university and an adjoining residential neighborhood, comprises two similar four-story buildings augmented by extensive below-grade construction. The strained relationship then existing between the university and the City of Cambridge is evidenced by the fact that four full years of intense negotiation and continuous design revision were required to obtain approval for the project to move forward.

Although one might assume that architecture would be the loser in such a process, in this case the extended negotiations and consequent reconsiderations created opportunities that led to improvements in design. One of my key objectives was to preserve a mid-block garden that had become one of the few landscaped open spaces successfully shared by residents and members of the university community. In order to save the garden, which in earlier proposals by others had been eliminated, two existing university-owned buildings were demolished, and spaces totaling more than 40 percent of the new construction—including a library, seminar rooms, and lecture halls—were placed underground. The two aboveground buildings, flanking a city street, are occupied almost entirely by faculty and research-center offices.

The transitional nature of the site, with large-scale university buildings on one side and wood-framed houses on the other, is acknowledged in both the materiality and the volumetric disposition of the buildings. The lower two floors are clad largely in terracotta, and an orthogonal geometry prevails; the upper floors are clad

1727
CAMBRIDGE
STREET
TOW ZONE
NO
STOPPING
2 HR
PARKING
TOW ZONE
NO PARKING
STREET CLEANING
SECOND TUESDAY
EACH MONTH

largely in glass, and a circular geometry prevails. The horizontal terracotta siding has a comfortable affinity for both the university's masonry buildings on one side and the neighborhood's clapboard houses on the other. The quasi-cylindrical forms of glass rising above do not have clearly defined tops: they simply evaporate into the sky, much as if they were the abandoned beginnings of planned but forbidden skyscrapers.

In retrospect, it can be seen that each of these university building projects, by virtue of its location within a large and architecturally disparate campus, compelled me to wrestle anew with the problem of language in architecture. It may also be observed that none of these projects, however extensive, equaled in scope the academic center at Fredonia, where we had been challenged to invent a new spatial structure and language of built form for an entire campus. That scope had allowed me to pursue and fulfill my totalizing vision of a monolithic architecture of reinforced concrete. Although no such opportunity would come my way again, the experience of Fredonia was nonetheless critically important to my subsequent work, launching my exploration of strategies for giving voice in architecture to the rich diversity of discourse that is the lifeblood of a university. Central to all such strategies is the deployment of language. Language, in architecture as in literature, is at once both an instrument of intellectual discourse that articulates ideas and an instrument of artistic discourse that transcends ideas. In both its aspects this instrumentality is fueled by imagination founded in knowledge. Those who practice architecture must always take care—and nowhere more attentively than on university campuses—that the instrumentality of its language not be degraded by either the folly of mimicry or the folly of incognizance.

THREE DIALECTICAL PAIRS

Statement, May 2017

An architect whose sensibility is closely attuned to particularities of place and occasion is by nature inclined to be skeptical of generalized theoretical propositions and ideological imperatives. Nonetheless, I acknowledge the insistent recurrence, throughout my nearly seven decades in practice, of questions posed by three dialectical pairs that are immanent in every projected work of architecture.

1. Singularity / Aggregation
Buildings are singular entities. Yet every building project requires the aggregation, be it horizontal or vertical, of multiple parts that are themselves singular entities. This poses a question for architecture: In what way and by what means should a built work, while affirming its holistic singularity, manifest also its accommodation of the multiple singularities aggregated therein?

2. Autonomy / Contingency
Buildings are physically autonomous entities. Yet every building project is inescapably contingent on the circumstances of its setting, be they natural or man-made. This poses a question for architecture: In what way and by what means should a built work, while affirming its self-determined autonomy, manifest also its contingency with respect to externalities that surround it?

3. Coherence / Contrariety
Buildings are functionally coherent entities serving defined programmatic goals. Yet intentions and aspirations incongruent with those goals are latent if not operative in every building project. This poses a question for architecture: In what way and by what means should a built work, while affirming its coherence of purpose, manifest also its vulnerability to underlying ambiguity, paradox, contrariety?

The questions posed by these dialectical pairs have been at the center of my life in architecture, and my considered if sometimes uncertain responses thereto are everywhere evident in my built works.

LANGUAGE

Conversation with Mark Pasnik
New York City, November 2017

Language in architecture is a reemerging question today, as evidenced in a renewed interest in post-modernism and in a neo-modernism fueled by digitized modes of form making. Your use of language shifts from your modernist beginnings to postmodern influences, and then again to the contemporary language you have been using over the past two decades. You explain the entire span of your career in terms of three dialectical pairs: singularity versus aggregation, autonomy versus contingency, and coherence versus contrariety. But among these, you make no reference to the important issue of language. Is this an oversight?
No, it's not an oversight. It's simply that language is one thing, and the territory defined by the dialectical pairs is something else. The three dialectical pairs pose questions for architecture; as such, they constitute the subject of our art. Language is the instrument for addressing those questions; as such, it is the substance of our art.

So the dialectical pairs are more foundational than language?
They're foundational in the sense that without a subject there can be no art. But we must not confuse the subject with the art. In architecture—as in literature, painting, or music—language is the substantive means by which the subject is not just addressed but transcended to become a work of art. Another way of getting at this distinction is to point out that formulating the questions posed by the three dialectical pairs is an ethical enterprise, whereas addressing them in the language of architecture is an aesthetic enterprise. I'd argue that both are indispensable to the work of art.

The exploration of language as a key aspect of your work is particularly visible in the middle years of your career in projects like the Portland Museum, which references its vernacular context, or your campus works, which engage earlier traditions and vocabularies. Why does language start to take greater hold for you in this middle period? Is the focus connected to the rise of postmodernism?
In my early years of practice, language—by which I mean the purposive coalescence of form, material, and detail—was sort of an open-and-shut case for me. I simply adhered to the language of high modernism as I had absorbed it in school. Although Place Ville Marie was quite forward-looking in its urban planning and spatial configuration, its architectural language was largely borrowed. I've often referred to the cruciform tower as having a body by Le Corbusier decked out in Miesian drag—a combination that would have made neither of them happy!

Why did you borrow like that?

Under the pressure of that extremely intensive design effort, which occupied me for three years from 1956 to 1959, I wasn't yet ready to develop and deploy my own language in such a large and complex built work. I needed to deploy a language that was readily at hand and appropriate to the occasion. By the time I got to Fredonia, however, I was eager to assert my personal identity as an architect, and I knew this would require that I somehow make language my own. The academic center at Fredonia provided me with that opportunity.

Would you say Fredonia was the first time your independent architectural voice was apparent?

Not really. Place Ville Marie was also very much my voice, but in terms of its language, it was an immature one, whereas I. M. Pei's work at that time already displayed a relatively mature voice, deploying a language that he had made his own. Observing this, I was naturally aware that I needed to develop my own version of that language, and in doing so to establish my individual identity within our firm. As a monolithic architecture of cast-in-place reinforced concrete, Fredonia is a product of the then-prevailing culture and modus operandi of our firm. And yet it couldn't possibly have come from Pei, because it's not his sensibility. It's my sensibility.

In what ways?

The diagonal spine that is the organizing element of the academic center—half landscape and half building—would be inconceivable coming from Pei. The formal development of Fredonia is also something both distinctly different from and certainly less sophisticated than Pei's work. Partly because of the limited budget and partly because of my own sensibility, there is not the same refinement in form, material, or detail. Yet there is a certain linguistic freshness, a sense of adventure, that permeates the academic center. It's interesting to me that you posed your earlier question as if language was not an issue for me until I got to Portland. That certainly was not the case.

In your early work the concern for language is more implicit than explicit.
No, it's really there from the beginning. You say it's there in Portland because you see the historicizing element of it, but that's not what language is about principally. There is no historicizing in Fredonia, yet it's very much an exploration of language. Hancock is an important building because it is a very refined linguistic exercise. Language is everything in Hancock.

"Minima" is the term others use for that type of language.
But the implication is that it's somehow deprived. What's deprived in Hancock is not language; it's the consequence of language. In other words, the architecture is limited because the language doesn't admit ruptures like, for instance, making a proper entrance. But in its deployment of language, Hancock is certainly the most fully realized work I have ever done, and that's why many people think of it as my most important building. There is a relentlessly disciplined purity in the language. It's so pure that it does—to make the literary analogy—begin to rise to the level of poetry.

Language articulates ideas. But language is also an instrument of artistic discourse, wherein it transcends ideas. The poet John Crowe Ransom expressed this well when he wrote that "the image cannot be dispossessed of a primordial freshness, which idea can never claim." In architecture as in literature, language has the capacity to transcend the ideological base from which we work and thereby make something else that we call poetry. It's extraordinarily difficult for me, as for most architects, to raise language to that level. I can make sense out of things, but when you want to be thrilled by a work of architecture, it's not just about making sense; it's about making something that goes beyond the idea. That usually requires a genius that I do not possess. If Hancock reaches that level, it's in part because I was by then the master of its language and in part because circumstance empowered and indeed required me to deploy that language with a discipline that rendered it transcendent.

Following the Hancock, how did you make such a dramatic shift to the language of Portland?

Portland was the first of our firm's commissions that came to me directly, and the issue of language took a turn. This was a deliberate choice by me, not one imposed by the client. I chose to pursue form, material, and detail that would resonate with the vernacular architecture of the context. I could have gone another way. There would have been no objection if I had cast the Portland Museum as a modernist icon. In fact, that might have been welcomed. But it was time for me to try something else.

It seemed to me that the site imposed on the building an absolute imperative to speak to Congress Square. The very first decision I made was to put a wall on the square, 120 feet long by 60 feet high. That decision immediately raised the problem of language in a way that I had never faced before. For the first time in my life, I was a making a facade. When I was a student in the late 1940s, *facade* was a dirty word—unspeakable. I spent months, literally months, on the facade of Portland, trying to figure out what to do. For me it was a high-stakes game. And you know, it's an interesting, provocative facade, even though it doesn't achieve a level to which I was aspiring.

Because it was new territory for you?
Totally new territory. It wasn't just that the brick was new; it was more the idea of the facade altogether that was new. Portland was a real struggle for me. Linguistically, you might say it is articulate, but it's not poetic.

In a short time you went from your exemplar of the Hancock to struggling with a new language and the issue of the facade. Why did you give up on the modern poetic? Did you feel pressure to change attitudes, given the postmodern discourses around you?
Let me step back for a minute. We've been coming to grips with language progressively. Starting with Place Ville Marie, the language is borrowed but not really an issue. Fredonia is where I really developed my own voice as an architect, and it's clear I am comfortable with that language. In Hancock the language is mature and is manipulated with a degree of assurance not previously seen in my built works. That then totally evaporates when we get to Portland, where there's a completely new kind of linguistic challenge with the facade, a self-imposed challenge. I certainly didn't feel any pressure from what you call the postmodern discourse. In fact, I was somewhat disturbed when Paolo Portoghesi published the Portland Museum, along with a number of other works, as a stellar example of the PoMo direction in which he wanted architecture to go. I was really upset about it.

Because of the other projects it was published with?
Yes. I did not see myself as residing in the PoMo camp. The volumetric organization of the Portland Museum was easy for me, because again, it's rooted in many of the things I had long been thinking about, most notably the problem of aggregation. The overall project in many ways is quite modernist and clearly shows the influence of Kahn, using a structure of parallelepipeds assembled, squares and rectangles assembled. On the garden side of Portland, there is no facade; there are only elevations and sections. It's still a very modernist schema.

And yet there is still the presence of the facade itself.
I believe I did the right thing in positing a facade. It's actually been very important for the city to have that facade as an affirmation of Portland's renascence, both cultural and economic, but I got myself into hot water with it because I wasn't really ready—and probably I'm still not ready.

Do you have lingering doubts about facades even today?
Yes, I'm very conscious of it. Maybe that's why I so admire Venturi and Scott Brown's Wu Hall at Princeton, because I see the linguistic genius in their manipulation of seemingly incoherent, incompatible elements somehow being brought together into a thrilling facade—completed, incidentally, the same year as my museum in Portland.

Wu Hall embraces the "complexity and contradiction" of Venturi's book. Was its publication influential on you?
I read it when it came out, in 1966. It's still the most important contribution to architectural theory published since World War II. Venturi succeeded in reanimating the classical language via mannerism, bringing a dead

language back to life. I looked at the book with some care. Ideas like using the conventional unconventionally were particularly compelling.

Your buildings were never conceived as "decorated sheds," a term used by Venturi and Denise Scott Brown. Your facades were never entirely independent of the interior content.
Exactly. For me it was vital that the facade in Portland reference the museum's internal structure.

In this way you were quite different from many of the postmodernists around you. When you were chair of architecture at Harvard, you were presiding over the school at the time when postmodern ideas were taking rapid hold.
My policy was to "let one hundred flowers bloom." When the Portland Museum was completed in 1983, which was in the middle of my term, Mark Angelil and Sarah Graham produced a postcard titled "Project for a Small Intervention," in which they superimposed the facade of Portland on the street elevation of Gund Hall. It was a humorous commentary on both my practice and my teaching. You have to understand, Portland appeared in the magazines at the same time that I was bringing Peter Eisenman and Daniel Libeskind to the school, so people found it totally confounding that I had done this facade.

You followed Portland with another facade in the competition for the Sainsbury Wing of the National Gallery in London.
Portland was the reason I was chosen as a finalist in London. Sainsbury was the first and only time that I've attempted to deploy the classical language in my work.

Clearly my proposal is an exercise-book kind of work. I hadn't made the language my own, as others pointed out—calling my Corinthian pilasters "lingerie." Sainsbury is all about a posture in the city, and the volumetric posture I chose was bold; but the language in which it was articulated was not of its time. In using the classical language straight—though with some mannerist gestures—I neither asked nor answered the questions about language that should have been raised at that time and in that place. Venturi and Scott Brown deserved to win because they made Wilkins's language their own in a clever way—employing ironic juxtapositions to carry his Corinthian pilasters onto their facade, where the pilasters and other fragments of the classical language then gradually evaporate into an almost modernist building envelope.

Let's shift focus to your university projects. In one of your more recent works, Butler College at Princeton, you were reacting to a predominant language in an existing campus environment.
That's correct. A few years earlier, I had been a finalist for a residential college at Princeton that the trustees decreed to be built in a historically accurate Collegiate Gothic style. I wasn't going to do straight-up Collegiate Gothic; so I submitted an essay in which I analyzed the qualities of Charles Klauder's splendid Collegiate Gothic dormitories and proposed to seek a contemporary analog that would exhibit without mimicking the qualities most valued in that style. As the essay put it, this approach could produce "a new residential college extending and honoring a great tradition by reinterpreting it in a form that invigorates the community it serves, while reminding its members that style is something other than the reincarnation of a 'style.'"

Of course, I didn't get the job. Demetri Porphyrios got it, and Whitman College is the result. But when the next dormitory came along, I was awarded the commission largely because my earlier proposition had not fallen on deaf ears. I was determined to make good on what I had written; and indeed Butler College is fundamentally a linguistic exercise, with the aim of developing an altogether fresh contemporary analogue to the Collegiate Gothic style.

***Style*: that's another taboo word in modernism. Why is that term held in such contempt?**
The polemical agenda of the modernist revolution was that it would liberate architecture from the tyranny of dead styles. In my early years as a design critic, I always refused to discuss architecture in terms of stylistic categories. Instead, I fell back on Whitehead's dictum that style is "the ultimate morality of mind." That was my way of closing the door on the subject of style.

Nonetheless, I have more than once been obliged to grapple with the question of stylistic conformity, especially on university campuses, where continuity with institutional tradition as embodied in architecture is a major issue. The Anderson School at UCLA is a very clear example. The school's site is a close neighbor to Royce Hall, the campus's first building, which was designed in the North Italian Romanesque Revival style. We developed a language for Anderson that employs brick matching that in Royce and cast-stone trim matching the color and texture of the older building's limestone trim. We also carried over the horizontal banding of stone and brick that characterizes Royce, but not the ornamental details. In this way, we established a linguistic harmony without mimicry, which allowed us to shape Anderson into altogether unprecedented contemporary forms while still remaining a good neighbor.

Anderson and Butler employ a similar palette. However, Butler is more adventurous linguistically, as evidenced by the episodically varied handling of limestone bands and undulations in its exterior wall. This more relaxed and exploratory attitude toward ornament is also evident in the curtain wall of the Koch Center of NewYork-Presbyterian Hospital. The building's facade is formed from triple-glazed panels of glass with a wooden screen inserted between the two outer layers to add warmth and a degree of privacy. A white frit pattern on the inner surface of the outermost layer of glass then adds a quietly flowing sense of movement. These linguistic elements together communicate the hospital's aspiration to be seen as a place of human sympathy and caring.

Above Detail, David H. Koch Center, NewYork-Presbyterian Hospital, New York City, 2018.

Thinking about the brick of Butler and the glass of Koch, it seems that you've developed two quite separate linguistic tracks in your later works, centered around these two materials. But in the Moakley Courthouse, both materials are present—brick on the street side and glass on the harbor. Was that a conscious synthesis of the languages?

There is also brick on the harbor side, behind the glass conoid. But you make a good point: there are indeed two linguistic tracks in play, a fact that Bob Campbell commented on with one of his wittiest critical remarks. Referring to the joining of the conoid to the brick, he said it is "like a blind date that isn't working." Whatever you think about that, the duality brings into focus my struggle to embody in architecture the predicament of judges who are expected to rely on precedent in reaching decisions about societal problems that are often entirely unprecedented. I wanted this predicament to be hinted at in the visitor's experience of the courthouse. It is what led me to the linguistic complexity that you mention. I acknowledge that the complexity is problematic, in that it precludes language from rising to the level of transcendent purity that you see in Hancock. But I'd argue that this sacrifice is appropriately offered in service to a higher goal: to make an architecture that illuminates the role of the federal judiciary in the life of the nation.

That's a long way from the Hancock Tower.
It's especially interesting to have the tower and the courthouse in the same city. Aside from their programmatic differences, two more linguistically divergent buildings would be difficult to imagine. So this discussion of my struggle with language, like so much else in my life, has inexorably brought us back once again to Boston.

FRIEDRICHSTRASSE, BERLIN

Quartier 206, Friedrichstadt Passagen, 1991–96
with Theodore J. Musho

The design for Quartier 206 on Friedrichstrasse had its origin in a competition organized by the Berlin Senate in the winter of 1991. Five developers were shortlisted from a total of twenty-two who had sought the opportunity to build a three-block-long, mixed-use project with the aim of revitalizing the street that had been, in the decades before World War II, the liveliest in Berlin. The rules of the competition required that each candidate submit three detailed design proposals, each authored by a different architect, for the entire development site. But when the jury was convened in May, its first act, even before looking at any of the fifteen submissions, was to decide that the project should be split up, with each block assigned to a different developer and a different architect. Inasmuch as our proposal, more than any other, was premised on the integrated development of all three blocks, we were astonished to be awarded the center block, Quartier 206. Unlike O. M. Ungers's premiated

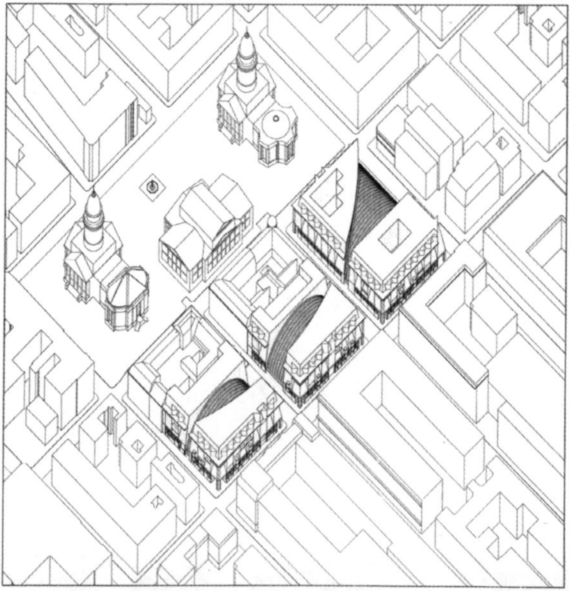

Top and Above Axonometric view and model, Friedrichstrasse competition proposal, 1991.

Top Perspective view along Friedrichstrasse, competition proposal. **Above** View along Friedrichstrasse. **Overleaf** View from intersection of Friedrichstrasse and Taubenstrasse.

proposal for Quartier 205 and Jean Nouvel's for Quartier 207, both of which had been designed as stand-alone buildings, our design for Quartier 206 was unintelligible in isolation from the two that flanked it. The highly integrated character of our scheme was clearly evident in our drawings and model and was emphasized in the accompanying text:

> We propose an architecture composed of two fundamental elements: an integrated set of Passagen and a highly articulated, episodically variegated street-wall. The programmed commercial and residential spaces are accommodated in buildings conceived simply as infill between these two bounding configurations. The space of the Passagen and the surface of the street-wall become the operative architectural elements of our project. Our Passagen are defined by the exceptional and aberrant nature of their interconnected spaces within the figural grid of streets. Our street-wall is defined by innovative surface strategies that provide variety and eventfulness within an underlying unity. The association of these two elements accomplishes the task of reanimating the grid…[giving] to both the Passagen and the adjoining streets an excitement that is attainable only at a scale unique to the vision of this enterprise: the simultaneous design of three contiguous blocks.

In the aftermath of the competition, we were obliged to radically rethink our project in order to acknowledge its new role—mandated by the jury—as one of three architecturally disparate (though functionally interdependent) entities within Berlin's reconstituted urban block structure. Our original concept of a dynamic spatial flow

traversing all three blocks was of necessity abandoned in favor of a reconfigured scheme that is, like its neighbors, essentially self-contained and self-centered. The project as built takes the form of a perimeter office block framing an internal courtyard at the first-floor level, beneath which a skylit atrium constitutes the spatial focus for shopping arcades at street and basement levels. The main feature animating both courtyard and atrium is a star-shaped glass roof, whose expansive geometry thrusts outward toward the enclosing courtyard walls.

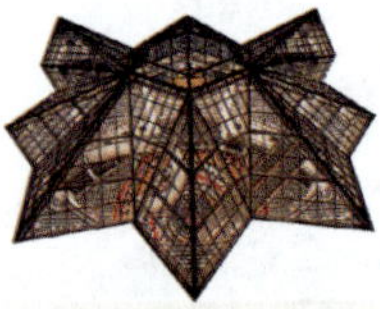

In reconfiguring the building's exterior surfaces, framing city streets, the original concept of a "highly articulated, episodically variegated street-wall" was retained, though its materialization was modified. The enabling element of this concept is an array of closely spaced horizontal bands of black metal, whose undulating profiles shape the rhythmically pleated and aberrantly eventful contours of the building envelope. Interstitial zones between these bands are filled with limestone or glass as appropriate to interior use. In thus activating the public facades of Quartier 206, we proceeded from our observation that because the blocks framing Friedrichstrasse are long and the street is relatively narrow, the street-wall is perceived sequentially rather than simultaneously and obliquely rather than frontally. Acknowledging these conditions, our design strategy sought to enhance, through architecture, the distinctive identity of that particular street in that particular city.

ETHICS AND ARCHITECTURE

Harvard Architecture Review 8 (1992)[1]

Ethics—that is to say, the science of morals—is a subject not much discussed in our profession, except at a rather superficial level bordering on the banal. Indeed, serious probing of ethical questions has been virtually taboo in contemporary architectural discourse, largely because it is presumed to be impossible to talk about morality without moralizing; and it is well established that moralizing is the death of art. Yet a head-in-sand attitude toward the ethical dimension of architecture has, in my view, significantly diminished the art of architecture in our time. Hence I am moved to offer a few observations with the aim of bringing into focus this inescapably problematic aspect of contemporary architectural practice. I begin by drawing on the authority of the *Oxford English Dictionary* to estab-

1 An earlier version of this essay was the introductory paper presented at a conference entitled "Ethics of Architecture: Building Without Thinking vs. Thinking Without Building," held at the Graham Foundation in Chicago on December 9 and 10, 1988.

lish the meaning of the two words that delimit the terrain of this discussion.

Ethics is defined as "the science of morals" and further as "the department of study concerned with the principles of human duty."

Architecture is defined as "the art or science of building or constructing edifices of any kind for human use."

Reducing these definitions to their essentials for our purpose here, when we speak of ethics in architecture we are speaking of principles of human duty as they may relate or apply to the art and science of building for human use. Now, the points of entry that one might select to begin an exploration of this very broad topic are virtually infinite in number, and I will make no special claim for the one I have chosen other than that it touches those aspects of the subject that I find most engaging as well as most accessible. I launch my probe with a question that momentarily expands the frame of reference: how do principles of human duty relate or apply to works of art? We can go a long way toward answering this question by referring to an aphorism of the poet-philosopher Paul Valéry: "We recognize a work of art by the fact that no idea it inspires in us, no mode of behavior it suggests we adopt, could exhaust or dispose of it."[2] This statement seems to me precisely correct. Though its eloquence be sacrificed, its meaning is not lost when we rephrase it as follows: a work of art always transcends those principles of human duty that it may embody or to which it may refer. Thus the work of art is alone among human productions in being privileged, indeed obligated, to escape the rule of human duty.

2 Quoted in Walter Benjamin, "On Some Motifs in Baudelaire," *Illuminations: Essays and Reflections* (New York: Schocken Books, 1969), 186–87.

Hence we can say that the only absolute duty imposed on a work of art is that of being *un*dutiful.

I have begun by making this briefly sketched argument for the intrinsic amorality of art for two reasons: first, I believe it to be the sine qua non shared by all works of art, including architecture; and second, it brings into focus the poignant, one may even say tragic, situation of architecture as the one art whose ethical dimension clearly cannot therein be satisfactorily encompassed. For it must be obvious that the duty to be undutiful, while true, is scarcely the whole truth about the role of ethics in architecture. Herein, then, architecture separates itself decisively from all other arts, and to understand the nature of that separation we need only refer back to the OED's definition: "Architecture is the art or science of building or constructing edifices of any kind for human use." The key words here are *human use*. These words place architecture under an ethical obligation from which other arts are specifically exempted: to wit, works of architecture are asked to be so constructed as to be useful—in other words, literally to accommodate the society that sponsors their construction. Hence a work of architecture is inescapably enmeshed in that system of ethical constraints, those principles of human duty, from which its art status demands with equal insistence that it be liberated. The reconciliation of these seemingly irreconcilable demands precisely defines, in my view, the ultimate task of the architect. And the difficulty of this task surely explains why it is so seldom fully accomplished, as well as why we so highly value those works of architecture in which we see evidence of its having been even partially accomplished. Furthermore, I would argue that a condition invariably prerequisite to such accomplishment has been the availability of well-established principles of human duty—that is to say, some system of ethics—to which architects have given their allegiance and which in turn has provided them with a reliable definition of *usefulness* on which to base their professional work.

You will have noticed that a new term—*professional work*—has suddenly appeared to complicate this discussion. I have purposely kept the word *professional* out of my remarks up to now in order to make it clear that I am not talking about "professional ethics" as conventionally defined. But having made that point, I am now obliged to speak of the architect's professional work, inasmuch as this is the only term that suitably encompasses all those ethical considerations—all those principles of human duty—that are embodied in his or her obligation to design edifices for human use. And this brings me at last to the heart of the matter that I set out to explore, which is not after all the general topic of ethics and architecture but the more specific problem of ethics as bearing on current practice. It seems to me that the question of what in fact constitutes usefulness has become the central ethical dilemma of contemporary architecture. Of course this dilemma has always existed, but in earlier periods of human history it was more or less successfully subsumed or sublimated within prevailing value systems—value systems that engendered a sufficiently strong consensus in any given society so that architects could clearly understand how buildings of various types should be designed in order to be acknowledged by that society as useful. But today many aspects of that consensus have vanished, and it is this circumstance, as reflected in the conditions of contemporary practice, that has, to quote a recent statement by Stanley Tigerman, "radically displaced ideals about ethical behavior." However, *displaced* seems to me not quite the right word, implying as it does a definitive shift one way or another. Rather, what we have witnessed, and what I have myself repeatedly experienced, is a kind of entropy of ethical principles—a dissolution brought about by the proliferation of conflicting value systems, with none having gained sufficient allegiance to constitute a consensus that could foster the elaboration of a reliable code of ethics governing professional conduct. By now I'm sure you understand that I am talking not about a code of ethics in the American Institute of Architects sense of the word, but about a much broader code embracing concepts of how architects ought to respond to the number and diversity of competing interests that cry out to be heard—and quite possibly should be heard—with respect to virtually every significant building project.

To put it another way, I cannot recall a single commission undertaken by my firm in the past forty years that has not required us to make difficult choices concerning how and to whom we render our professional service and how and to whom the intended building will make itself useful. These choices are difficult because the numerous constituencies whom we as a matter of professional responsibility see ourselves as serving—the client institution, the building's users, its neighbors, and so on—are often fiercely committed to widely divergent and deeply conflicting principles of human duty. This is especially true in the large-scale urban building projects that have always constituted a significant component of our practice. Hence a disquieting ambivalence with respect to ethical issues—a pervasive uncertainty about how best to fulfill my duty as a professional—is a nearly perpetual state of mind for me, as surely it must also be for every architect in practice today whose work significantly touches or shapes the public realm. And although the anxiety felt by architects as a result of such uncertainty is perhaps a matter of merely private concern, there is another much more troubling consequence for architecture that stems directly from this contemporary ethical predicament. For just as entropy in physics invariably entails a diminishment of available energy in the affected system, so the phenomenon of entropy in ethics has measurably diminished the architect's capacity to shape a positive outcome from the always problematic encounter between architecture and power.

Now, it is surely true that all the arts, through the institution of patronage, are to some degree instruments of power. Nonetheless architecture, owing to the expenditure of labor and material required for its production, is clearly the art most inextricably enmeshed in the belief systems and institutional mechanisms that govern human culture and society. Hence the uncomfortably intimate embrace between architecture and power: an embrace to which architecture often passively submits, within which it occasionally struggles, from which it never escapes. Neither the supine posture of surrender nor the futile dream of deliverance has yet produced a significant built work of architecture. But the struggle of architecture to speak and act within and against the embrace of power has resulted in some of the most fascinating and profoundly moving manifestations of human intelligence. It has produced buildings wherein overt allegiance to power, clear mastery of technique, and explicit dedication to use have been subtly combined by the architect's skill so that these edifices for human use become, marvelously, instruments for speculative thought—instruments that relentlessly, if covertly, challenge the conventions, the preconceptions, and finally the very powers that brought them into being. Then indeed, if all too rarely, does architecture reach the highest realm of art. That the science of morals, however beset by uncertainty, is as indispensable to this attainment as is the science of building seems to me beyond question. Without the latter a work of architecture perhaps will not stand, but without the former it surely cannot *mean*.

COURTHOUSE: A CHALLENGE AND OPPORTUNITY FOR ARCHITECTURE

Responses to Questions Posed to Finalists for the Commission to Design a New Federal Courthouse in Boston, March 1991

How do you envision a building of this scale, with its central civic purpose, fitting into the existing context of Boston?

"Glory be to God for dappled things." The poet was speaking of the natural world, but had he been thinking of cities, he might well have found downtown Boston worthy of his praise. No other city in North America displays a physiognomy so engagingly idiosyncratic, so "fickle, freckled," so curiously fragmented, so picturesquely disordered—in sum so vividly and ineradicably contaminated by a contentious altercation, played out across three and a half centuries, between topography and human settlement.

Construction of a new federal courthouse will surely engender a fascinating encounter between this highly particularized urban context and the most idealized of societal institutions. The courthouse will succeed architecturally and urbanistically only if *both* agents of the encounter are suitably acknowledged, indeed celebrated, in its design. By this I mean that the courthouse must assert in its posture an appropriate balance between autonomy and contingency: it must embody the separateness and rigorous probity of due process, without alienating itself from its neighbors; and it must respond sympathetically to its urban context, without being tyrannized by circumstance. I want to make it clear that I do not see this balance being achieved through a compromise requiring the suppression of one or both agents in the encounter. On the contrary, I believe that an appropriate posture for this building must be at once strongly autonomous and strongly contingent. It should, in sum, both fit in and stand out.

To what degree should this U.S. courthouse be modern?
It should be thoroughly modern in the sense of being up to date in all its facilities, but not modern in the sense of a style that turns its back on history. Even though this courthouse is in many respects without precedent, its design can and should be informed by an understanding of the classical tradition. This does not mean a pastiche of elements borrowed from styles of the past. Rather, it means a passionate and authoritative reinterpretation of the classical tradition, drawing on its inexhaustible capacity not just to preserve memory but equally to nourish invention. This is my definition of a modern architecture.

What symbolism should this courthouse incorporate?
The central importance of symbolism in courthouse design derives from the essential *formality* of due process. To be sure, the seat of due process is the courtroom itself, where functional and symbolic forms have been so highly integrated as to be virtually inseparable. But the

need for symbolism in the service of due process extends well beyond the courtroom into those spaces and settings that constitute the access system mediating between the sanctity of the courtroom and the outside world. This access system has traditionally been shaped by architectural elements dense with symbolic meaning. Stairs, porticoes, loggias, architraves, vestibules, rotundas: these are but a few of the devices employed to create the desired processional leading from the loosely ordered public realm of the street to the tightly ordered public realm of the courtroom. The shaping of this interstitial public realm between street and courtroom thus constitutes an extraordinary opportunity for architecture as metaphor and symbol.

The new federal courthouse should convey in every aspect of its design those qualities—probity, permanence, clarity, restraint—that are embodied in the administration of justice. Another quality that I would wish to see in its architecture cannot be well expressed in words; it must be demonstrated in stone. But an analogy that may be relevant is evidenced in the portraits that adorn the walls of the present First Circuit courtroom. As paintings, all are competent, but few are interesting. Only one—Gardner Cox's painting of Judge Bailey Aldrich—stands out as immediately engaging. I have never met Judge Aldrich, but this portrait makes me *want* to meet him. It is suggestive, in the best sense of the word. That is to say, it stimulates one's interest in the person portrayed and engenders respect for his character and for the quality of his mind. What the portrait does for the judge, the new federal courthouse must do for justice.

Above Gardner Cox, *Judge Bailey Aldrich*, 1978.

FAN PIER, BOSTON

John Joseph Moakley United States Courthouse, 1991–98

with Ian Bader, Ellsworth Kelly (artwork), Laurie D. Olin (landscape)

Out of deference to its neighbor, the Hancock Tower is as silent as any building can be, so that the voice of Richardson's great church can continue to be heard. This self-imposed silence perhaps explains why, when it was announced in 1991 that a new federal courthouse was to be built in Boston, I so eagerly sought the commission to design it. For while the skyscraper had been obliged to remain mute, the courthouse, so I believed, would be invited to speak. And I longed for the opportunity to build in my erstwhile hometown a truly public building—a building to be experienced not just externally as object but internally as space, and a building that not only need not but clearly must not remain speechless.

Well, I got my wish. And then, standing on that splendid site overlooking the harbor and a city so transformed as to be scarcely recognizable as the Boston of my childhood, I faced the question, "What should this building say?" Luckily, I could turn for help to Judges

Top and Above Aerial views of downtown Boston, 1930 and 1990 (Moakley U.S. Courthouse site outlined in red).

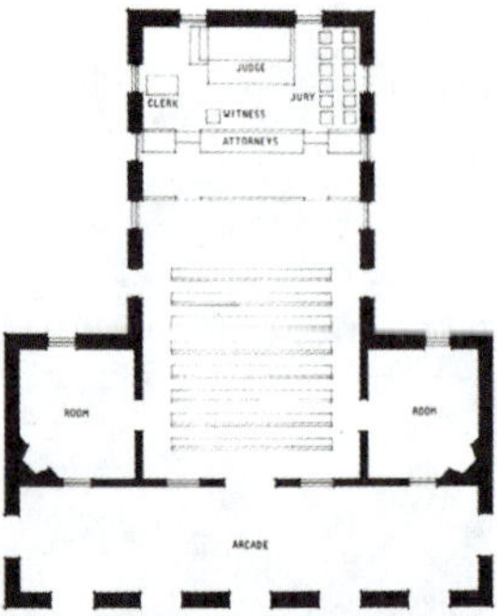

Top Hanover County Courthouse, Virginia, 1735.
Above Left Courthouse plan. **Above Right** George Cooke, *Patrick Henry Arguing the Parson's Cause at Hanover Courthouse*, 1834.

Stephen Breyer and Douglas Woodlock, two superb mentors who took me in hand and generously instructed me in the elements of American jurisprudence. Together the judges and I looked for relevant precedents among twentieth-century American courthouses, in both modern and classical modes. Dissatisfied, we found ourselves going back in time, hoping to encounter a courthouse embodying those qualities that we sought: probity, clarity, and restraint, together with an unequivocal declaration of openness to the public being served.

We found these qualities present at last in one of the nation's oldest courthouses still in use for that purpose, the Hanover County Courthouse in Virginia, built in 1735. Here, in December 1763, Patrick Henry argued the Parson's Cause. And as a well-known painting vividly suggests, the courthouse was at that time the center and symbol of its community, playing an important public role that Stephen Breyer, in particular, was eager to recover in a form appropriate to contemporary civic life.

But then we had to face the really hard question: How is it possible to transpose those qualities, so perfectly embodied in this one-room courthouse, to a huge structure housing twenty-seven courtrooms embedded in three-quarters of a million square feet of bureaucratic support space? Our response took the form of an L-shaped building, with courtrooms arrayed on three levels behind a glass-walled atrium overlooking Boston Harbor. In envisioning this courthouse, we sought to make a building that would be perceived as appropriately emblematic, yet open and accessible to all.

Judges Breyer and Woodlock explained to me at the outset that aside from its spectacular waterfront setting, a key factor in their selection of the Fan Pier site was its perceived appropriateness to the status of the federal

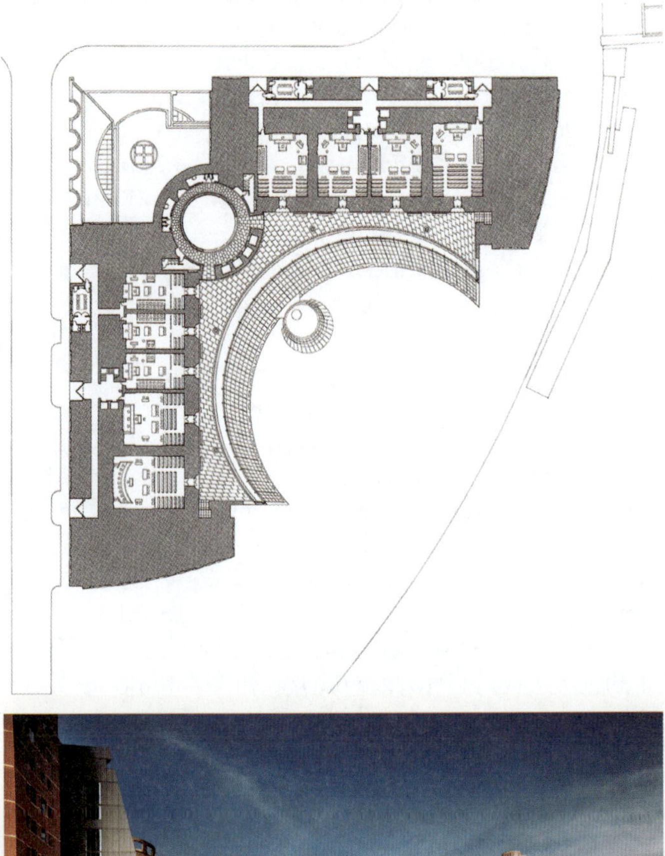

Top Plan of typical courtroom floor. **Above** Courthouse and Harborpark overlooking downtown Boston. **Opposite Top** Main entry and cupola. **Opposite Bottom** Rotunda with Ellsworth Kelly's *Boston Panels*.

Top Gallery with courtroom entries on left, conoid glass wall on right. **Above** District Courtroom with stenciled ornament. **Overleaf** Half-dome at courtroom entry.

courts as both part of and apart from the local communities they serve. And early on, they also drew my attention to another interesting paradox—that while the courts must rely extensively on precedent in adjudicating the cases before them, those cases often require them to address societal problems that are entirely unprecedented. It is no exaggeration to say that this courthouse embodies our shared intention to acknowledge and indeed to celebrate in architecture the opposing terms of these two paradoxes. While this intention is clearly evident in the building's exterior, with its reference to the traditions of its place on the one hand and its emblematic departure from them on the other, it is in the experience of its interior spaces that our preoccupation with these dualities is most explicitly revealed.

Having passed through a monumental entry arch, one proceeds through the skylit reception hall to a central rotunda that seems to affirm unequivocally the separateness of the judicial process from the everyday life of the street—a separateness embodied both in the serene autonomy of its cylindrical form and in the equally serene abstraction of the Ellsworth Kelly paintings on its walls. But when, upon arriving at one of the upper floors, one emerges into the gallery that gives access to the courtrooms, a panoramic view of the city and its harbor offers a vivid reminder that the courts are not so separate after all—that indeed they exist to serve the contemporary needs of the ever-changing world beyond their walls. Then, turning toward the courtroom, separateness and respect for precedent are again suggested by the half-dome entrance and further reaffirmed within the room itself, where large arches dignify equally all participants in the judicial process—judge, jury, witnesses, and the interested public—while the domed ceiling declares the

1

1

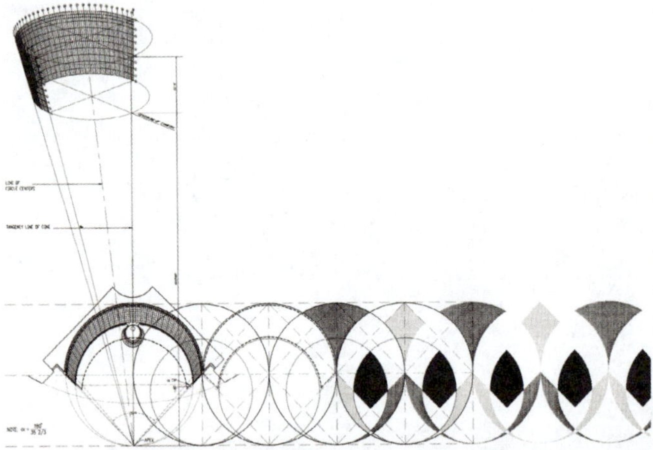

Top Diagram showing derivation of courtroom stencil ornament from conoid geometry. **Above** Harborpark as seen from courtroom gallery. **Overleaf** Courthouse at dusk.

centrality of the litigants to the proceedings taking place therein. Here also the duality between respect for precedent and openness to the unprecedented is embodied in the stenciled ornament, which recovers a traditional New England craft in a new pattern derived from the structurally innovative form of the conoid glass wall enclosing the galleries—a wall through which, upon emerging from the courtroom, one encounters once again the life of the city in all its splendid diversity.

Finally, after descending to ground level, one may enter the Harborpark, and perhaps pause to read some words carved in granite that were once spoken by Justice Breyer: "This most beautiful site in Boston does not belong to the judges; it does not belong to the lawyers; it does not belong to the federal government; it does not belong to the litigants; it belongs to the public."

In the Harborpark, one may relax among friends and enjoy the water's edge in company or in solitude. And here, as dusk falls, one may turn toward the courthouse to see affirmed in architecture the principle that every citizen shall have equal access to the law and to the guarantee of due process embodied in an independent judiciary. For despite our preoccupation with ambiguity and paradox, the unambiguous assertion of this principle—that the courthouse and Harborpark belong to the public, and the courts and their proceedings are open to all—was from start to finish our most important goal in the design of this building. And I dare to hope that one may also sense here an echo of the voice that inspired us—the voice of the little one-room courthouse in Hanover County, Virginia.

REPRESENTATION

Conversation with Paolo Conrad Bercah
New York City, February 1998

You have spoken of architecture as a representational art. Most people think of painting as representational, but not architecture. In what sense can architecture be representational?

Historically, the value placed on the art of architecture has flowed in large part from its capacity to characterize the intended relationships between individual human beings, their institutions, their communities, and the natural world. That is what I mean by architecture as a representational art, though obviously I am talking about a form of representation that is metaphorical, not literal. Underlying the statement is a stubborn humanism: I mean simply that if there were no human beings, and no institutions, and no communities, and no natural world, there would be no architecture. All four elements are necessary. In my insistence on this tetrad, I do not mean to preclude the kind of formal explorations that are explicitly anti-humanist, such as those conducted by Peter Eisenman. I am not at all opposed to such adventures; as a matter of fact, I specifically endorse experimental procedures that exclude one or more elements from the equation for the purpose of acquiring a deeper understanding of our discipline. But in the end I believe that none of these elements can be excluded or neglected, and that were architecture to lose its capacity to represent those relationships or simply fail to do so, it would very soon lose legitimacy as an art form. It would become trivial and superfluous.

All this reflects my view that the importance of architecture to the culture—like that of any other art—derives from the fact that it is indispensable, by which I mean that no other form of expression can communicate what it does. If writing could communicate what music does, we would not need music. If painting could communicate what architecture does, we would not need architecture. That is why I am skeptical of ideologically based prescriptions in architecture. It is self-defeating to think that architecture is simply a manifestation of ideas that can be expressed in another form.

Architecture, in other words, must speak for itself. Nonetheless, it would be helpful if you could be more specific about the sort of ideas that public buildings have the potential to express.

The best way to do this is to take a look at a specific type of public building—for example, the courthouse. Many institutional buildings in our society, including those serving the administration of justice, while having a public function that should enrich public life, have actually become so encumbered by bureaucratic support systems that the capacity of these building types to give voice to their public roles and the values underlying them has been suppressed, suffocated, muted. A vivid illustration of the problem is to be found in the sad history of the American courthouse, particularly in the twentieth century. The challenge the modern courthouse offers to architecture is twofold. First, if you have to build a courthouse with thirty courtrooms instead of one, how do you do it in such a way that each of those thirty courtrooms remains valuable and retains its dignity to the same extent as the courthouse in which there was only one courtroom? How can you, in other words, prevent the devaluation of the courtroom and, by implication, of the administration of justice that this aggregation implies? And second, when those courtrooms are embedded in bureaucratic support space whose floor area is more than ten times that of the courtrooms they serve, how can you prevent the courthouse from becoming just another big office building?

In a curious way, the problem of aggregation that the demands of society have placed on the system of justice are different but nonetheless part of the same problem of aggregation that architects have to face in the design of the tall building. The difference is that while one can accept, let us say, the reduction of commercial offices to anonymous space housed in a more or less attractive but inexpressive volume, one absolutely cannot accept that solution for a courthouse—as occurs, for example, in one of Mies van der Rohe's late buildings, the courthouse in Chicago, which looks exactly like the office building next to it. No matter how handsome the building may be—and in that case it is very handsome indeed—this kind of swallowing up of all distinctions of use is precisely what accounts for the skepticism that many people feel about architecture in our time, because too many buildings fail to give meaningful expression to their relationships with the institutions that shape their lives.

So this is a capacity that architecture used to have but now has lost, probably because of modernist whirlwinds. Yes, owing to an overly literal and entirely uncritical interpretation of programmatic requirements, the courthouse was allowed to become just another bureaucratic building. And indeed the system of justice does require a huge bureaucratic apparatus to support what goes on in the courtroom. That apparatus cannot be made to go away; it is necessary. But its scale is so much larger than the scale of the courtroom that the courthouse tends to become an office building containing just a few special spaces, and those spaces may not even be discernible from the outside. Yet, as I said, this explains only half the problem; the other half has to do with the need to aggregate a large number of courtrooms together, which implicitly devalues the singularity of the courtroom. Why is that singularity important? Because the whole system of justice in our society rests on the principle that each person can have his or her own problem heard and adjudicated as an individual. The administration of justice, as opposed to the other branches of our government, does not deal with society en masse; it deals with society in terms of problems brought to it by individuals. To the extent that architecture can characterize or represent that role, it can do so only insofar as the individual courtroom is celebrated and does not become devalued by aggregation.

I can see why the external appearance of a public building is all the more important in a context of high-rises. Yet there are internal challenges as well.

One particular problem for courthouses is security, which is so stringent that the building is forced to become a sealed box. How do you deal with that?

To answer that question, I have to go back to our discussion of education and modernism versus the classical tradition. The one thing Beaux-Arts training was very good at was teaching people how to deal with problems of aggregation—that is, how to assemble many things into one thing. If you look at Durand's studies of idealized plans, you realize that in the evolution of the École des Beaux-Arts there is a long history of the study of that very problem. This is the way in which I feel that architecture was blinded by modernism, in its total refusal to learn anything from what was, admittedly, an exhausted if not bankrupt approach to architecture, but one from which there was still something to be learned. How do you aggregate a number of identical parts in a structure so that it has a kind of richness and is not reduced to being a closed box on the street? In fact, richness can be created through arcades, passages, foyers, *salles des pas perdus*—all those structures of public space. That was the strongest part of the Beaux-Arts tradition, the idea of a sequence of spaces that mediate between the public space outside the building and what goes on inside.

The weakness, however, of the discipline of the École des Beaux-Arts—and arguably the reason it had to be rejected—was that it became formulaic and rule bound. Yet it did not have to be as rule bound as it was, and I think that some of the renewed interest in the classical language is driven precisely by a sense that the classical language still has the potential to respond to new needs, that it can change and is not frozen in time or in a system of rules from which it cannot escape. But it was our sense of its being frozen in a system that led to our rejection of it, and by rejecting it out of hand, my generation deprived itself—or more accurately was deprived by our mentors—of any knowledge of it. We were not to be exposed to it; we were not to be infected by knowledge of the history of our discipline, which was presumed to be dangerous—literally dangerous.

This explains some of the weaknesses of modernism, particularly in terms of public buildings. Such buildings were what the École des Beaux-Arts was all about. The total rejection of the Beaux-Arts discipline and the failure, particularly of the Gropius school, to replace it with anything other than the vague idea of "basic design" and the so-called new objectivity—which was like rejecting the whole history of the culture and going back to kindergarten—now seems perverse in the extreme. At the same time, you have to acknowledge that the blame for this appalling lacuna lay not just with the modernists but also with those who clung to the classical tradition. They became more and more defensive, more and more rigid, more and more inflexible, and less and less capable of showing persuasively how the classical tradition in architecture could respond to contemporary needs.

In the Boston courthouse, then, my main goal was to recover the capacity of architecture to declare, clearly and unambiguously, the publicness of a public building. To this end, the building embodies a very explicit processional sequence that acknowledges the Beaux-Arts principle that there is value in the successive experience of an articulate space between the street and the destination. The courthouse is an attempt to show that architecture can effectively address both the issue of aggregation, so that the value of each courtroom is not diminished by the fact that many courtrooms are assembled together, and the issue of the apparatus of bureaucracy, so that the presence of bureaucracy does not overwhelm the sense that the building is open, available, accessible, and transparent to the public. The bureaucratic space is cast in a solid that enhances and dramatizes the experience of the building as a public building. The two wings around the central rotunda, which are opaque from the street, set the stage—like the wings of a theater—for a procession that begins on the street and leads one through a succession of spaces into an internal public realm. And that internal public realm acquires power from the fact that it unexpectedly and dramatically opens a vista to an even larger public realm than that of the street—a realm embracing the entirety of downtown Boston and its harbor.

So the way the building engages the public—on the street side as well as the water side, where it addresses the whole city—is the essence of its architecture.
Yes. That was my intention from the very start. When the project was announced, it was immediately obvious to me that if we were awarded the commission, it would give me the opportunity to make a speaking architecture in Boston as a complement and counterbalance to the mute architecture of the Hancock Tower.

What was your strategy for getting the job?
In the winter of 1991, the seven short-listed architects were told of four possible sites for the courthouse: three were in the heart of downtown, and the fourth was Fan Pier. During the selection process, which was an extended one, we were asked to respond in writing to a number of questions, and I gave a lot of thought to the issues involved while preparing my reply (page 410). Retrospectively, it is clear to me that my response, combined with the presentation I made at the interview,

is what secured the commission. It was not because of our reputation or the work we had done, although that was a necessary background. The reason we got the job was that my understanding of the issues matched the judges' aspirations. Rather than speculating on possible design solutions or the relative merits of the four sites, in my presentation I gave a brief history of courthouse architecture in this country from colonial times to the present day. I reflected on the alarming decline in the capacity of federal courthouses to communicate, first, the values underlying the American system of jurisprudence, and second, the role of the federal courts in the American judicial system. I said that architecture had somehow lost the capacity to express—or, you might say, to represent—these values, and I committed myself unreservedly to the task of recovering that capacity. The judges responded positively to my presentation, and we got the job.

On the day that the selection of the architect was announced, it was also announced that Fan Pier had been chosen as the site for the courthouse. This had not been known to me or anyone else except the judges. What that choice made emphatically clear was the judges' intention to put this courthouse on stage. You would only choose such a site if you had the intention, as the two judges did, of proving that a courthouse could be once again a public building in the emblematic, experiential sense, not just in the sense of its use. That choice of site, combined with the judges' aspirations and my own analysis of the problem, laid the foundation for the scheme to emerge.

In the course of competing for the commission, you wrote that the Boston courthouse should exhibit,

among other things, a respect for precedent. Would it be fair to say that the building attempts to establish a dialogue with Bulfinch's State House, and that the gesture embodied by the conoid can be seen as a contemporary reply to his dome?

Yes and no. On the face of it, the conoid is a rhetorical gesture, and that gesture is essential to achieving the goal of dignifying the aggregation of courtrooms, because without it, all you have is three balconies in front of twenty-seven courtrooms. The conoid, in combination with the cupola, is the rhetorical element; it is the formal means of making that affirmation. What the conoid is trying to do is express the relationship between this institution and its community in as explicit and precise a way as the golden dome expresses the relationship between the institution it houses and its community. The presence of the dome on the State House compels one to think hard about the specific contribution the building makes in giving people a sense of the role of government in society. Underneath the golden dome there is a legislature; underneath the dome in Washington there is a legislature. The legislature is the seat of representative power. The power to act on behalf of the people as a body is housed in a statehouse under a golden dome, and that is a very emblematic and wonderful thing.

But the role of the federal court is not the same as that of the legislature. The federal courts have an extraordinarily interesting and ambiguous relationship to the communities in which they are housed. What they represent is the responsibility of the federal government to adjudicate matters that are deemed beyond the reach of the state government for one of two reasons. Either the matters being adjudicated are more than local—between two states, say—or the matters being adjudicated involve federal statutes, including the federal Constitution, that transcend local statutes. This is a very important role that should never be confused with the role of local government in the city or state. And it is an intrusive role. The federal courts are both part of and apart from the communities in which they reside. They are part of them because they help to adjudicate issues that have a local origin, but they are apart from them because they bring to those issues matters that transcend the local origin. For example, the conflict over school busing, which convulsed Boston for more than a decade in the 1970s and '80s, was adjudicated in the federal court because it arose from a conflict between the expressed will of the local community and an interpretation of the U.S. Constitution that declares school busing to be constitutionally mandated.

If you compare an architect to a novelist, this is my storyline. Just as a novelist makes literature out of a story, the architect makes architecture out of that story. This is what I mean when I say that architecture is a representational art. It is about enriching in every citizen his or her sense of citizenship by communicating, through architecture, the role of this particular institution in a civil society. The most explicitly representational element of the Boston courthouse is the cylindrical cupola, which occupies a central position when viewed from both street and harbor sides and is crowned by twelve square openings, declaring the primacy of a jury of peers as the fundamental principle of our judicial system. That said, nothing is more important to fulfilling the communicative purpose of this courthouse than the conoid glass wall. What the conoid does—and I do not know of any device in the classical language that could do this, though there may be such—is to affirm the significance, the dignity, and the transparency of the activity that is arrayed behind it. And most important, the eccentricity of the conoid declares unequivocally that this activity is not self-centered but is related and responsive to the city it faces. The Harborpark embraced by the conoid belongs not just to the courthouse but to the harbor and the city. The eccentricity of the form declares this. If you did not have that, the building would become an isolated, self-referential object.

Why does the conoid end the way it does, with those acute angles?

The geometry of the conoid produces the angles. They are true to the conoid. If it were a simple cone, you would get a half-circle, which would end in ninety-degree angles but would be formally counterproductive; it would be self-centered. The important thing about the conoid is that it reaches out and embraces the park. It is dynamic, not static. The park belongs to the courthouse, but it also belongs to the city, and in order for that duality to be acknowledged, the conoid is essential.

This brings me to another important aspect of the Boston courthouse—namely, the modesty, the probity, the resistance to excess that should be embodied in a building dedicated to the administration of justice. The building has to be rhetorical, because if it were not, it would be only bureaucratic. But in giving it a rhetorical quality, one has to be very careful. As you know, judges are not supposed to engage in rhetoric. Above all, they are not supposed to become poetic. They are supposed make things clear, not seduce people. So while the rhetorical device of the conoid is crucial to the posture of the building, that rhetorical device must not be seen as compromising the probity of the courtroom's process. That process is separate. The interior brick wall tells you that even when you are inside the gallery, you are still outside the courtroom. In fact, to extend your comparison, the gallery is the equivalent of Bernini's colonnade at St. Peter's. When you are in the gallery, you feel that you are not yet in the courthouse, just as when you are in the colonnade, you feel you have not yet entered the church.

Achieving this delicate balance is not simple. A courthouse is not a museum or a restaurant or a church. It is a very specific activity, and architecture should assume the obligation of helping people understand their relationship to that activity and the relationship of that activity to the larger community. The Boston courthouse has all four components: the individual, the institution, the community, and the natural world. It is therefore an extraordinarily rich problem, and all the resources of architecture have had to be called upon here. For the most part, not much of that is terribly explicit. But the way you are greeted, the sense you have as you pass through the space that you have been set apart from the city but are being reintroduced to it in a different way, and the manner in which you proceed to the courtroom—all that is very explicit. The explicit experience is intended to help people understand and enjoy being there, even though it is hard to imagine people enjoying being in a courthouse. They can enjoy it in the sense that they respect the institution, and it becomes a significant part of their lives; they are not simply alienated by a monolith and swallowed up in a process they do not understand.

What lies behind your decision to use brick?
That goes back to the issue of modesty and probity, to an acknowledgment of the location and the traditions of the place, to the fact that the building does not seek to set itself apart. Some people criticize the building for being too absorbed into the city fabric; they believe that a federal courthouse should set itself apart. But a courthouse is too large an object to set itself apart. That may have been appropriate when it was a one-room building, but now it is too large, too encumbered with bureaucratic space. The best approach was to absorb it into the city on the street side and set it apart through a dramatic gesture on the water side. In this case, it was better to dramatize the elements rather than the volume, which becomes merely the frame for the entrance pavilion. As for the brick, it amounts to a kind of polemic on my part. One of the things for which public buildings—and courthouses specifically—have been criticized lately is their materiality. People say, "It's a courthouse, so it should be in stone." But then they get upset about the cost and ask why we need to spend so much money. In my view, the priority in a public building is not the richness of the material but the richness of the experience of the space. That is the purpose of architecture, and you do not need marble to do that. What you do need is a material that is durable and permanent, and that embodies in the way it is assembled a sense of craft, which is emblematic of the care that goes into judicial work.

The choice of brick was natural for several reasons.

First of all, it is indigenous to this part of town. Secondly, it is modest, it is inexpensive, it embodies the idea of craft, and it is also very beautiful. So why not? And finally, the brickwork is carried into the interior of the building to make explicit the idea that you haven't really entered the courthouse—you are still, metaphorically speaking, outdoors—until you pass under the half-dome of brick at the entrance to each courtroom. The brickwork is allowed to permeate the building in a way that declares its publicness internally as well as externally.

You have said, in reference to the Hancock Tower, that architecture is a critique of culture carried out through the language of forms. Does this maxim apply to the courthouse?
Definitely.

In what way?
If you believe that the courts are important to the well-being of the society, then it is ethically mandatory for a courthouse to be able to say something about that. It is okay for the Hancock Tower to remain mute, but it is not okay for the federal courthouse to remain mute. That is an ethical position. I do not think that you can justify or explain these two buildings without reference to the ethical position that underlies them. Ideally, the architecture of the courthouse will cause people to reflect on the role played by an independent judiciary in our society and the relationship between individual human beings, the system of justice, and the larger world of which they are a part. Even if it succeeds only partially in this, the Boston courthouse is certainly one of those projects that for me have made life worth living.

INDEPENDENCE PARK, PHILADELPHIA

National Constitution Center, 1998–2003
with Ian Bader, Laurie D. Olin (landscape)

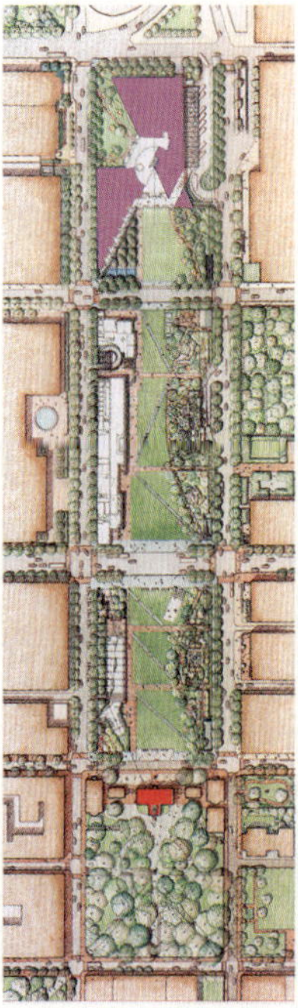

The mission statement of the National Constitution Center declares that its building is "the first-ever structure built to honor and *explain* the Constitution." But can this be literally true? Architecture has always been practiced and perceived as an art of celebration, while *explanation* is a task traditionally left to other arts that may inhabit or embellish a building. Indeed, those other arts are amply represented in the exhibitions, lectures, films, and live performances that visitors encounter within this building. Nonetheless, I believe that architecture can and must make its own contribution to *explaining* as well as honoring the Constitution.

The conceptual wellspring of our design was an understanding that the purpose of the National Constitution Center is not to enshrine that document as an object of worship but to proclaim its active engagement with the ongoing life of the people and nation it serves. Our task then was to so shape the building—its exterior forms and interior spaces—so that it can communicate to visitors a sense of that engagement while at the same time appropriately celebrating its place of honor at the northern end of the newly renovated Independence National Historical Park, facing Independence Hall at the opposite end.

Our design strategy is exemplified in the way the National Constitution Center presents itself to a visitor approaching from the south across the generous greensward of the park. The central feature of this most prominent face of the building is a monumental porch, 40 feet high and 140 feet wide, axially situated and offering a complementary gesture to the distant cupola of Independence Hall. Flanked to the east by a limestone and granite wall upon which is emblazoned the preamble to the Constitution, this porch shelters a glass wall through which the eye is drawn into a lofty skylit hall, with the

Top Lobby and grand stair, National Constitution Center. **Above** South facade. **Overleaf** Grand Hall Lobby.

flag of the United States suspended in its center and the flags of all fifty states arrayed nearby. Thus does architecture help to *honor* the Constitution.

But as the visitor crosses Arch Street and strolls up a gentle slope toward the welcoming porch, the asymmetrical composition of the building becomes increasingly apparent, suggesting that it offers more than just a static terminus to the park's north-south axis. Indeed, this asymmetry deliberately contradicts any misconception that the National Constitution Center embodies a definitive end to the story begun in Independence Hall. For upon arrival beneath the roof of the great porch, the visitor discovers a space within that is vividly transparent, inviting the eye along a diagonal path straight through the building and out to the city beyond. This dynamic spatial gesture serves to remind the visitor that our Constitution continues to shape and be shaped by the civil society for which it provides the structure of government. Thus does architecture help to *explain* the Constitution.

One country, one Constitution, one destiny
DANIEL WEBSTER
1837
The people themselves must be the ultimate makers of their own Constitution
THEODORE
1912

THE ANNENBERG CENTER
FOR EDUCATION AND OUTREACH
IOWA
1848
CALIFORNIA REPUBLIC

PARIS, CHICAGO, MADRID, NEW YORK, ISTANBUL, NEW YORK

Skyscraper as Citizen: Six Office Towers

From 1997 to 2015, I contributed annually as a guest lecturer to a course at the Harvard Graduate School of Design entitled Issues in the Practice of Architecture, a groundbreaking pedagogical initiative launched by Carl Sapers, the eminent attorney and specialist in construction law whom I had helped bring to the school during my chairmanship in the early eighties. My talk was titled "The Skyscraper as Citizen: Reflections on the Public Life of Private Buildings." Although its central topic was the saga of the Hancock Tower (page 110), this was preceded by introductory remarks that are equally appropriate here as a preamble to discussion of several more recent office towers.

> I will begin by offering a few general observations about a building type, not unjustly ill-reputed, that is always and everywhere a subject of controversy. I mean of course the tall office building, which I

propose to consider here not in functional or technical terms but rather as a presence in the city—or to state my concern more precisely, the skyscraper as citizen. I should explain, as you may not be aware of it, that this building type has been a persistent and relentlessly demanding presence in my own professional life. Indeed, there has been scarcely a day in the life of our practice when my colleagues and I have not been engaged in the design of one or more office towers. Added up, they total at least forty in all, of which about three dozen have actually been built in an almost equal number of cities across North America and around the world. I hasten to assure you that I don't intend to review all these projects here. I mention the number only to make it clear that I cannot hope to approach this topic with the cool detachment of a scholar or critic. Rather, my remarks must be understood as those of an interested, not to say implicated, party, and my attempts at self-criticism as the expression of a deeply felt ambivalence about a building type to which I have devoted perhaps too much of my life.

"Architecture," as Roland Barthes succinctly remarked, "is always dream and function, expression of a utopia and instrument of a convenience."[1] This double meaning is indeed a profound attribute of our art, but its manifestation in office towers is especially vivid, it seems to me, owing to the paradoxical situation of tall buildings in the spatial fabric of the city. To understand this, we need only observe that while the tall office building inescapably intrudes itself as a dominant presence in the public realm, it is

1 Roland Barthes, *The Eiffel Tower and Other Mythologies* (New York: Farrar, Straus and Giroux, 1979), 6.

essentially a very private building, virtually inaccessible to the general public except at street level—and since 9/11 often inaccessible even there—and housing no public function that could begin to fulfill the expectations aroused by its assertive bulk and form. Thus, however effective the office tower may be as a beacon of corporate or entrepreneurial achievement, its programmatic limitations would seem to condemn it a priori to the status of a monument without meaning and a symbol without substance—an enormous and indigestible object that is inescapably banal, exploitative, alienating, inhumane. Now, the effort to overcome this condition, to humanize the tall building and give it the demeanor of a good citizen, has preoccupied American architects for a century and a half, indeed preoccupies us still.

Yet ironically, the underlying cause of the problem—that is to say, the office tower's poverty of program—has actually proved useful in the search for remedies. For the mass of anonymous office space out of which a tall building is made—space that is isotropic, homogeneous, repetitive, and conceptually limitless—constitutes a relatively neutral and quite malleable body that architects have been able to manipulate more or less at will, shaping it into an amazing variety of forms, clothing it in every conceivable stylistic garb, and conjuring up every imaginable utopian vision that might engender at least an illusion of higher aspiration in this quintessential instrument of convenience. Thus the very vacuity that has made the tall office building so problematic has actually invited and supported a great diversity of strategies for civilizing it.

But to return to the theme of architecture's double meaning, the important point I want to make is that all of these diverse design strategies, as applied to the office tower, are virtually independent of the building's actual use, so that to a greater extent than in any other building type, dream and function are apt to be unrelated, each operating in its own realm—one public, the other private—and according to its own dictates. I would further argue that on account of this disjunction between the two levels of meaning, the tall office building is inherently eclectic and destined always to serve as a clotheshorse *par excellence* for the superimposed expression of cultural value. And it is in this sense, as an insistent and inescapably intrusive reminder of successive shifts in our priorities, our tastes, and our values, that I believe one is justified in viewing the tall office building as the preeminent monument of the late-twentieth-century city, not just in North America but around the world.

In previous chapters I have discussed the cruciform tower at Place Ville Marie (1956–62) in Montreal, John Hancock Tower (1967–76) in Boston, and Fountain Place Tower (1982–86) in Dallas. Among the dozen or so tall building projects that punctuated my first half-century of practice, these three were especially instrumental in shaping as well as embodying my evolving sensibility and intentions as an architect. Two of the three, the Montreal and Dallas towers, may be classified as formally *autonomous*: that is to say, the posture of each as a work of architecture is principally determined by imaginative interpretation of the *internal* systemic disciplines—spatial, circulatory, structural, mechanical—that govern the design of every tall office building. Owing to the often

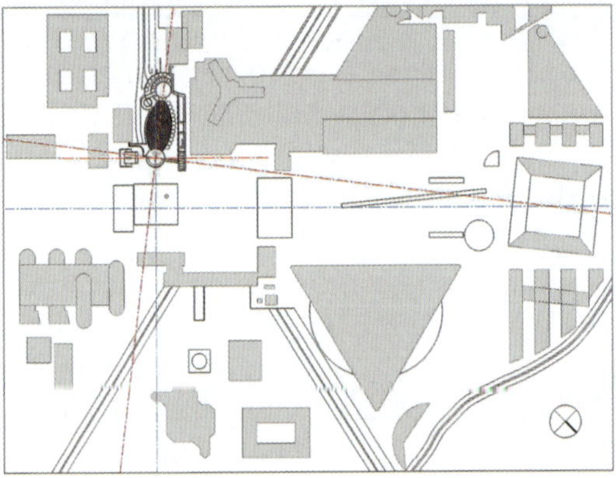

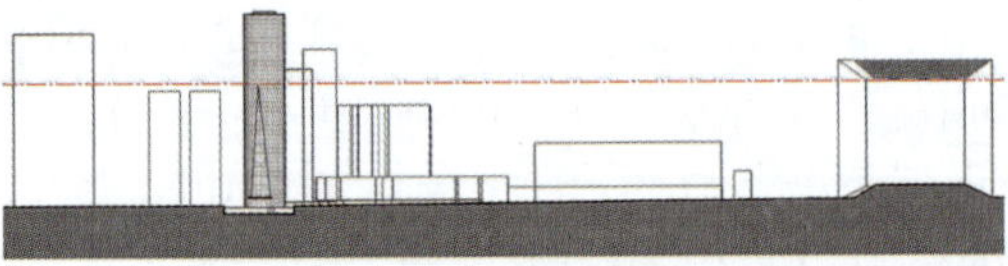

Top Left and Right Tour EDF at La Défense.
Above Site plan and elevation showing axial relationship to Grande Arche. **Overleaf** Entrance canopy and plaza.

entirely unchallenged hegemony of such disciplines, the majority of tall office buildings around the world may be so classified. By contrast, the Hancock Tower may be classified as formally *contingent*: that is to say, its posture, while accommodating internal systemic imperatives, is principally determined by imaginative response to particular *external* circumstances in its urban setting. Although the distinction here made between autonomous and contingent postures seems to me both self-evident and profoundly significant, I have been astonished to discover how little understood it is among my colleagues in the profession and how little interest it has aroused even when understood. For me, however, this distinction has been a persistently recurring preoccupation ever since I first confronted what I felt to be a moral obligation to devise a radically contingent posture for the tower in Copley Square. Among the six office towers to be considered here—all completed since the turn of the century—the postures of those in Chicago, Madrid, and Istanbul may be classed as autonomous, while the Paris tower and both New York towers may be classed as contingent.

The first of the contingent towers, **Tour EDF** (1996–2001, with Michael D. Flynn), stands on a prominent site close to the statue of La Défense de Paris and fronting on a broad pedestrian promenade that leads to the nearby Grande Arche, marking the western end of the great urban axis that begins eight kilometers to the east in the courtyard of the Louvre. The distinctive form of this forty-story office tower has its origin in my belief that the privilege of building on this key site carries with it a corollary obligation to enrich the public realm of La Défense. To this end, we sought to transform the tower from an autonomous into a contingent presence by modifying its symmetrical form, shaped by the intersection of two

quarter-circles, in such a way as to make it responsive to the specific circumstances of its urban context. The tower's orientation is canted to acknowledge a seven-degree shift introduced by the skewed axis of the Grande Arche. Its prow, located precisely on the centerline of the Grande Arche, is cut away so that it does not stand aloof but rather makes an engaging gesture toward the Parvis de La Défense, celebrating the monument in front of which it stands. At the base of this conical incision, a circular marquise, twenty meters in diameter, creates a gathering place where passersby are invited to pause and enjoy the axial view of the Grande Arche from a sheltered vantage point beneath the canopy of stainless steel and glass. Thus does this entirely private building—it serves as headquarters for Electricité de France—become the occasion for shaping a memorable public space.

Although the lozenge-shaped plan of **71 South Wacker** (2001–05, with Peter Schaudt, landscape), located at the western edge of Chicago's Loop, is typologically similar to that of Tour EDF, its emphatically autonomous posture makes no gesture to anything in its surroundings. Instead, this forty-eight-story tower is shaped in response to the very precisely defined internal requirements of the law firm that was its prospective major tenant. The firm's insistence that all partners' offices be identical relieved us of the normal corporate requirement for hierarchical corner offices and invited the windowless splayed end walls that give the tower its distinctive identity and desired vertical emphasis. Careful appraisal of the long, narrow site suggested two important benefits to be gained from curving the tower's major faces: first, the curved profile opens up diagonal views from the interior past neighboring towers hemming it in on both sides; and second, at street level the curved

Top 71 South Wacker.

Above Block-long garden viewed from above.

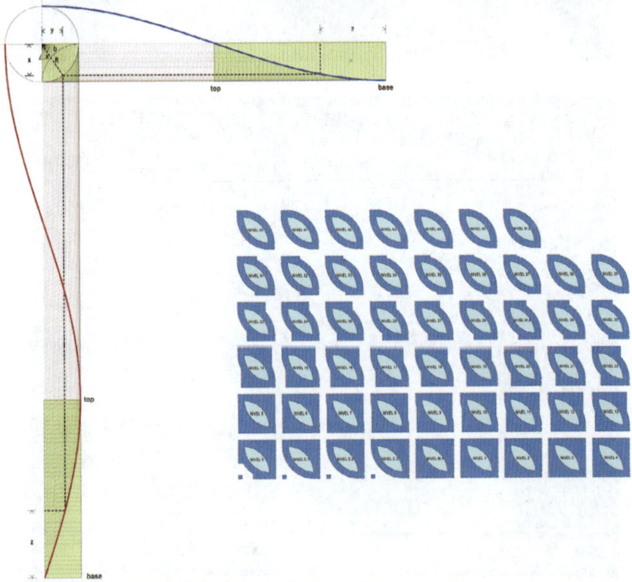

Top Torre Espacio as seen from different viewpoints.
Above Diagram illustrating evolution of floor plans from base to crown, as determined by cosine curve.

profile creates an important public amenity in the form of a garden stretching along the entire block-front on Monroe Street. Thus even this rigorously autonomous tower acknowledges its contingency on the shape of its site and the character of its urban setting.

In contrast to the dense urban fabric that encases 71 South Wacker, **Torre Espacio** (2001–08, with José Bruguera) is the northernmost of four widely spaced towers, each designed by a different architect for a different developer, that rose more or less simultaneously on a prominent site at the northern end of the Paseo de la Castellana in Madrid. Here the adjacency to other towers in an otherwise vacuous urban context advocated an autonomous posture, and the client's desire for a memorable image invited a metamorphic design strategy, wherein the tower's form changes continuously as it rises in accordance with preestablished geometric parameters. Like the earlier tower in Dallas, this fifty-story building presents varied profiles when seen from different points of view. But in this case, owing to the slenderness of the tower and its curvature in both plan and section, its gesture is at once more vigorous and more graceful—if perhaps not as instantly recognizable—than that in Dallas. Torre Espacio evolves from a square in plan at its base to a curved lozenge, formed by the intersection of two quarter-circles, at its crown. The geometric mechanism—or in today's parlance, the parametric function—for accomplishing this evolution in a constructible form is a cosine curve that defines and rationalizes the points of intersection between the two curved surfaces, thus facilitating fabrication and assembly of the curtain wall. The size and shape of each office floor is different from every other—a feature unacceptable to most American developers but embraced with enthusiasm by our client in Madrid, who declared it to

be "very Latin!" An important characteristic of the cosine curve is that its rate of curvature is not constant but rather decreases gradually as it rises from base to crown. This gives the resulting tower form its distinctive sense of lift, almost as if it were a living organism that had sprung from the earth on which it stands.

Sharply contrasting with the self-referential autonomy of Torre Espacio is the radically contingent posture of **200 West Street** (2004–10, with Michael D. Flynn, Jay L. Berman; Ken Smith, landscape; Preston Scott Cohen, canopy), a forty-five-story tower occupying a large but oddly shaped site catercorner from New York's One World Trade Center. This massive office building was built to house the programmatically complex global headquarters of Goldman Sachs. Here a mandated setback combined with other constraints had conspired to produce an overbearing and ungainly zoning envelope. Seeking to animate this lifeless mass without depriving our client of the very large floor plates it required, we noticed that Broadway and Vesey Street define one urban grid and West and Murray Streets another, with both grids intersecting to form the boundaries of the building site. We then seized on this circumstance to generate the formal articulations that enliven the building volume on its eastern side. These, combined with the shaping of its western face into a sweeping curve, are the modest but nonetheless effective means by which this two-million-square-foot building acquires a presence that is palpably responsive to its specific place in the urban fabric of Lower Manhattan. And it should be noted that in doing so, 200 West Street emulates and affirms a familial bond with its charming neighbor just across the street, Ralph Walker's Barclay-Vesey Building of 1927. I invite those who remain skeptical of my preoccupation with posture

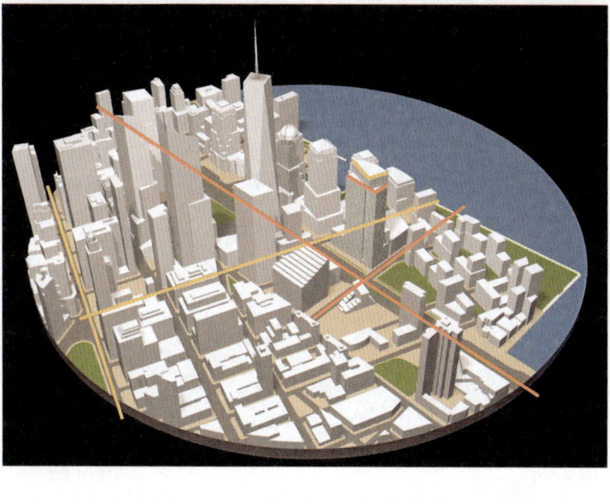

Top Left 200 West Street. **Top Right** Ralph Walker, Barclay-Vesey Building, 1927. **Above** Model of Lower Manhattan showing intersecting street grids.

Top Soyak Kristalkule Finansbank Headquarters as seen from different viewpoints. **Above** Sky garden in crown.

to notice that the contingent postures adopted by 200 West Street and Barclay-Vesey have enabled both buildings to assert their civic identities in works of architecture that joyously and effortlessly hold their own in the presence of their gigantic neighbor, the emphatically autonomous One World Trade Center.

Soyak Kristalkule Finansbank Headquarters (2005–14, with José Bruguera) rises on a prominent site in Istanbul's newly developed central business district, nine kilometers from the historic center in the Golden Horn. In this spatially disordered and architecturally inchoate urban scene, which did not invite a contingent response, the

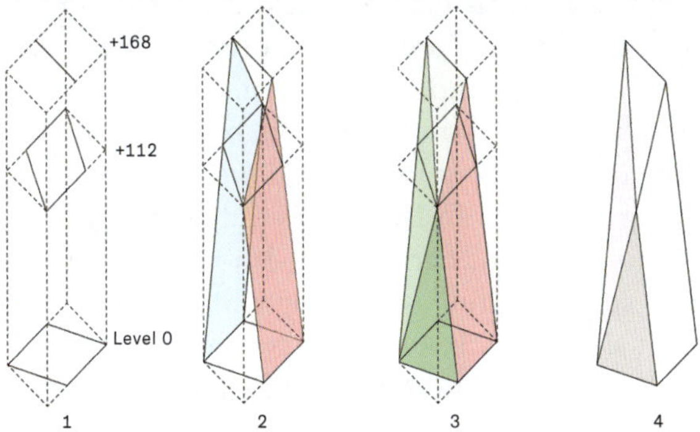

autonomous posture of this thirty-five-story tower is the product of a rigorously disciplined subtractive process governed by precise geometric parameters applied to an imagined orthogonal volume measuring 50.4 meters by 33.6 meters in plan and 168 meters in height. In step one, three horizontal figures are inserted into the volume: a parallelogram at level zero, a reverse parallelogram at level 112, and a line bisecting the top at level 168. In step two, trapezoidal surfaces are inscribed in the two long vertical sides of the volume, connecting the orthogonal edges of the two parallelograms to the line at the top. In step three, six sloping triangular surfaces, three on each side, are formed within the orthogonal volume by the intersection of planes extending along the sloped edges of the two vertical surfaces: upward from the diagonal edges of the parallelogram at level zero, upward and downward from the diagonal edges of the parallelogram at level 112, and downward from the line at level 168. In step four, the imagined orthogonal volume and inscribed figures are removed, revealing the form of the tower as defined by steps one, two, and three. Like its predecessors in Dallas and Madrid, this metamorphic tower presents radically different appearances when seen from different points of view. At its apex, Soyak Kristalkule dissolves into a line from which, by means of an operable hatch, the window-washing equipment from time to time emerges like a jack-in-the-box to surprise the onlooker below.

Very different from the chaotic urban scene surrounding the tower in Istanbul is the highly ordered context of 7 **Bryant Park** (2010–16, with Yvonne Szeto), a thirty-story building occupying a block-long site on the west side of Sixth Avenue between Thirty-Ninth and Fortieth Streets in Midtown Manhattan. Although a zoning-mandated setback at the tenth-floor level would seem to mark this as an unexceptional Manhattan office building, its catercorner relationship to Bryant Park invited an articulation of the otherwise ordinary volume with the aim of enabling the building to speak to the park. This was accomplished by two conical incisions—one pointing up, the other down, with their apexes touching at the setback level—that together animate the building volume while celebrating its specific place in the city. As at Tour EDF in Paris, a circular canopy at the base of the lower cone further dramatizes the tower's gesture while providing a sheltered gathering place

Top 7 Bryant Park at dusk, with Empire State Building at left. **Above** Corner detail. **Overleaf** Tower as seen from Bryant Park.

where pedestrians are invited to pause and admire one of New York City's most treasured landscapes.

Varied as they are in character and setting, all six of the buildings discussed herein fall within a definition of architecture once proposed by the philosopher and architect manqué Ludwig Wittgenstein. "Architecture," he wrote, "is a *gesture*. Not every purposive movement of the human body is a gesture. Just as little as every functional building is architecture."[2] Wittgenstein's observation is especially relevant, in my view, to the design of tall buildings. For is it not, in the end, the quality of its *gesture* that most concerns us when we speak of the skyscraper as citizen? But an affirmative answer to this question begs another: which type of posture—autonomous or contingent—is likely to foster the most satisfying gesture in a tall building? For me the answer is not in doubt: however memorable an autonomous presence may be, the gesture fostered by a contingent posture is more likely to contribute to a meaningful built environment; a contingent tower's gesture is not self-referential but respects and responds to the specific character of the urban setting in which it is embedded. And that is my definition of good citizenship.

2 Ludwig Wittgenstein, *Culture and Value*, 2nd ed. (Oxford: Blackwell, 1998), 49.

THE EVENTS OF 9/11

Remarks at a Meeting Convened by the Architectural League of New York, Great Hall at The Cooper Union September 25, 2001

The New York Times

Sunday, August 31, 2003

Arts & Leisure

Section 2

PICTURING THE NEW GROUND ZERO

Finding Comfort in the Safety of Names

Lists of the Dead Have Practically Become a Requirement of Memorials. But Really, What's in a Name?

Every moment in the life of a city is a moment appealing simultaneously to three realms of consciousness: a memory of the past, a preoccupation with the present, a dream of the future. In the ongoing and inescapably contentious discourse among these three realms—a discourse that defines the very essence of human civilization—the city is both the principal arena of debate and the cumulative, absolutely authentic, minutely accurate record of its outcome. This is why we can confidently affirm that despite all the miracles wrought by our sciences, the city remains, in the words of Claude Lévi-Strauss, "*the* human invention, *par excellence*."[1]

Two weeks ago, a moment in the life of *this* city was shattered by acts of violence that have changed all of our lives in ways more profound than we can yet fully comprehend. As we in the design professions struggle to come to terms with the memory of horror beyond belief, we must take care not to neglect, in our necessary preoccupation with the immediate tasks of healing, our larger obligation to dream a dream. For is this not in fact the very essence of our art? Architecture tells us not what human beings *were* at any time or place, but what they *dreamed*. Now, in the aftermath of tragedy, we are urgently summoned to dream *our* dream.

1 Claude Lévi-Strauss, *Tristes Tropiques*, trans. John Russell (New York: Criterion Books, 1961), 127.

Opposite Ellsworth Kelly, *Ground Zero*, 2003.

LOWER MANHATTAN, NEW YORK CITY

Seven Stems, 2002
with Guy Nordenson

In the summer of 2002, Herbert Muschamp asked the engineer Guy Nordenson to envision a replacement for the telecommunications and broadcast tower that had been lost in the destruction of the World Trade Center. Guy invited me to collaborate with him in giving form to his structural concept, and our design proposal was published in a special issue of the *New York Times Magazine* commemorating the first anniversary of 9/11. The aspect of this project that both Guy and I found most engaging was the opportunity it offered to rethink the gesture of a very tall structure. Until now, such structures have always been conceived as compact vertical shafts terminating in a single apex, even when sometimes rising from multiple bases, as in the Eiffel Tower, for example. Such structures are inherently autonomous, hierarchical, and self-referential. In proposing this tower, intended to be the world's tallest man-made structure, for New York City, we shaped it in a way that sends a different signal—expressing interdependence rather than autonomy, equality rather than hierarchy, and openness rather than exclusivity.

Seven Stems, as we call our project, is imagined to rise from a small plaza occupying less than half an acre of ground just south of the New York Stock Exchange

NYC

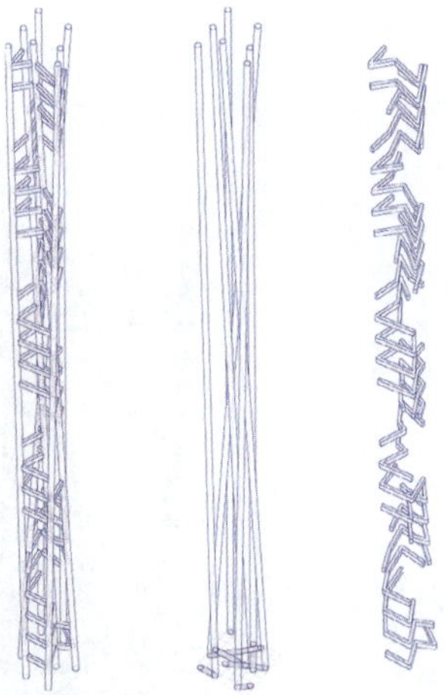

Top Left Axonometric views of tower, stems, and outriggers. **Top Right** Model detail. **Middle** Photomontage of Seven Stems as seen from Brooklyn. **Bottom** Plans of tower's thirty levels.

building in the heart of Lower Manhattan. The cylindrical stems, each fourteen feet in diameter and 2,100 feet high, are set in a loosely ordered arrangement within a square measuring 140 feet on each side. All but one of the stems tilt slightly in various directions within the underlying square, so that their relationships to one another change as they rise. At vertical intervals of seventy feet, outrigger beams connect the stems so as to form a variety of patterns but without creating a closed figure at any one level. The structure thus conceived is highly efficient yet entirely nonhierarchical: it sets in motion a conversation among equals wherein no one voice overrides any other, thus embodying a principle of civil discourse that we believe to be appropriate, indeed arguably necessary, at this time and in that place.

Shortly after the publication of Seven Stems, we issued the following supplementary statement.

> We have been asked to explain why our proposed telecommunications and broadcast tower is composed of seven stems. The primary reasons for this decision are: (1) Seven is a prime number. (2) Experimental data show that the human mind can normally absorb no more than seven objects at a glance, and that short-term memory normally includes seven items. (3) Personal experience leads us to believe that seven is the maximum number of persons who can participate fruitfully in a single conversation. (4) On the surface of the earth there are said to be seven seas and seven continents—the latter already celebrated in New York Harbor by the seven points in the crown of the Statue of Liberty.

ENDS AND MEANS, THEN AND NOW

Excerpt from the Kassler Lecture
Princeton University School of Architecture
April 24, 2002

In addressing architects of *your* generation, an architect of *my* generation faces two difficulties. First, he—or in my generation only very rarely she—has a lot of explaining to do, if he wants to account for his inevitably flawed performance during half a century or more of professional practice. Second, and perhaps even more daunting, he is likely to find his audience not much engaged by such explanations. For we architects, of whatever generation, are inclined to think associatively and anecdotally—habits of mind that disincline us to take an interest in discussions of past events that may not seem directly relevant to matters preoccupying us in the present. Yet I do believe that something worthwhile can be communicated to young architects by someone fully two generations their elder, not necessarily, or even preferably, through the customary presentation of "recent and current work" but rather through a more reflective account that may reveal how the sensibility of an architect in practice evolves over time, shaped by and perhaps occasionally itself shaping the stream of history that inescapably engulfs it. To be sure, the effect of such an account may be more cautionary than inspirational, but I will be perfectly satisfied if you learn from me at least something useful about how you may *not* wish to conduct your professional lives.

I referred a moment ago to the stream of history, and I want to begin this talk—which has two distinct though perhaps not entirely unrelated parts—by dipping into that stream to pluck out a pair of artifacts in which we may discover some sense of shared enterprise, I hope serving to bridge as well as illuminate the gulf between your generation and mine. One of these artifacts conveniently fell into my hands at the meeting of this school's advisory council last December, when I was presented with a copy of *306090*, issue number 01. This exceptionally engaging document, subtitled *A Journal of Emergent Architecture and Design*, caused me to recall the excitement I felt back in 1948 upon receiving the first postwar issue of *Task*, a journal then edited by students at the Harvard Graduate School of Design. I was doubly thrilled on that earlier occasion because I had contributed to *Task* as both an editorial assistant and an author.

Now, one never forgets one's first published work, however forgettable it may be, and this no doubt explains the twinge of nostalgia accompanying the other pleasures that I found in turning the pages of *306090*. As it happened, at the same advisory council meeting, I also learned of Beatriz Colomina's initiative in launching the Center for Media and Modernity here at Princeton, and this provoked me to wonder whether a comparison of these two publications, *Task* and *306090*, might somehow prove relevant, even if only marginally, to the fascinating field of inquiry that Beatriz and her colleagues have opened up to exploration. Thus inspired, I have set them here side by side, and I propose to take a brief look at both, with the aim of seeing what they can tell us about ends and means, then and now. In this way, you and I, youth and old age, may gain some sense of how we are joined as well as separated by the turbulent stream of history.

Even a cursory glance at the front covers and spines tells us that these are the products of very different eras and very different intentions, reflecting very different values. We will return to these covers later on, but for the moment I would simply observe that the only thing they have in common, aside from a compact format of similar size and thickness, is the word "architecture." We already know, then, even before we turn a page, that however different their perspectives may be, the editors of both publications believe that their purposes include, inter alia, discussion of the particular manifestation of human culture that the OED defines as "the art and science of designing structures for human use."

A closer look at the spine of *Task* hints strongly at what we'll find inside: this journal is about *planning* as well as *architecture*, and the order of the words is significant. It implies what the contents amply confirm: that its editors conceive of planning as the fundamental discipline governing the design of human settlements, and that the value of architecture derives mainly from its capacity to give form to intentions defined by planning. Opening now to the masthead and table of contents, the source of this bias becomes immediately apparent when you understand that the editor and both associate editors of *Task* were indeed students in the department of city and regional planning at the Graduate School of Design. Some of you will no doubt recognize the name of Martin Meyerson, who subsequently went on to a distinguished academic

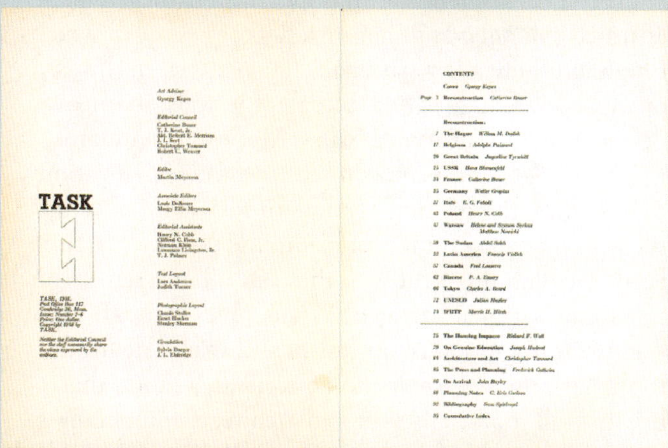

Top Cover of *Task*, issue number 7/8, designed by György Kepes.

Above Masthead and table of contents.

career, culminating in his presidency at the University of Pennsylvania.

What we see listed in the table of contents tells us exactly what we get in this issue of *Task*: that is to say, a few broadly thematic essays appended to a series of articles devoted to purportedly objective reporting of postwar reconstruction in cities and countries around the world. I say "purportedly," because the fact is that *Task* embodied in its editorial posture, in most of its contents, and indeed in its very title, a powerful ideological agenda. This was the proposition that planning and architecture are interdependent disciplines jointly dedicated to providing human societies with adequate shelter in well-planned communities conducive to the development of human culture. The eminent housing specialist Catherine Bauer affirmed this agenda in her introductory essay, of which I highlight here a key passage. "The material in this issue of *Task* is extremely varied, but all of it deals, in one way or another, with universal issues. Minimum standards, neighborhood norms, new towns and the revivification of old cities, the relation of modern social and physical science to architectural expression, the political dynamics of the planning process—these are all questions which transcend national barriers." What comes through in this statement is a mood of optimism and shared dedication to the task then perceived to be at hand, a mood that briefly—all too briefly—united architects and planners around the world in the years just following World War II.

A glimpse of the drawings and photographs that accompanied some of the articles accurately conveys the aspirations embodied in their texts. As you can see, the focus was on ambitious, often visionary planning accompanied by markedly less ambitious architecture, although Le Corbusier's as-yet-unbuilt Unité d'Habitation does make a cameo appearance in model form. And it should also be noted that although *Task* is clearly biased toward planning and housing, with architecture seen as servant rather than master, it nonetheless includes Joseph Hudnut's passionate plea for the humanities as meriting precedence over the sciences in education, and Christopher Tunnard's equally passionate plea for architecture as an art in which aesthetics must take precedence over functional and technical considerations.

This leads me to note a curious fact about this issue of *Task*: although it was edited and produced by Harvard students, its authors were, with one exception, distinguished practitioners in their respective fields, including the architect Walter Gropius, the planner Jacqueline Tyrwhitt, the historian Charles Beard, and the scientist Julian Huxley. In the entire book there is only one article written by a student, and it is mine, wherein I report my findings during a two-week visit to Poland in August of 1947. "The people of Poland," I wrote, "have undertaken a bold experiment in democratic planning. Through careful correlation of immediate reconstruction work with long-range schemes for redevelopment, Polish planners hope to establish the social, economic, and physical framework for a free and prosperous national life." These words, proclaiming the boundlessly uncritical enthusiasm of a twenty-one-year-old, were all too soon rendered moot when events tragically canceled the Polish experiment before it had even begun to bear fruit. Only months after my article appeared, Poland was effectively annexed by the Soviet Union, its government was taken over by hard-line Stalinists, and the dream of one world dedicated to the arts of peace, so eloquently expressed by Catherine Bauer at the conclusion of her essay, was obliterated by the onset of the Cold War.

Turning now to *306090*, we find in its subtitle clues to its editorial posture as telling as those found in the subtitle of *Task*. The key word here is "emergent," applied as a modifier to "architecture and design." It is worth noting that "planning" is a word to be seen neither on the cover nor, so far as I have been able to discern, anywhere else in the pages of *306090*.

Opening to the masthead and table of contents, we see clear evidence of the editors' insistence on both the randomness and the complex interrelatedness of their notably heterogeneous offerings—an affirmation that would have seemed both unnecessary and irrelevant to the editors of *Task*, whose table of contents offers the reader a simple listing of reports presented as contributions to a single overarching theme.

Moving on to the editors' introduction, we discover in its very first paragraph that the social agenda evidenced in *Task* has been supplanted here by a *cultural* agenda, the centerpiece of which is the concept of "multidisciplinary practices crossing the conventional boundaries of creative impulse." Confirmation of this agenda is abundantly evident in the selection of student work, as exemplified by the thesis project of Janette Kim and in the projects by young professionals, of which my own favorite is the delightful In-Door house by the group practicing under the acronym L.E.FT. Interlaced with these presentations is the e-mail correspondence between students that runs across the bottom of many pages, offering a variety of pithy comments and raising some interesting questions about the current state of theory and practice.

Yet another editorial strategy for making connections is seen in the cross-referencing that occurs in the right-hand margin of the opening spread for each article, in this case linking Alexander Briseno's interesting essay on "loosely defined order" to the work of Elena Bresciani that precedes it and the interview with Philip Nobel that follows.

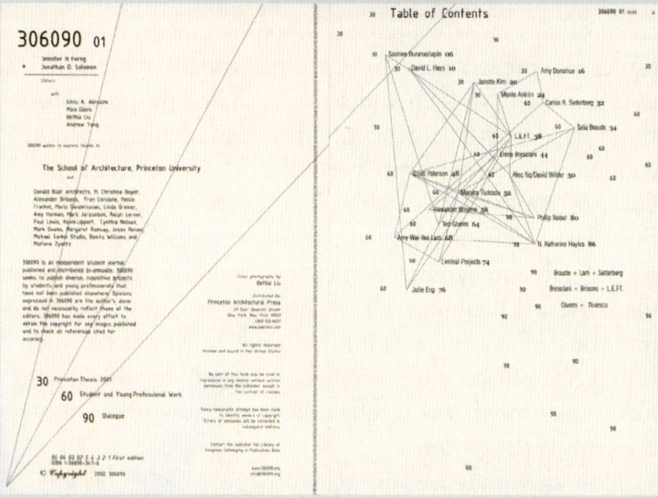

Top Cover of *306090*, issue number 01.

Above Masthead and table of contents.

I confess that I was not much engaged by the latter, which is full of yesterday's news about architectural education, together with old-hat truisms delivered in words that would have been more persuasive had they been less patronizing.

But the concluding interview with Katherine Hayles, dealing with the impact of media technology on the processes and products of design, is both informative and thought-provoking. I'm sure it is no accident that the editors chose to bring issue 01 to a close with her quote from Tom Stoppard's *Arcadia*: "It's the best time to be alive, when everything we thought we knew is wrong."

Returning now to the two covers, each seems perfectly emblematic of what we have found within. The cover of *Task*, with its powerful graphic design by György Kepes, eloquently proclaims not just the thematic content but the optimism and sense of shared purpose, albeit short-lived, that energized planners and architects worldwide in the aftermath of World War II. Conversely, the cover of *306090*, while also graphically compelling, is as mystifying in its message as the other is clear. By dint of considerable research, aided by a network of spies, I have discovered the subject of the photograph, but I have no intention of sharing this information. I will only say that it makes no discernible reference to anything within, and I must assume that this reflects a deliberate intention on the part of the editors.

How then may we summarize a comparative review of these two publications? First, I would define the differences as follows. Whereas the editorial mode of *Task* is reportorial and objective, that of *306090* is speculative and subjective. Whereas *Task* is focused on serving needs, *306090* is focused on exploring possibilities. Whereas *Task*'s outlook is comprehensive, that of *306090* is anecdotal. *Task* is socially charged, whereas *306090* is culturally charged. The tone of *Task* is authoritative and didactic, whereas that of *306090* is skeptical and conversational. *Task* sees the world as ordered, determinate, and actual, whereas *306090* sees it as random, indeterminate, and virtual.

While these differences are striking, they should not blind us to a few equally striking similarities. Both publications proclaim a global outlook linked to aspirations that are global in scope. In 1948 this global outlook was a groundbreaking innovation; today we take it for granted. Both publications proclaim their passionate commitment to the task of shaping human settlements, however differently they may interpret the meaning and purpose of that task. Both are ahistorical, in the sense that they largely neglect historical studies as a resource that could be relevant or useful in addressing contemporary problems. It strikes me that this neglect is even less justifiable today than it was in 1948, especially here at Princeton, with its uniquely strong dual role as a center of both design education and advanced scholarly research.

This observation leads me to conclude my overview with a pair of questions. Could not you, the editors of *306090*, find some way to engage doctoral students in your splendid journalistic enterprise? And conversely, could not you, the doctoral students, offer some substantive response to the editorial initiative of your colleagues in the master's degree program? It seems to me that there is an opportunity here that ought not to be missed—an opportunity to demonstrate the very great importance of a vigorous discourse, nourished in this school more fruitfully perhaps than in any other, between the history, theory, and practice of architecture.

JAMES INGO FREED

Introductory Remarks at a Memorial Tribute
American Academy of Arts and Letters
New York City, February 15, 2006

Henry N. Cobb

Good afternoon. Thank you for joining us on this occasion, when we gather to remember and celebrate the life of James Ingo Freed.

As one of Jim's partners, I was privileged to keep company with him for almost half a century. On the twentieth of February, 1956, having completed his military service and a subsequent brief stint working for Mies van der Rohe on the Seagram Building, Jim joined the still-fledgling practice that had been launched six years earlier by I. M. Pei under the auspices of William Zeckendorf, Sr. Four decades later, in his interview for the Chicago Art Institute's oral history project, Jim recalled that our group seemed to him then "like merry pranksters. I felt immediately that I was not in a very pure place architecturally…[in part] because I took offense at the stair rail running down the circular staircase in Zeckendorf's office." Now, as the hapless designer of that very same staircase, I can attest that it certainly merited his disapproval, revealing as it all too clearly did that its Harvard-trained author entirely lacked the tectonic rigor, instilled by five years at IIT, that Jim Freed would immediately and forcefully bring to our practice. Later on it would be precisely those confining Miesian strictures that he would turn away from and then set out to transcend—an adventure movingly recorded in the numberless sketchbooks that together constitute nothing less than a graphic autobiography spanning the last thirty years of Jim's life.

But this thumbnail history begs a question: Inasmuch as partnerships between autonomous designers, though surely not unheard of, rarely endure for more than a few years, what then accounts for the unusual staying power of this particular partnership—Pei, Cobb, and Freed—so that it could serve as the vehicle for Jim's entire

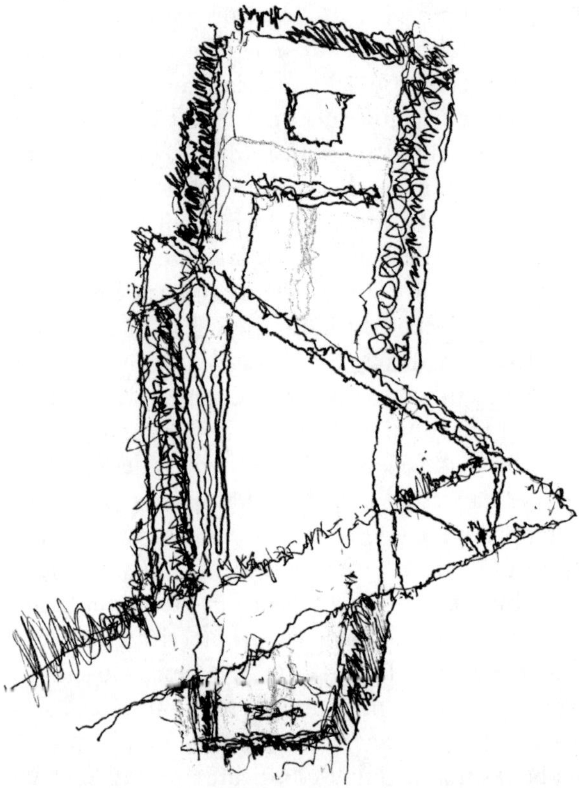

Above James Ingo Freed, sketch plan for United States Air Force Memorial, Washington, D.C., circa 2002. **Page 488** James Ingo Freed at Los Angeles Convention Center, 1993.

professional life? In retrospect, it seems clear that our long association was fostered and sustained by shared values that are certainly prerequisite to any fruitful collaboration, and by equally essential differences of sensibility that made every encounter between us interesting, challenging, and fun. Yes, we shared the ambition to practice architecture at an urban scale; we shared a desire to tackle what Jim called "difficult public buildings"; and we shared a commitment to unstinting care for the expressive qualities of material and detail. Yet these shared values coexisted with profound differences in temperament and habit of mind—differences that, by mutual agreement, we chose not to suppress but rather to accept, indeed to celebrate, as our practice matured.

And this brings me back to Jim's sketchbooks. My colleagues and I believe these to be so distinctive and so central to his persona that we have decided to exhibit a few of them on this occasion, together with some photocopies of pages from the nearly one hundred similar books already consigned to the Freed archive at the Library of Congress.

In speaking about his sketches, Jim described them as "seeping out like steam from a pressure cooker…not intended to hold together, least of all as public documents…[but to] be seen as what they are: an ongoing open dialogue with myself." And what a fascinating dialogue it is! But that is not all. Throughout his difficult last years, Jim continued indefatigably to fill new sketchbooks, giving voice to a soul that against all odds never ceased—if I may borrow a trope from Yeats—to "clap its hands and sing, and louder sing for every tatter in its mortal dress," while disclosing to us, line by trembling line, unpremeditated "monuments of its own magnificence."

GARIBALDI REPUBBLICA, MILAN

Palazzo Lombardia, 2004–13
with Simon Hsu, José Bruguera, Matteo Milani

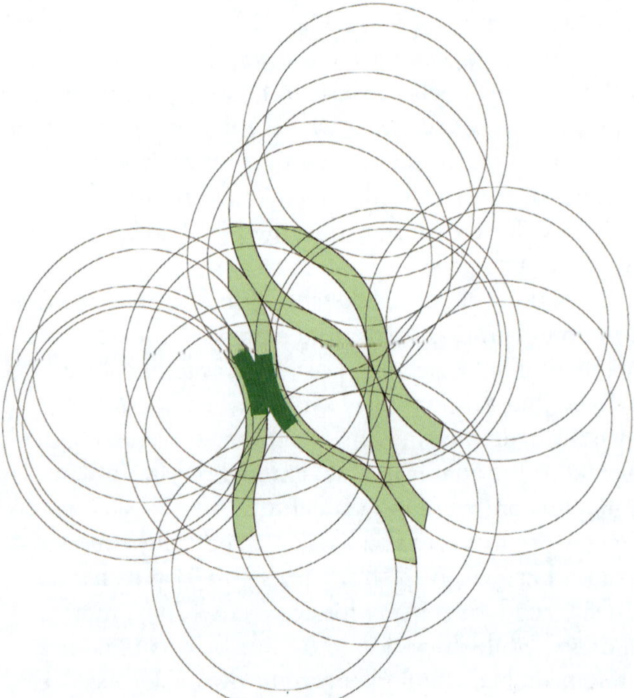

The site of Palazzo Lombardia is located some distance from the city's historic center, in a long-neglected district that is nonetheless remarkably well served by public transport and therefore well suited to the current program of sustainable urban regeneration in which Palazzo Lombardia plays a central role. The rather disordered arrangement of neighboring residential buildings is the natural result of a confluence of unrelated street grids, with none achieving clear primacy. The challenge, then, was to envision on this oddly shaped urban site a work of architecture that could provide nearly 90,000 square meters of floor area above grade, while also shaping attractive public spaces and fitting comfortably into a neighborhood of mid-rise buildings.

We began by imagining a podium structure comprising sinuous interweaving strands of linear office space, seven to nine stories high, whose modest scale relates well to the adjoining residential neighborhood, while their curvilinear forms make reference, here in the heart of the city, to the mountains, valleys, and rivers of Lombardy. Although seemingly random, these strands are actually the highly disciplined products of a geometric order made up of twenty-two circles arranged to form eleven identical intersecting rings. Fragmentary arcs embedded in two of these intersecting rings then rise to form a slender bifurcated tower. At a height of 161 meters, the tower contributes an emblematic presence on the skyline that is explicitly complementary to the neighboring Pirelli Tower, heretofore the tallest building in Italy. Whereas the form of Gio Ponti's great work is singular, convex, and closed, the new tower engages it in conversation with a form that is dual, concave, and open. While the former meets the ground as a solid shaft, the latter virtually dissolves into the curvilinear strands of the podium below.

The upper floors of this tower shaped by intersecting arcs comfortably house the offices and reception room of the president and other senior executives of the Lombardy regional government, while its lower floors, just above the podium, are dedicated to conference and reception rooms. Nine floors above the street, a major transition occurs, from the exceptionally small tower floor plate of just 1,120 square meters to the podium floor plate of 12,500 square meters—surely among the largest of any office building in the world—where we see now that the interweaving strands are responsive not only to the urban condition of the site but also to our client's need for space that is exceptionally flexible and hence readily adaptable to the evolving organizational structure of the relatively new regional government it houses.

The end walls of the podium are clad in stone so as to fit in harmoniously with neighboring residential buildings. I am especially fond of the stone employed in these walls, which is called Ceppo. It is quarried only in the Lombardy region and can be seen in many notable Milanese buildings, such as Muzio's Ca' Brutta and Portaluppi's Villa Necchi.

Within the intersecting strands of the podium, the fourteen-meter-wide office floors are consistently laid out with smaller private offices along the concave sides and larger group workplaces along the convex sides. At each point of inflection in the curvilinear strands, a spiral stair facilitates circulation between floors, and at each point of contact between two strands, there is an entry lobby flanked by elevators and service spaces. In addition to providing clear and convenient points of access for staff and the general public, these circulatory elements also create almost limitless flexibility for rearrangement of government departments over the life of the building.

Top Left Tower at Palazzo Lombardia. **Top Right** Gio Ponti, Pirelli Tower, 1960. **Above** Site plan showing high-rise and low-rise components, with Pirelli tower in red.

Above View from Viale Francesco Restelli showing Ceppo-clad street-walls. **Overleaf** Piazza Città di Lombardia.

The interweaving strands of the podium office floors shape a variety of open spaces before terminating in the stone end walls that dramatize the encounter between those strands and the surrounding city streets. It is also worth noting that our design concept made it possible for a holdout apartment house to remain in place without compromising the functional and architectural integrity of Palazzo Lombardia.

In terms of its influence on the architecture of Palazzo Lombardia, by far the most significant of its many sustainable features is the active climate wall enclosing the curvilinear faces of office floors in both podium and tower. The one-meter-wide cavity between the inner and outer layers of glass houses retractable vertical blinds that rotate to provide shade from the sun while maximizing transparency of the building envelope. Air is drawn from the interior into this cavity, from which it is then recirculated with the addition of fresh air—a system that provides exceptionally effective and energy-efficient climate control for the office spaces and their occupants in all seasons.

Exemplary as it is of green building practices, Palazzo Lombardia equally embodies the regional government's commitment to *social* as well as ecological sustainability in contemporary urban development. To fulfill this commitment, a central public open space—Piazza Città di Lombardia—is sheltered by a transparent ETFE roof so as to be habitable in all weather and all seasons. This major gathering place, made memorable by the curvilinear walls that enclose it, is open at ground level in all directions to the surrounding city, from which it invites entry through generous landscaped passages shaped by the curvilinear strands of the podium. Complementing this permeability, the ground floor of the building is enlivened with shops, restaurants, galleries, and a large

Protocollo →

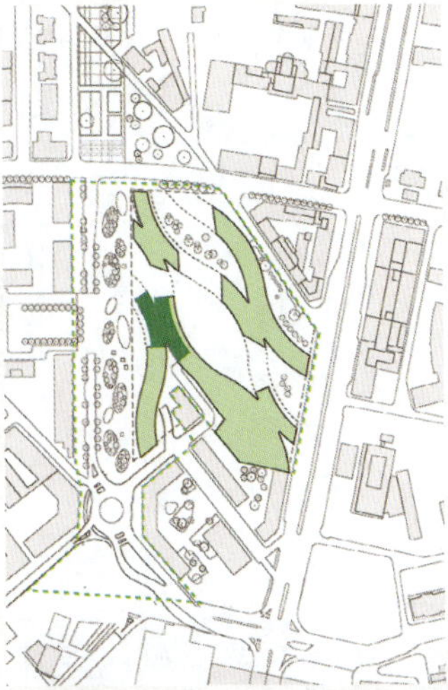

Top Left Ground-floor plan. **Top Right** Palazzo Lombardia in urban context. **Above** Piazza Città di Lombardia. **Opposite** Piazza at night.

auditorium. The piazza, which is open twenty-four hours a day, has already proved hospitable to a great variety of activities—be they ceremonial, celebratory, athletic, promotional, cultural, or simply casual.

Finally, if we now place the ground-floor plan of Palazzo Lombardia into its larger urban context, we can see how the concept of interweaving strands has sponsored a formally coherent transition from tower above to podium below and thence to the sequence of street-level open spaces that join the central piazza seamlessly to the city around it. The transfiguration thus accomplished, from emblematic object on the skyline to emblematic space at street level, is the most important contribution offered by Palazzo Lombardia to the advancement of critical thinking about tall buildings in the urban habitat. And although its geometric order is more fluid, its language more mature, and its intervention in the city more gracious, Palazzo Lombardia may nonetheless correctly be seen as a late-career manifestation of the same urbanistic aspirations that motivated the design of Place Ville Marie in Montreal, completed half a century earlier.

REFLECTING ON A CHAIRMANSHIP

Introductory Remarks at a Conference on Education and Practice, Harvard Graduate School of Design
November 3, 2006

First I want to remind you that more than twenty-one years have passed since my chairmanship ended in the spring of 1985. My recollections of that era are not always clear, and even if clear, they are perhaps not entirely reliable. For it is well known that with the passage of time, fading memories are often reborn as deceptively vivid myths. On at least one point, however, my memory does not deceive me, and it is this: I had a lot of fun being chairman, even though or perhaps precisely because those turbulent five years were full of anxiety and uncertainty.

I was the first chair of architecture to serve under Dean Gerald McCue, and my appointment clearly signaled his desire to forge stronger ties between this school and the practicing profession. But from the outset, both he and I were aware of the potential downside of that strategy—namely, that the school could become a mere instrument of training for practice. That's why, in my inaugural lecture, I emphasized my intention to promote open debate and searching inquiry—activities that I argued would prove in and of themselves more useful, more invigorating, more consequential than any array of answers that might ensue. In the same talk, I went on to specify four qualities that I hoped would characterize our teaching program: these were coherence, rigor, openness, and audacity.

During the first two years of my chairmanship, in my eagerness to instill the coherence and rigor that I had found lacking, I filled several faculty positions with people who very capably did exactly that. But halfway into my second year, I discovered to my dismay that I had brought coherence and rigor at the expense of openness and audacity. I also sensed an impending complacency and self-satisfaction that I found profoundly disturbing. The coherence and rigor of the core program was doing exactly what Alfred North Whitehead was worried about when, in *The Aims of Education and Other Essays,* he wrote, "necessary technical excellence can only be acquired by a training which is apt to damage those energies of mind that ought to direct the technical skill." I saw that the core program was threatening to stifle the imagination and the will to discover one's own voice. Of course, I had never intended coherence to produce that result. In the same inaugural lecture I had said that I saw the metaphor for coherence as a structural frame, not an enclosing wall; not something you find yourself trapped in, but an open framework upon and against which both students and faculty could find their own way. Coherence was supposed to be a means of getting somewhere, not a destination. When I saw that it was becoming closed, I felt an urgent need to act quickly and decisively.

Now, as everyone here knows, rapid course correction is difficult to achieve in the academic world, but for me it happily was possible because of the freedom of action and unfailing support that I received from Jerry McCue, who throughout my tenure made a practice of giving me more than enough rope to hang myself many times over. From the beginning, I had brought visitors to the school, but during my final three years—most often with Jerry's encouragement, sometimes with his amused toleration, and very occasionally with his unamused toleration—I accelerated and greatly diversified my game of throwing foreign bodies into the soup. Some of those foreign bodies are here this evening, and they know who they are. This initiative, which created a good deal of discomfort among both students and faculty, arose from my fervent desire to create a condition of disequilibrium, and it was this that ultimately emerged as the core of my pedagogical strategy, if indeed such a desire can be dignified by that name. I wanted students and faculty to experience first-hand the disequilibrium that then characterized the culture of architecture, and I wanted the GSD to be not just a scene of debate but the center of debate. In pursuing this goal, while it was not my purpose to make people uncomfortable, I was willing to make them uncomfortable if that was a necessary side effect of creating disequilibrium and provoking debate.

I could not have gotten away with the destabilizing, not to say explosive, mix of opposing viewpoints that I sponsored during the second half of my term if I had not had the strong though certainly not uncritical support of the dean and a few other key people—Michael McKinnell comes especially to mind—who shared my belief that the culture of architecture was at stake in this initiative. I was certainly not creating this mess for the sake of instrumental training. On the contrary, had that been my main concern, I would have kept on doing what I had done in the first two years. That was a very solid program of professional training, but it was only confirming Frank Lloyd Wright's famous remark—uttered in my presence, as a matter of fact—that schools of architecture are places into which young people enter as perfectly good plums and from which they emerge as perfectly good prunes. That is what I saw beginning to happen at our school, and I dedicated the remaining years of my chairmanship to making sure that it would not happen.

In retrospect, it seems to me that my role at the GSD can best be characterized as that of impresario rather than teacher, let alone ideologue. Other than my midterm shift toward disequilibrium, I can recall only two instances during those five years when my own pedagogical convictions entered decisively into policymaking. The first was my insistence that the thesis be reinstated as a degree

Investigations in Architecture
Eisenman Studios at the GSD: 1983–85

Henry N. Cobb

requirement. This was indeed the only clear preconception that I brought with me to the chairmanship. And the second was my advocacy of a senior faculty appointment in history, with a focus in the Renaissance or Baroque period. Postmodernism was reaching its apogee in the early eighties, and I believed that it was the obligation of our school to make sure that the debate thus engendered would be informed not just by polemics but also by serious scholarship.

I am happy now to turn this discussion over to Rafael Moneo, just as I was happy in 1985 to turn the chairmanship over to him. He is a great teacher as well as a great architect, and there can be no doubt that he arrived just in time to bring a needed new sense of direction to a teaching program that by then was perhaps beginning to suffer from an overdose of Dr. Cobb's disorienting medications.

Opposite Publication containing work by students in Peter Eisenman's studios at Harvard Graduate School of Design.

SCI-ARC GALLERY, LOS ANGELES

Hypostyle Installation, 2015

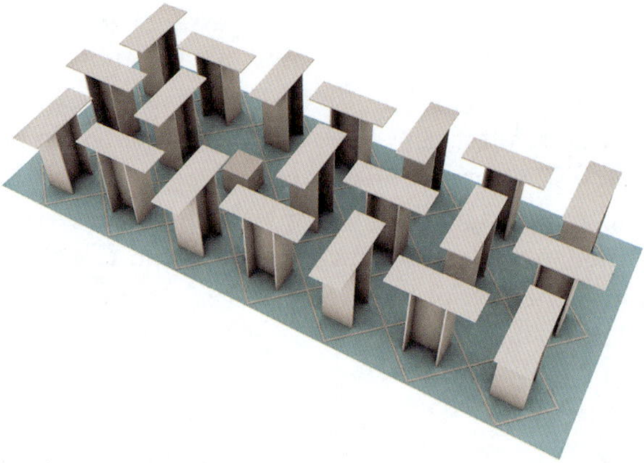

This gallery installation, conceived in response to an invitation from SCI-Arc director Eric Owen Moss, was built by thirty-one SCI-Arc students under the direction of faculty member John Southern and was on view from April 2 to May 17, 2015. My statement introducing the installation reads as follows:

> This hypostyle is an experiment. Far from being intended to demonstrate or test a general theory, its purpose is simply to discover the experiential consequence of populating a hypostyle not with historically conventional columnar solids but with planar elements joined to form vertical constructs that shape figural spaces both within and between them. Each of the twenty constructs comprising the installation is composed of four 3-by-8-foot, 1¾-inch-thick hollow-core doors: three joined to form an H-shaped vertical that is then capped by a fourth roofing the space below. Rotation of the constructs in alternating rows sequentially in both directions introduces a larger-scale order, further enhancing a complex interplay that blurs the distinction between solid and void, open and closed. One construct in the center row is omitted to create a gathering space within an otherwise uninterrupted array. A hypostyle thus constituted is without precedent, and its effect on the occupant cannot be fully predicted by drawings: it must be experienced.

Opposite Top Axonometric view of hypostyle installation. **Bottom** Author in conversation with Eric Owen Moss and SCI-Arc students, April 2, 2015. **Overleaf** View of gallery installation.

THE TYPOLOGICAL TOWER

Conversation with Paolo Conrad Bercah
New York City, February 1998

We have talked about the tall building as a unique object. But could such a building ever serve as a type, something that could be repeated many times over?
The only tall building that I'm aware of that could credibly be replicated to make a livable city is the tower in the form of a Doric column that Adolf Loos proposed for the 1922 Chicago Tribune competition. What uniquely characterizes this project is the emphatic definition of a nine-story-high cubic base with a two-story stepped top, from which a fluted column then rises as a separate entity. While I once dismissed Loos's proposal as trivial and outré, I have since come to appreciate it as a profound meditation on the problem of the tower in the city.

The typological purity of Loos's column is its strongest feature. It's unambiguous. Within the cubic base there are monumental openings addressing the street. Superimposed on the base there is a twenty-story columnar building of less mass. It is only above the base that the figure of the building becomes dominant, but acceptably so, as its circular plan occupies only a fraction of its site. Replication of the tower posits a field of figural objects in the form of columns rising from cubic volumes that define the figural space of an urban grid. You could imagine a pretty wonderful city made up entirely of such buildings.

Are you suggesting that through such strategies, tall buildings could be made less transgressive?
Yes. In a city made up of Loos columns, the buildings would not be transgressive at all. When you were in the street, they'd be seen as nine-story blocks; you'd scarcely even notice that the columnar towers were there.

It is curious, though, that the Loos column has always been perceived as highly transgressive.
Considered as a singular object, it is indeed transgressive, but that's because our modernist sensibility is offended by what we see as the misappropriation of classical elements deployed at a gigantic scale.

The materiality of Loos's building might also be considered transgressive. It was supposed to be polished black granite.

That would be beautiful. I don't want to imply that the transgressive aspect of the tall building is entirely negative. The density of the contemporary city requires buildings of a scale that is inescapably transgressive. The problem for architecture is to make something positive out of that transgression. This is why I have come to a new appreciation of the Loos column.

Postscript

Seventeen years after this conversation took place, in conjunction with the Hypostyle gallery installation at SCI-Arc, I finally found an opportunity to test my speculation about the merit of multiplying the Loos column to form a city that I called Loosville. The model that I placed at the center of the hypostyle portrayed a sixty-four-block city populated by fifty-six Loos columns, with the remaining eight blocks devoted to a four-block central park flanked by four one-block parklets.

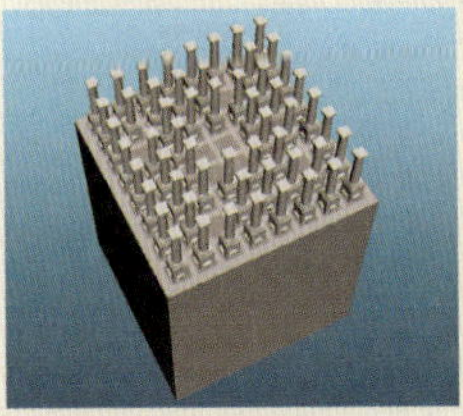

Every building in my imagined Loosville contains a mix of uses: shops, restaurants, art galleries, or theaters on the ground floor; offices on the upper floors of the cubic base; recreational amenities on the two setback floors; and residences in the columnar floors above, topped by building services in the crowning capital. It's a surreal, profoundly disturbing, yet arguably quite livable city.

When I contemplate the more than three dozen tall office buildings designed by our firm in the past six decades, only one built work could be seen as approaching the serenely self-referential authority of the Loos column. Library Tower in Los Angeles (1983–89, with Harold Fredenburgh) has indeed a Loos-like iconic presence, with its overlapping concentric geometries that govern the varied shapes of floor plates as the tower rises. However, because it lacks an orthogonal base, a city composed of such towers would be intolerable. Whether on account of its status as the tallest building in North America west of the Mississippi, or its distinctive crown, or its perceived position of privilege in downtown Los Angeles—probably on account of all three—Library Tower seems to have captured the imagination of the makers of horror films. It was the first building to be vaporized in *Independence Day* (1996) and more recently was crushed in the coils of a monster snake in *Dragon Wars* (2007). Eat your heart out, Adolf Loos!

Above Left Library Tower, 1989.
Above Right *Dragon Wars*.

GADSDEN'S WHARF, CHARLESTON

International African American Museum, 2014–20
with Matteo Milani, Guy Nordenson (structure), Walter Hood (landscape)

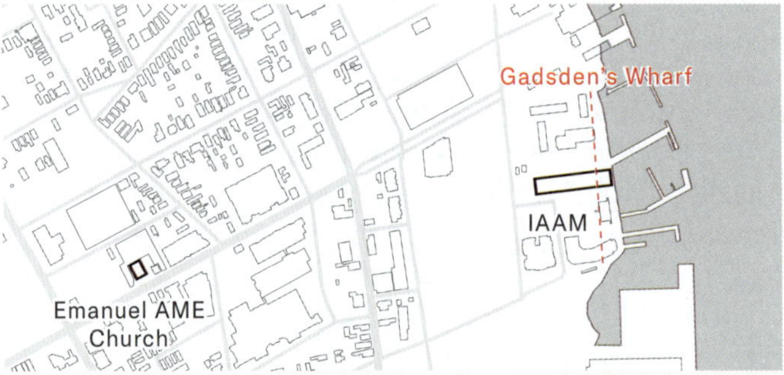

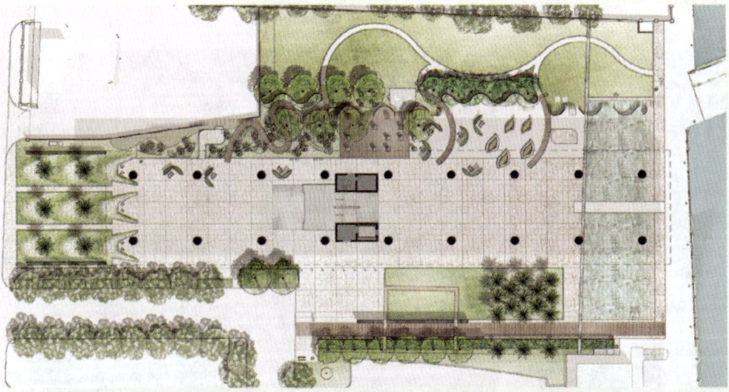

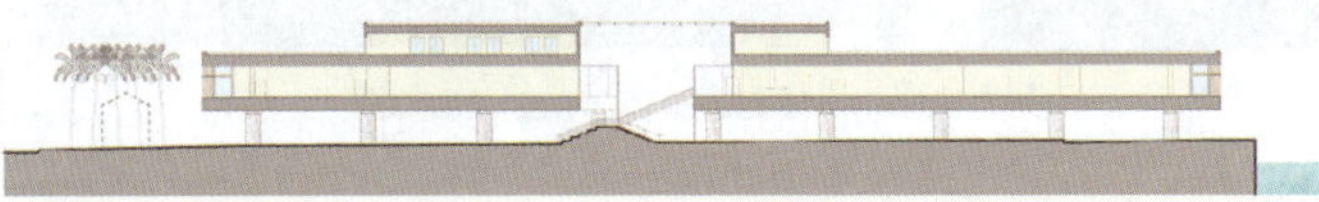

It has been estimated that 80 percent of African Americans alive today are descended from enslaved forebears who survived the Middle Passage to disembark in chains at Gadsden's Wharf. Traces of the original seawall still exist, as do foundations of a nearby warehouse in which new arrivals were held while traders awaited a rise in prices at Charleston's slave market. As the place at which many thousands of Africans from diverse cultures first set foot in North America, Gadsden's Wharf is not just the right place to tell this story; it is hallowed ground. Hence the special design challenge of the International African American Museum: to build on this site without occupying it.

The one-story museum takes the form of an elongated parallelepiped hovering thirteen feet above the ground and supported on eighteen cylindrical pillars of oyster-shell tabby that rise from a pavement of the same material, thus leaving the entire ground plane open except for service cores framing a central skylit stairway. The building's long side walls are clad in pale yellow brick, while the glazed end walls are framed by African sapele louvers directing views at the eastern end to the Atlantic and at the western end to downtown Charleston.

At ground level, Walter Hood's splendidly imagined African Ancestors Memorial Garden embraces the entire site, deploying elements of low-country landscape as it celebrates the arts, the crafts, and the labors of African Americans. The garden is bounded on one side by a shallow pool—a metaphor for the Atlantic—whose sharply defined western edge marks the original seawall of Gadsden's Wharf, while its soft eastern boundary evokes the limitless ocean beyond.

Here, then, a purposefully unrhetorical work of architecture quietly affirms the power of place as it shelters and frames a richly articulated work of landscape art.

BACK BAY, BOSTON

Belvidere Dalton Development, 2012–19
with Roy G. Barris, Gary Johnson (Cambridge Seven Associates), Michael Van Valkenburgh (landscape)

In tracing the history that led to construction of the Hancock Tower (page 110), I recounted how railway lines laid down in 1838 had prompted the filling of the Back Bay, and how their crossing had created the topographic predicament out of which Copley Square eventually emerged. Further to the west, the influence of the same railway alignments is evident in the shape and distinctive street layout of a twenty-acre zone in the form of an equilateral triangle bounded by Massachusetts Avenue, Huntington Avenue, and Belvidere Street. In 1905 Mary Baker Eddy, the founder of Christian Science, vigorously reaffirmed this unique topographic condition when she directed that the expansion of the Mother Church, located in the center of this zone, be built on a similar triangular ground plan. Six decades later, our firm was engaged to prepare a master plan for redevelopment of surrounding church-owned properties and subsequently to design the Christian Science Center, completed in 1973. My then-partner Araldo Cossutta was the principal author of this major urban regeneration project, comprising a group of boldly formed and finely crafted reinforced concrete buildings framing a 670-foot-long, granite-paved reflecting pool.

In 2010 the church gained approval for an amended master plan permitting the sale and development of three vacant parcels of land at the northern edge of its property, directly across the street from the Prudential Center. Two years later a new ownership consortium engaged our firm, together with Cambridge Seven Associates, to envision a mixed-use development on these parcels, which also enjoy adjacency to a quiet residential neighborhood within the Christian Science precinct. We set aside one parcel at the intersection of Dalton and St. Germain Streets for a small urban park that Michael Van Valkenburgh was commissioned to design. On a second parcel, with its

Top One Dalton as seen from Christian Science Center Plaza. **Above** One Dalton podium. **Preceding** Plaza with One Dalton and 30 Dalton beyond.

long side fronting on Belvidere Street, construction of a twenty-five-story residential tower, **30 Dalton**, was completed in 2016. On the third and largest parcel, shaped as an equilateral triangle, a sixty-story mixed-use tower—**Four Seasons Hotel and Private Residences One Dalton Street**—is scheduled for completion in 2019.

While the shape of this parcel clearly invited a tower form that would reaffirm the distinctive geometry of the district in which it stands, the vertical extension of an unmodified equilateral triangle would produce a built form with broad surfaces and sharp corners, making it an overbearing and ungracious neighbor. We therefore shaped the tower into a soft triangle with gently curved sides and rounded corners—a form well suited to its several occupancies, the varied natures of which are clearly indicated in the articulation of its exterior wall. The lower four floors, containing lobbies and other quasi-public rooms, are clad in Chelmsford granite framing large areas of clear glass. Above this podium, whose street walls match the height of adjoining buildings in the Christian Science Center, the slender tower's twenty floors of hotel rooms are clad entirely in gray-tinted glass. The remaining thirty-six floors of condominium residences, though also clad in the same glass, are distinguished by vertical incisions that enliven the surface of the tower while creating corner windows with operable sashes in all perimeter rooms of every apartment. By thus explicitly acknowledging the tower's residential component, this articulation of the exterior wall further celebrates the aggregation of multiple occupancies within the singularity of One Dalton, while also clearly distinguishing it from neighboring office towers. In my view, making these distinctions is now more than ever a matter of the first importance for architecture. As

Above One Dalton as seen from St. Germain Street.

Opposite One Dalton curtain-wall detail and plan.

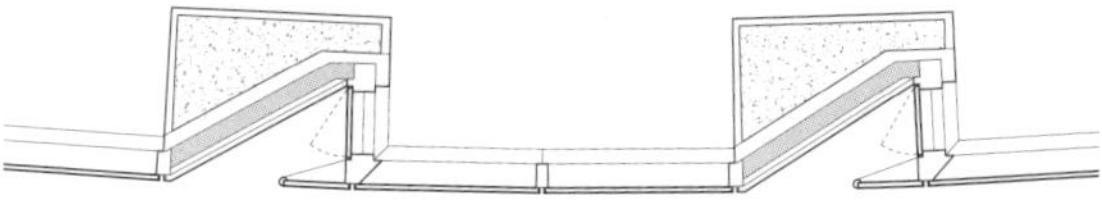

the world becomes ever more urbanized and cities ever more densely populated with tall buildings, we need to find the means to give voice in architecture to the rich diversities of occupancy, activity, and culture that bring a city to life—diversities that ought to be celebrated in our buildings, not suppressed behind masks of uniformity.

An especially rewarding aspect of this commission has been the opportunity here afforded to create a pair of buildings framing a small park that offers the delights of an intimate landscape while mediating the disjunction in scale between the new towers and their townhouse neighbors. In my Harvard thesis proposal for residential towers on Boston's waterfront (page 16), I rejoiced in liberating myself from the fabric of what I then saw as a moribund city. Seven decades later, in the Back Bay, I now rejoice in immersing myself in the fabric of what I have since come to see as a vibrantly living city.

THE VOICE OF ARCHITECTURE

A Talk to Colleagues at Pei Cobb Freed & Partners
New York City, April 7, 2016

Standing as I do on the threshold of the tenth decade of my life, and having entered my sixty-seventh year in the design practice of which I am one of the founders, I naturally find myself in a reflective frame of mind, provoking me to recall some thoughts about architecture that I've put forward previously in other contexts and would like to offer now to you with whom I am privileged to share this enterprise.

What is it that fuels our shared commitment to a design practice, in the face of all its concomitant difficulties and frustrations? Without doubt it is our shared understanding that architecture, like every art, has its own voice. That is to say, architecture commands the means of expression by which a built work, having satisfied all requirements of use and technique, may yet illuminate and give meaning to the human condition while giving shape to the physical world. And as with every art, it is the distinctive revelatory power of that voice—something not flowing from any other source—that ultimately validates architecture's claim on our attention, its appeal to our imagination, and its authority as an indispensable manifestation of our culture.

Now, a characteristic feature of the human condition to which the voice of architecture has always been eloquently responsive is the occurrence of ambiguity, paradox, and contrariety in the programs and purposes that buildings are asked to serve. As a matter of fact, the need to acknowledge and often to celebrate the coexistence of divergent and apparently irreconcilable intentions or ideas is a theme recurring throughout the entire history of Western architecture. To give substance to this claim and bring it into sharper focus, let's consider a few well-known built works that are in this respect paradigmatic.

The church of **Hagia Sophia** in Istanbul, designed by Isidore of Miletus and Anthemius of Tralles, was built by command of the emperor Justinian and dedicated in the year 537. The richly orchestrated spatial drama of this great church arises from its hybrid nature—the superimposition of a domical building form on a basilican ground plan. Structurally, Hagia Sophia is a brilliant tour de force. But this accolade does not begin to explain the emotive intensity of its interior. What stirs us in this extraordinary polyphonic composition is the bringing together of two powerful but opposite intentions: stability, absolutism, wholeness, and symmetry juxtaposed with asymmetry, incompleteness, anxiety, and aspiration. Each of these two opposing value systems is rendered eloquent by the presence of the other. And they are synthesized in a way that greatly intensifies the dialogue between them. Here architecture has given voice to St. Augustine's conception of love as a dynamic and energizing force—a forward movement of the mind. And yet here we also see this characteristic Christian impulse—this anxiety of spirit—brilliantly joined with its opposite, a reassertion of absolutism and immutability in the temporal affairs of mankind.

Among the works of the sixteenth-century architect Andrea Palladio, one of my favorites is the **Palazzo Chiericati** in Vicenza. Here we see the resolution in architecture of a different kind of paradox. Are we to read this masterful array of superimposed orders as the projecting porch of a private house, or as the colonnaded enclosure of a public square? Marvelously, it is both, and this splendid ambiguity gives the building a richness and poignancy that is entirely owing to the architect's skill in simultaneously acknowledging these entirely opposite intentions. The key invention here is the audacious clustering of columns—a breathtakingly brilliant device—by which the otherwise evenly spaced colonnade has been articulated and given its double meaning, at once a public arcade and a private entry. The miracle is that the architecture of the building is in no way compromised; rather, it draws its particular vigor from the necessity of simultaneously promoting two very different readings of its posture in the city's public realm.

In the seventeenth-century church of **San Carlo alle Quattro Fontane** in Rome, Francesco Borromini gave entirely new meaning to the discourse between dome and basilica first evidenced in Hagia Sophia. Here both forms have been radically reshaped so as to produce a dynamic and highly integrated spatial construct wherein the aspirational and the immutable are joined to form a geometrically complex and infinitely suggestive whole. The indispensable operative element in this great work is the undulating entablature that distorts the array of columns below while forming a base for pendentives that then make the transition to oval dome above. The discourse thus engendered redefines the nature of the struggle between aspiration and absolutism: what in Hagia Sophia is presented as an unresolved conflict between church and state is here declared to be an unresolved conflict within the church itself—a conflict brought vividly to life by the genius of the architect.

The **Carpenter Center for the Visual Arts** at Harvard, completed in 1964, is Le Corbusier's only built work in North America. This small but exceptionally complex and highly charged building masterfully addresses the disconcerting ambiguity of intent reflected in a seemingly hopeless disjunction between the aspirations of its program and the limitations of its site. The stated purpose to be served by the building was the integration of the visual arts, both their appreciation and their practice, into the everyday life of the college. But instead of being granted a suitably prominent place in Harvard Yard, with its spacious quadrangles crisscrossed by diagonal paths, the Carpenter Center was relegated to a cramped and altogether marginal site hemmed in by preexisting buildings. The architect's response to this dilemma was to compress the absent space of the campus into a single diagonal path in the form of an open-air ramp plunging straight through the building and offering views into the studios at its heart. This extraordinary invention—the architectural equivalent of nuclear fusion in its compaction of energy—does not try to conceal but instead vividly dramatizes the building's awkward predicament, while at the same time artfully achieving the programmatic goals that this predicament would seem to have placed out of reach.

The **Salk Institute for Biological Studies** in La Jolla, California, almost exactly contemporary with the Carpenter Center, is one of Lou Kahn's finest works. This building complex embodies a splendid solution to a characteristic problem of our time—the need to accommodate the conflicting demands of community and privacy within a single institution. To be specific, the very bright individuals who are the users of the building want to enjoy all the benefits of being in a group without sacrificing any of their much-prized sense of individuality. Kahn's resolution of this paradox is rigorously ordered yet superbly uncontrived. The very simple, symmetrical, and unpretentious arrangement of parts in the ground plan sows the seed that then flowers in the spare but enormously rich interplay of volumes and spaces. The progression, from each side toward the center, starts with service cores on the perimeter, then laboratories for group work, then the scientists' private studies flanking a central courtyard that is open at both ends. The courtyard is literally and symbolically the unifying element of the scheme, bringing together in subtle balance the identity of the individual scientist with that of the institution and reconciling them both in a shaft of space—noble and austere—that links them to the world at large. Thus boldly but with remarkable economy of means, the building reconciles without suppressing the conflicting intentions inherent in its program, giving voice to a delicately balanced social contract between the individual, the institution, and the natural world.

Seen from a distance on the skyline of Boston, the **John Hancock Tower**, designed by our firm and completed in 1976, may appear at first glance as yet another relentlessly self-centered affirmation of corporate achievement and power, governed entirely by its internal needs and systems. But a closer look reveals two striking aspects of this tower's form that call into question its self-referential autonomy. First, the end walls are skewed so as to produce a notched rhomboid rather than a rectangular plan-form. While this deviation has been accomplished in a way that is coherent with systemic elements of the plan, it nonetheless cannot be explained by reference to any identifiable internal need. And second, on the lower eight floors of the tower, one long side of the rhomboid has been rotated outward to form a trapezoid. These peculiar geometries become explicable only when one takes note of the building's urban setting. The rhomboid tower rising from its trapezoidal base is then immediately perceived to be a response to the particular external situation of the Hancock Tower, most notably its adjacency to Copley Square and H. H. Richardson's Trinity Church.

By virtue of its rhomboid shape and reflective surface, the tower is effectively disembodied as seen from the square, and this huge monolith, so assertive on the skyline, here pays homage to its much smaller neighbor, so as to become the contingent satellite in a composition of which the church is unequivocally reaffirmed as the autonomous center. Thus, as a work of architecture, the Hancock Tower is defined entirely by its preoccupation with the task of reconciling without suppressing two entirely opposite intentions: affirming the power of private enterprise, while unequivocally declaring the primacy of public buildings and civic space.

The **Caltrans District 7 Headquarters** in downtown Los Angeles—one of Thom Mayne's most provocative built works, completed in 2003—invites a question similar to that raised by Palazzo Chiericati: Is the enormous void in this building's otherwise impenetrable volume to be understood as a gathering place for its employee occupants or as an extension of the city's public realm? And as with Palladio's great work, the answer is "yes" to both readings. But whereas in Vicenza this double reading is accomplished through the subtle articulation of a colonnaded porch, in Los Angeles it is the product of a boldly forceful voiding of the building volume and a complementary extension of a secondary volume so as to frame a civic space that oscillates between conditions of interiority and exteriority. This altogether thrilling space, further dramatized by Keith Sonnier's light installation, resolves without suppressing the paradoxical predicament of a public-service bureaucracy grown so large that only a perfect act of architecture, as here performed, can make its presence not only tolerable but intensely meaningful to the public it serves.

Diverse as they are in size, character, and purpose, all seven of the buildings we've just seen vividly exemplify the remarkable capacity of architecture to illuminate ambiguity, paradox, and contrariety as they occur in the programs and purposes that buildings are asked to serve. And as my inclusion of the Hancock Tower suggests, in the course of my own quite long professional life, I have faced a number of challenges that invited, indeed compelled me to call on that same capacity. There is much more to be said on this subject, but I will conclude this talk now by reminding you that despite all our recent advances in digital technology, we still face two fundamental conditions of practice that have remained unchanged across the fifteen centuries since Isidore and Anthemius responded to Justinian's command.

The first of these—and here I quote from a talk I gave some years ago—is that:

> Architecture, owing to the expenditure of labor and material required for its production, is…inextricably enmeshed in the belief systems and institutional mechanisms that govern human culture and society. Hence the uncomfortably intimate embrace between architecture and power: an embrace to which architecture often passively submits, within which it occasionally struggles, from which it never escapes. Neither the supine posture of surrender nor the futile dream of deliverance has yet produced a significant built work of architecture. But the struggle of architecture to speak and act within and against the embrace of power has resulted in some of the most fascinating and profoundly moving manifestations of human intelligence…edifices for human use [that] become, marvelously, instruments for speculative thought—instruments that relentlessly, if covertly, challenge the conventions, the preconceptions, and finally the very powers that brought them into being.

The second unchanged condition of practice, corollary to the first, is that ours remains an art of indirection. That is to say, as architects we do not make the building; rather, we make an elaborate set of instructions that direct the work of others who actually make the building. Hence every built work of architecture is inescapably institutionalized, not just in the purposes it serves but equally in the modes of its production. For between our intention and the materialization of a building, a multitude of institutional mechanisms intervene—of finance, of law, of industry, of trade—that inexorably shape, encrust, encumber, and threaten to suffocate both the process and the product of our art.

Why, then, have I persisted for six and a half decades in a profession so relentlessly burdened? Simply because the practice of architecture is for me inseparable from the act of building: it is an enterprise not just of envisioning but of accomplishing a built work, with the intention, as I said earlier, that such a work may illuminate and give meaning to the human condition while giving shape to the physical world. And it is worth noting, finally, that the intrinsic merit of this enterprise was persuasively affirmed more than a century ago by the novelist Henry James. "Viewed in this way," he wrote, "a great building is the greatest conceivable work of art. More than any other it represents difficulties annulled, resources combined, labor, courage, patience."[1]

1 Henry James, "From Chambéry to Milan," in *Foreign Parts* (Leipzig: Bernhard Tauchnitz, 1883), 74.

AFTERWORD

With a Note on Authorship

The reader will have discovered in this book, as its title promises, a miscellany of lectures, writings, and conversations commingled with expositions of built works and unbuilt projects. In assembling this selection of words and works, which together define the arc of my professional life, I have sought to illuminate the predicament of an architect, and by extension of architecture, across seven decades since the end of World War II—an era that has witnessed the triumph and exhaustion of modernism, the rise and eclipse of postmodern historicism, and the emergence of a neo-modernism both energized and enervated by the limitless possibilities immanent in digital modes of form making.

The built works discussed herein, chosen because of their relevance to questions posed by the three dialectical pairs set forth on pages 382–83, constitute approximately half of those for which I have been principally responsible as a lead designer within the group practice of which I am a founding partner. That practice—launched by I. M. Pei at mid-century and vigorously led by him until his retirement in 1990—has been titled successively I. M. Pei & Associates (1955–65), I. M. Pei & Partners (1965–89), and Pei Cobb Freed & Partners (1989–), the name it still bears. A salient feature of the practice has been the remarkable diversity of expression evidenced in its built works. Quite aside from the effects of professional maturation and sociocultural evolution over time, this diversity is also the natural consequence of a modus operandi whereby principal responsibility for each project has typically been assumed by one (or sometimes two) of the design partners. These have included Pei (1955–90) and Cobb (1955–) as founders, then Araldo Cossutta (1963–73) and James Ingo Freed (1980–2005), later Ian Bader and Yvonne Szeto (1999–), and most recently Jay Berman, Michael Bischoff, and José Bruguera (2009–). It cannot be left unsaid that I have benefited greatly from my long and close association with all of these individuals, and also with Michael Flynn, our partner in charge of building technology, whose expertise, discerning eye, and judgment have helped shape almost every one of our built works over the past half-century.

As acknowledged in the relevant chapters, a number of the works discussed herein have been designed in collaboration with one or another of the abovementioned partners. Also noted are other colleagues in the practice and design professionals in related disciplines (planning, landscape, structure, lighting) with whom I have shared close collaborative relationships and whose contributions have therefore been so much more than merely instrumental.

Finally, in recognizing the collective nature of authorship, I would be seriously remiss were I not to take note of the resources, intellectual as well as material, that clients have contributed not just to the realization but to the conceptualization of built works. Institutional clients have been identified by name in project titles; individuals whose guidance I have found to be especially meaningful have been mentioned from time to time in the relevant texts.

ACKNOWLEDGMENTS

An author whose book has been in gestation for nearly a quarter-century must first acknowledge the patience as well as the support of his ever-faithful publisher. More than half a decade after our initial agreement had expired, Gianfranco Monacelli graciously agreed last year to reopen a conversation with me. In addition to his long-standing friendship, I am especially grateful to him for his willingness to accommodate my idiosyncratic preference for a page size (matching that adopted by Edmund Wilson) that is unusually compact for any book and unheard of for one so densely illustrated as mine. Editor Alan Rapp then took on the task of keeping me on track and on message. His constructive criticism of the manuscript, together with his diligent attention to the multitude of details that give the book its distinctive character, have placed me ever in his debt.

Because I envisioned a book in which text and images would be intimately commingled, I wanted to receive editorial and design advice from a single source, rather than from separate entities. When I noticed that *Heroic*, recently published by The Monacelli Press, had been written, edited, and designed by the principals of over,under, a Boston-based interdisciplinary practice, I sensed that I had happened on the right team. Mark Pasnik and Chris Grimley have more than fulfilled my expectations—the former principally as editor and the latter principally as designer, but both collaborating intensively to shape the book in form and content. It has been a great pleasure to work with these gifted and accomplished advisers, who have been ably assisted by their colleagues Shannon McLean and Anna Driscoll in composing the layout of text and images.

It is entirely unimaginable that this book could have come into being without the unfailingly thoughtful critical commentary, editorial guidance, and patient encouragement—stretching across two decades—that I have received from Emma Cobb. Throughout the many years during which my alternating moods of enthusiasm and self-doubt left the project always at risk of abandonment, she persisted in the burdensome preparatory work that gave the book an ever more credible substance and motivated its author to keep the project going. Hence, in many respects, this book is as much hers as it is mine.

CREDITS

Reprinted from *306090*, no. 01 (2001), courtesy of Jonathan D. Solomon 485
Aerial Photos International 177 bottom
Aerial Photos of New England 70, 75 top
Aerial Photo Services 358 bottom right
Dorothy Alexander 220
© 2015 Pavel Bendov 467 bottom
Boston Athenaeum 112
Boston Public Library, Print Department [Detroit Publishing Company, postcard no. 10636, *Copley Square, Boston, Mass.*, 1906] 118–19
Charlotte Brooks, photographer, LOOK Magazine Photograph Collection, Library of Congress, Prints & Photographs Division [LC-L9-56-6581-D, no. 27] 52
Canada Post Corporation 55 top
Tony Cho/Pei Cobb Freed & Partners 468–69
Henry N. Cobb ii–vii, 16, 23 bottom, 24–28
Henry N. Cobb/Pei Cobb Freed & Partners 113 top and bottom left, 120, 124 top right, 129 top right, 166 top, 415 top, 416 bottom left, 463 top right, 513 right, 514–516
Pamela Cobb Photography viii, 360–61, 424 bottom
Conway Library, The Courtauld Institute of Art, London 306 left
George Cserna Collection, Avery Architectural & Fine Arts Library, Columbia University 51, 64–65, 84–90, 110 top, 127 top, 128, 129 bottom left, 536
Photograph Robert Damora © Damora Archive, all rights reserved 123 top, 127 bottom, 541
Courtesy of the Dumbarton Oaks Research Library and Collection, Washington, D.C. 531
© F.L.C./ADAGP, Paris/ Artists Rights Society (ARS), New York 2018 23 top right, 34 top, 534
Scott Frances 444–47
James Ingo Freed/Pei Cobb Freed & Partners 490
Freestyle Releasing 517 right
Bill Gallery/Harvard University Graduate School of Design 268
Gorchev & Gorchev 113 bottom right
Andre Gorcynski/Pei Cobb Freed & Partners 75 bottom
Jim Griwach 533
Reprinted from Victor Gruen Associates and Larry Smith & Company, *Patterns for Progress: General Neighborhood Renewal Plan for Downtown Portland, Maine* (1967) 166 bottom
Fernando Guerra 458 top, 464, 495 top left, 496–99, 500 top right and bottom, 501
Miguel de Guzmán 460–61
Steve Hall © Hedrich Blessing 457
Harvard University Graduate School of Design 212, 502, 506
Historic England 305 bottom
Thomas Hoepker/Magnum Photos 245 top right
Hood Studio 518 middle
Naquib Hossain, licensed under CC BY-SA 2.0 537
Houghton Library, Harvard University [MS Typ 10097, no. 51] 117 top
© Wolfgang Hoyt/Esto 211 right
Simon Hsu 454–55
Allen L. Hubbard, Library of Congress, Prints & Photographs Division [HABS ME, 3-PORT, 3-7] 165 bottom right
Timothy Hursley 362 bottom, 364–65
IK's World Trip, licensed under CC BY 2.0 495 top right
Stanley Jesudowich 210 top
Alan Karchmer 442 right
Ellsworth Kelly Foundation [Ellsworth Kelly, *Ground Zero*, 2003, newsprint collage, 11½ × 13½", Whitney Museum of American Art, New York, gift of the artist and an anonymous donor, 2003; image by David Allison, courtesy Whitney Museum of American Art] 473
Chuck LaChiusa 532
Langford Studios 58
Robert LaPrelle © 2013 Kimbell Art Museum, Fort Worth 93
Richard Levine/Alamy Stock Photo 463 top left
Library of Congress, Prints & Photographs Division [LC-DIG-ppmsca-51972] 513 left
Fred Licht 488
Jane Lidz 517 left
Courtesy of the Frances Loeb Library, Harvard University Graduate School of Design 23 top left
John Loengard/The LIFE Picture Collection/Getty Images 44
Collections of Maine Historical Society 165 top
Marcok, licensed under CC BY-SA 3.0 328

Norman McGrath 243 top left
MICA Architects 200
Joseph Molitor Collection, Avery Architectural & Fine Arts Library, Columbia University 56, 61 bottom, 69
Gérald Morand 452 top left and right
© The Museum of Modern Art, licensed by Scala/Art Resource, NY 33
Theodore J. Musho/Pei Cobb Freed & Partners 403
© National Gallery, London 293 bottom, 298 bottom
© National Gallery, London, licensed by Art Resource, NY [The Wilton Diptych (English or French, *Richard II Presented to the Virgin and Child by His Patron Saint John the Baptist and Saints Edward and Edmund*), circa 1395–99, egg tempera on oak, 53 × 37 cm] 336–37
© Nicholas Nixon, courtesy of Fraenkel Gallery, San Francisco 150
Guy Nordenson and Associates/Pei Cobb Freed & Partners 475–76
Paul Stevenson Oles/Pei Cobb Freed & Partners 172 bottom, 248, 293 top, 303, 357
Osher Map Library 169
José Oubrerie 436
over,under 508 top, 518 top
© Richard Pare, courtesy of Canadian Centre for Architecture, Montreal 416 top
Richard Payne 243 top right
Pei Cobb Freed & Partners 40, 42, 55 bottom, 61 top, 62, 73, 76, 79, 80, 82, 110 bottom, 113 bottom left, 123 bottom, 124 top left, 129 bottom right, 131, 145–46, 162, 182–184, 186 bottom, 196–97, 240, 245 diagrams, 245 bottom right, 247, 259, 293 middle, 295 top, 298 top, 304, 308–09, 325, 330–31, 333, 354, 362 top and middle, 366 bottom right, 371 bottom left, 372 top, 397–402, 415 bottom, 418 top, 424 top, 442 left, 452 bottom, 458 bottom, 463 bottom, 465, 492, 495 bottom, 500 top left, 518 bottom, 520–21
Pei Cobb Freed & Partners/Cambridge Seven Associates 524–29
Jacqueline Poggi 306 right
Portland Museum of Art [Albert Sands Southworth, *The Reverend Mr. Ichabod Nichols, D.D.*, circa 1850, daguerreotype, 8½ × 6½", gift of Henry Nichols Cobb, 1980] 165 bottom left
RIBA Collections 291, 305 top
John Roemer 366 top, 368–69
Steve Rosenthal 129 top left, 170, 172 top, 174–75, 177 top, 178, 180–81, 186 top, 187–89, 208 bottom, 210 bottom, 211 left, 418 bottom, 419–23, 426–27
Salk Institute for Biological Studies 535
Scala/Art Resource, NY [Michelangelo Buonarroti, *Bacchus*, 1496–97, marble, 203 cm, Museo Nazionale del Bargello, Florence] 350
Eric Schiller 358 top
Courtesy of SCI-Arc 508 bottom
Sky's the Limit 206
Stuart Smith 96
© Ezra Stoller/Esto 39, 208 top
Mary Ann Sullivan 205
Reprinted from *Task*, no. 7/8 (1948) [http://nrs.harvard.edu/urn-3:GSD.loeb:10140534, seq. 309–408] 481
taylorphoto.com 366 bottom left, 371 top and bottom right, 372 bottom, 374–75
Wes Thompson 242, 243 bottom
Dmitry Tonkonog, licensed under CC BY-SA 3.0 320–21
Trinity Church Archives 114 bottom
Judith Turner 203
United States Courts, Portrait Collection, John Joseph Moakley United States Courthouse, Boston 413
Brian Vanden Brink 376, 378–79, 381
Peter Vanderwarker 130, 148–49
Reprinted from Mariana Griswold Van Rensselaer, *Henry Hobson Richardson and His Works* (New York: Dover Publications, 1969) 117 bottom
Michael Van Valkenburgh Associates 522
© Albert Vecerka/Esto 394, 467 top, 470
John Vincent 295 bottom
Virginia Historical Society 416 bottom right
Joshua White/JWPictures.com 358 bottom left, 510–11
© 2018 Frank Lloyd Wright Foundation, Scottsdale, Arizona. All rights reserved. The Frank Lloyd Wright Foundation Archives (The Museum of Modern Art | Avery Architectural & Fine Arts Library, Columbia University, New York) 34 bottom

Library of Congress Control Number: 2018940980

ISBN 978-1-58093-514-2

10 9 8 7 6 5 4 3 2 1

Printed in China

Edited by Mark Pasnik and Emma Cobb
Designed by Chris Grimley, Shannon McLean, and Anna Driscoll
OverUnder

The Monacelli Press
6 West 18th Street
New York, New York 10011

www.monacellipress.com